The ultimate stats and facts guide to
English League Football

Steve Pearce

B📷XTREE

First published in 1997 by Boxtree, an imprint of Macmillan Publishers Ltd, 25 Eccleston
Place, London SW1W 9NF and Basingstoke

Associated companies throughout the world

ISBN O 7522 2229 5

Design by Ian Piercy.
All photographs by Professional Sport.
Statistics supplied by Final Score RSL. Tel 01277 632070. Fax 01277 632080

9 8 7 6 5 4 3 2 1

A CIP catalogue record for this book is available from the British Library

Printed by Mackays of Chatham plc, Kent

SHOOT magazine is published weekly by IPC Magazines Ltd, King's Reach Tower, Stamford St,
London SE1 9LS. Subscription enquiries: Quadrant Subscription Services, FREEPOST CY1061,
Haywards Heath, West Sussex RH16 3ZA. Tel: 01444 445555.

*Every effort has been made to ensure that the statistics in this book are correct at the time of
going to press. Any omissions are entirely unintentional.

Contents

Thanks

SHOOT would like to thank Final Score RSL for their editorial and technical expertise in putting this publication together and Ian Cruise, Tim Barnett, Ian Piercy, David Prole, Wendy Hems, Chris Peck, Tony Grimsey and Emma Mann for their invaluable assistance to the editor.

Introduction

Manchester United might be the most successful club in English League football during the 1990s but who else has dominated the football scene in this country down the years?

SHOOT, Britain's most famous football magazine, looks back over the history of the Football League since The Invincibles of Preston won the first Championship trophy back in 1889.

Our *Ultimate Stats and Facts Guide to English League Football* is packed with information including every League table since football began. There's also an extensive look at the Champions through the years and the stars that have lit up the English soccer scene.

We salute the double-winning Aston Villa side from the early years, the Tottenham team that conquered all in the swinging sixties, the mighty Liverpool of the 1970s and 80s, led by the genius of Ian Rush and Kenny Dalglish, up to Alex Ferguson's awesome Manchester United of the 1990s.

There are special spotlights on some of the biggest names in the game with Eric Cantona, Tony Adams, Gary Lineker and Bobby Charlton just four of the stars we focus on in our Pro-Files section.

And if that's not enough - then take a look at our A-Z of League clubs capturing some amazing stats and facts about YOUR team

Take in the added ingredient of football funnies from around the world of English League football and you have a comprehensive package that will keep any soccer fan happy.

DAVE SMITH
SHOOT SPECIAL PROJECTS EDITOR

1888-1909

THE INVINCIBLES

The Football League was founded on March 22, 1888 at a meeting at Anderson's Hotel in Fleet Street, London and was the brainchild of William McGregor. At the time, the game was in a mess. International football was well established, the FA Cup was flourishing and professionalism had been legalised, but friendlies were cancelled at will for a variety of reasons, and games would often be called off as late as Saturday morning.

Clubs with high wage bills would sometimes find themselves without a game - and therefore no income - for two or three weeks and fixture lists were meaningless. So McGregor wrote a letter to several clubs to suggest that ten or 12 of the biggest clubs arrange a home-and-away fixture and at that meeting in London, and a second in Manchester soon after, plans were drawn up.

Twelve clubs were asked to become members of the Football League, six from Lancashire - Preston North End, Bolton, Everton, Burnley, Accrington Stanley and Blackburn Rovers - and six from the Midlands - Aston Villa, West Brom, Wolves, Notts County, Derby and Stoke. McGregor was appointed as the first president.

Preston became the first Champions and they did so without losing a match. They also won the FA Cup without conceding a goal. It was widely accepted that North End were ahead of their time and for that reason they were nicknamed 'The Invincibles'. They retained the title in 1889-90 and finished runners-up for the next three seasons.

Strange but true!

The League was extended to 28 clubs in 1892, with Test matches to decide promotion. Notts County and Accrington were relegated, but Manchester United, the bottom team, were not, and Birmingham, top of Division Two did not go up.

In the net

In 1891 the first goal nets were introduced and seven years later promotion and relegation was brought in for the first time.

Strange but true!

The 1901-02 season was remarkably close. Only 12 points separated the top 15 of the 18 clubs, they all won at least ten games, and all lost at least ten except Champions Sunderland's nine.

Sunderland and Aston Villa dominated the 1890s - Sunderland winning three titles and Villa five - and as the Victorian era ended the League was expanded to two Divisions of 18 clubs each, including for the first time a southern club, Woolwich Arsenal. Football was, indeed, really booming and blooming.

LEAGUE TABLES 1888-89 to 1909-10

1888-89
DIVISION 1

1 Preston	40
2 Aston Villa	29
3 Wolves	28
4 Blackburn	26
5 Bolton	22
6 West Brom	22
7 Accrington	20
8 Everton	20
9 Burnley	17
10 Derby	16
11 Notts Co	12
12 Stoke	12

1889-90
DIVISION 1

1 Preston	33
2 Everton	31
3 Blackburn	27
4 Wolves	25
5 West Brom	25
6 Accrington	24
7 Derby	21
8 Aston Villa	19
9 Bolton	19
10 Notts Co	17
11 Burnley	13
12 Stoke	10

1890-91
DIVISION 1

1 Everton	29
2 Preston	27
3 Notts Co	26
4 Wolves	26
5 Bolton	25
6 Blackburn	24
7 Sunderland*	23
8 Burnley	21
9 Aston Villa	18
10 Accrington	16
11 Derby	15
12 West Brom	12

* Two points deducted for fielding an illegible player

1891-92
DIVISION 1

1 Sunderland	42
2 Preston	37
3 Bolton	36
4 Aston Villa	30
5 Everton	28
6 Wolves	26
7 Burnley	26
8 Notts Co	26
9 Blackburn	26
10 Derby	24
11 Accrington	20
12 West Brom	18
13 Stoke	14
14 Darwen	11

1892-93
DIVISION 1

1 Sunderland	48
2 Preston	37
3 Everton	36
4 Aston Villa	35
5 Bolton	32
6 Burnley	30
7 Stoke	29
8 West Brom	29
9 Blackburn	29
10 Nottm For	28
11 Wolves	28
12 Sheff Wed	27
13 Derby	27
14 Notts Co	24
15 Accrington	23
16 Man Utd	18

DIVISION 2

1 Birmingham	36
2 Sheff Utd	35
3 Darwen	30
4 Grimsby	23
5 Man City	21
6 Burton Utd	20
7 Northwich Vic	20
8 Bootle	19
9 Lincoln	17
10 Crewe	15
11 Port Vale	15
12 Walsall	13

1893-94
DIVISION 1

1 Aston Villa	44
2 Sunderland	38
3 Derby	36
4 Blackburn	34
5 Burnley	34
6 Everton	33
7 Nottm For	32
8 West Brom	32
9 Wolves	31
10 Sheff Utd	31
11 Stoke	29
12 Sheff Wed	26
13 Bolton	24
14 Preston	23
15 Darwen	19
16 Man Utd	14

DIVISION 2

1 Liverpool	50
2 Birmingham	42
3 Notts Co	39
4 Newcastle	36
5 Grimsby	32
6 Burton Utd	31
7 Port Vale	30
8 Lincoln	28
9 Arsenal	28
10 Walsall	23
11 Middlesbro Iro	20
12 Crewe	19
13 Man City	18
14 Rotherham T	15
15 Northwich Vic	9

1894-95
DIVISION 1

1 Sunderland	47
2 Everton	42
3 Aston Villa	39
4 Preston	35
5 Blackburn	32
6 Sheff Utd	32
7 Nottm For	31
8 Sheff Wed	28
9 Burnley	26
10 Bolton	25
11 Wolves	25
12 Birmingham	25
13 West Brom	24
14 Stoke	24
15 Derby	23
16 Liverpool	22

DIVISION 2

1 Bury	48
2 Notts Co	39
3 Man Utd	38
4 Leicester	38
5 Grimsby	37
6 Darwen	36
7 Burton W	35
8 Arsenal	34
9 Man City	31
10 Newcastle	27
11 Burton Utd	25
12 Rotherham T	24
13 Lincoln	20
14 Walsall	20
15 Port Vale	18
16 Crewe	10

CHAMPIONS
Preston North End 1888-89

It was Preston's ritual hammerings of friendly and Cup opponents - such as their famous 26-0 victory over Hyde - that helped prompt the Football League into existence in 1888. William McGregor, the main force behind the League idea, persuaded sceptics that it would lead to a wider spread of talent, increasing the game's popularity around the country. He was to be proved right, but not at once, for the Preston 'Invincibles' won the first Championship with 40 points out of a possible 44, as well as winning the Cup without conceding a single goal! They certainly lived up to their nickname.

WHAT A STAR ⭐ BILLY McCRACKEN

Not many players cause a rule to be changed, but Billy McCracken did. His use of offside tactics as a full-back for Ireland and Newcastle was so frequent and frustrating that the game's rulers altered the law so that only two opponents, rather than three, needed to be nearer the goal-line when the ball was last played. McCracken was a good player as well as a clever one, winning two Championship medals and one FA Cup medal, and 16 caps between 1902 and 1923. He later managed Hull to an FA Cup Semi-Final, and was scouting for Millwall when in his eighties.

1895-96

DIVISION 1
1	Aston Villa	45
2	Derby	41
3	Everton	39
4	Bolton	37
5	Sunderland	37
6	Stoke	30
7	Sheff Wed	29
8	Blackburn	29
9	Preston	28
10	Burnley	27
11	Bury	27
12	Sheff Utd	26
13	Nottm For	25
14	Wolves	21
15	Birmingham	20
16	West Brom	19

DIVISION 2
1	Liverpool	46
2	Man City	46
3	Grimsby	42
4	Burton W	42
5	Newcastle	34
6	Man Utd	33
7	Arsenal	32
8	Leicester	32
9	Darwen	30
10	Notts Co	26
11	Burton Utd	24
12	Loughboro'gh	23
13	Lincoln	22
14	Port Vale	18
15	Rotherham T	17
16	Crewe	13

1896-97

DIVISION 1
1	Aston Villa	47
2	Sheff Utd	36
3	Derby	36
4	Preston	34
5	Liverpool	33
6	Sheff Wed	31
7	Everton	31
8	Bolton	30
9	Bury	30
10	Wolves	28
11	Nottm For	26
12	West Brom	26
13	Stoke	25
14	Blackburn	25
15	Sunderland	23
16	Burnley	19

DIVISION 2
1	Notts Co	42
2	Man Utd	39
3	Grimsby	38
4	Birmingham	37
5	Man City	35
6	Gainsboro T	32
7	Blackpool	31
8	Leicester	30
9	Arsenal	30
10	Darwen	28
11	Walsall	27
12	Loughboro'gh	25
13	Burton Utd	24
14	Burton W	20
15	Lincoln	12

Strange but true!

Sunderland, elected in place of bottom club Stoke in 1890, got off to a bad start. They had two points deducted for fielding an ineligible player.

1897-98

DIVISION 1
1	Sheff Utd	42
2	Sunderland	37
3	Wolves	35
4	Everton	35
5	Sheff Wed	33
6	Aston Villa	33
7	West Brom	32
8	Nottm For	31
9	Liverpool	28
10	Derby	28
11	Bolton	26
12	Preston	24
13	Notts Co	24
14	Bury	24
15	Blackburn	24
16	Stoke	24

DIVISION 2
1	Burnley	48
2	Newcastle	45
3	Man City	39
4	Man Utd	38
5	Arsenal	37
6	Birmingham	36
7	Leicester	33
8	Luton	30
9	Gainsboro T	30
10	Walsall	29
11	Blackpool	25
12	Grimsby	24
13	Burton Utd	21
14	Lincoln	17
15	Darwen	14
16	Loughboro'gh	14

1898-99

DIVISION 1
1	Aston Villa	45
2	Liverpool	43
3	Burnley	39
4	Everton	38
5	Notts Co	37
6	Blackburn	36
7	Sunderland	36
8	Wolves	35
9	Derby	35
10	Bury	35
11	Nottm For	33
12	Stoke	33
13	Newcastle	30
14	West Brom	30
15	Preston	29
16	Sheff Utd	29
17	Bolton	25
18	Sheff Wed	24

DIVISION 2
1	Man City	52
2	Glossop NE	46
3	Leicester	45
4	Man Utd	43
5	New Bright'n T	43
6	Walsall	42
7	Arsenal	41
8	Birmingham	41
9	Port Vale	39
10	Grimsby	35
11	Barnsley	31
12	Lincoln	31
13	Burton Utd	28
14	Gainsboro T	25
15	Luton	23
16	Blackpool	20
17	Loughboro'gh	18
18	Darwen	9

Villa Thrillers

Aston Villa 9 Notts County 1 was the highest score in the first League season.

Oh Stanley

Eleven of the 12 founder members of the new League are still in action. Accrington, the only exception, withdrew because of financial problems in 1961-62.

WHAT A STAR ⭐ STEVE BLOOMER

He scored 297 League goals and 32 Cup goals for Derby, plus 55 in the League and three in the Cup for Middlesbrough, and 28 goals in only 23 games for England - the latter record stood for nearly 50 years. Yet he did not win a Championship or a Cup, with appearances in the losing FA Final teams of 1898 and 1899 being the closest he went to glory in his 22-year career. Bloomer was slightly built and deathly pale, but had a strong, instantaneous shot and was almost foolhardy in his bravery when facing beefy opponents. A born scorer and one of the best players of his generation.

1899-1900

DIVISION 1

1	Aston Villa	50
2	Sheff Utd	48
3	Sunderland	41
4	Wolves	39
5	Newcastle	36
6	Derby	36
7	Man City	34
8	Nottm For	34
9	Stoke	34
10	Liverpool	33
11	Everton	33
12	Bury	32
13	West Brom	30
14	Blackburn	29
15	Notts Co	29
16	Preston	28
17	Burnley	27
18	Glossop NE	18

DIVISION 2

1	Sheff Wed	54
2	Bolton	52
3	Birmingham	46
4	Man Utd	44
5	Leicester	43
6	Grimsby	40
7	Chesterfield	38
8	Arsenal	36
9	Lincoln	36
10	New Bright'n	T35
11	Port Vale	34
12	Walsall	32
13	Gainsboro T	25
14	Middlesbro	24
15	Burton Utd	24
16	Barnsley	23
17	Luton	18
18	Loughboro'gh	8

Not very Common!

Alf Common became the first £1000 transfer between League clubs when he left Sunderland to join Middlesbrough in 1905

1900-01

DIVISION 1

1	Liverpool	45
2	Sunderland	43
3	Notts Co	40
4	Nottm For	39
5	Bury	39
6	Newcastle	38
7	Everton	37
8	Sheff Wed	36
9	Blackburn	33
10	Bolton	33
11	Man City	32
12	Derby	31
13	Wolves	31
14	Sheff Utd	31
15	Aston Villa	30
16	Stoke	27
17	Preston	25
18	West Brom	22

DIVISION 2

1	Grimsby	49
2	Birmingham	48
3	Burnley	44
4	New Bright'n	T42
5	Glossop NE	38
6	Middlesbro	37
7	Arsenal	36
8	Lincoln	33
9	Port Vale	33
10	Man Utd	32
11	Leicester	32
12	Blackpool	31
13	Gainsboro T	30
14	Chesterfield	28
15	Barnsley	27
16	Walsall	27
17	Stockport	25
18	Burton Utd	20

Ton Up

Darwen were the first club to concede a century of goals, 112, when bottom in 1891-92. On the last day of the following season Sunderland became the first club to score a century of goals, reaching exactly 100 with a 3-2 win at Burnley.

1901-02

DIVISION 1

1	Sunderland	44
2	Everton	41
3	Newcastle	37
4	Blackburn	36
5	Nottm For	35
6	Derby	35
7	Bury	34
8	Aston Villa	34
9	Sheff Wed	34
10	Sheff Utd	33
11	Liverpool	32
12	Bolton	32
13	Notts Co	32
14	Wolves	32
15	Grimsby	32
16	Stoke	31
17	Birmingham	30
18	Man City	28

DIVISION 2

1	West Brom	55
2	Middlesbro	51
3	Preston	42
4	Arsenal	42
5	Lincoln	41
6	Bristol City	40
7	Doncaster	34
8	Glossop NE	32
9	Burnley	30
10	Burton Utd	30
11	Barnsley	30
12	Port Vale	29
13	Blackpool	29
14	Leicester	29
15	Man Utd	28
16	Chesterfield	28
17	Stockport	23
18	Gainsboro T	19

1902-03

DIVISION 1

1	Sheff Wed	42
2	Aston Villa	41
3	Sunderland	41
4	Sheff Utd	39
5	Liverpool	38
6	Stoke	37
7	West Brom	36
8	Bury	35
9	Derby	35
10	Nottm For	35
11	Wolves	33
12	Everton	33
13	Middlesbro	32
14	Newcastle	32
15	Notts Co	31
16	Blackburn	29
17	Grimsby	25
18	Bolton	19

DIVISION 2

1	Man City	54
2	Birmingham	51
3	Arsenal	48
4	Bristol City	42
5	Man Utd	38
6	Chesterfield	37
7	Preston	36
8	Barnsley	34
9	Port Vale	34
10	Lincoln	30
11	Glossop NE	29
12	Gainsboro T	29
13	Burton Utd	29
14	Blackpool	28
15	Leicester	28
16	Doncaster	25
17	Stockport	20
18	Burnley	20

Strange but true!

Loughborough Town, bottom of the Second in 1899-1900, conceded only 26 goals in 17 home games but 74 away, including seven on Good Friday and 12 on Easter Monday.

1903-04
DIVISION 1

1	Sheff Wed	47
2	Man City	44
3	Everton	43
4	Newcastle	42
5	Aston Villa	41
6	Sunderland	39
7	Sheff Utd	38
8	Wolves	36
9	Nottm For	31
10	Middlesbro	30
11	Birmingham	30
12	Bury	29
13	Notts Co	29
14	Derby	28
15	Blackburn	28
16	Stoke	27
17	Liverpool	26
18	West Brom	24

DIVISION 2

1	Preston	50
2	Arsenal	49
3	Man Utd	48
4	Bristol City	42
5	Burnley	39
6	Grimsby	36
7	Bolton	34
8	Barnsley	32
9	Gainsboro T	31
10	Bradford	31
11	Chesterfield	30
12	Lincoln	30
13	Port Vale	29
14	Burton Utd	29
15	Blackpool	27
16	Stockport	27
17	Glossop NE	26
18	Leicester	22

1904-05
DIVISION 1

1	Newcastle	48
2	Everton	47
3	Man City	46
4	Aston Villa	42
5	Sunderland	40
6	Sheff Utd	40
7	Birmingham	39
8	Preston	36
9	Sheff Wed	33
10	Arsenal	33
11	Derby	32
12	Stoke	30
13	Blackburn	27
14	Wolves	26
15	Middlesbro	26
16	Nottm For	25
17	Bury	24
18	Notts Co	18

DIVISION 2

1	Liverpool	58
2	Bolton	56
3	Man Utd	53
4	Bristol City	42
5	Chesterfield	39
6	Gainsboro T	36
7	Barnsley	33
8	Bradford	32
9	Lincoln	31
10	West Brom	30
11	Burnley	30
12	Glossop NE	30
13	Grimsby	30
14	Leicester	29
15	Blackpool	28
16	Port Vale	27
17	Burton Utd	20
18	Doncaster	8

1905-06
DIVISION 1

1	Liverpool	51
2	Preston	47
3	Sheff Wed	44
4	Newcastle	43
5	Man City	43
6	Bolton	41
7	Birmingham	41
8	Aston Villa	40
9	Blackburn	40
10	Stoke	39
11	Everton	37
12	Arsenal	37
13	Sheff Utd	36
14	Sunderland	35
15	Derby	35
16	Notts Co	34
17	Bury	32
18	Middlesbro	31
19	Nottm For	31
20	Wolves	23

DIVISION 2

1	Bristol City	66
2	Man Utd	62
3	Chelsea	53
4	West Brom	52
5	Hull	44
6	Leeds City	43
7	Leicester	42
8	Grimsby	40
9	Burnley	38
10	Stockport	35
11	Bradford	34
12	Barnsley	33
13	Lincoln	30
14	Blackpool	29
15	Gainsboro T	28
16	Glossop NE	28
17	Port Vale	28
18	Chesterfield	28
19	Burton Utd	26
20	L.Orient	21

1906-07
DIVISION 1

1	Newcastle	51
2	Bristol City	48
3	Everton	45
4	Sheff Utd	45
5	Aston Villa	44
6	Bolton	44
7	Arsenal	44
8	Man Utd	42
9	Birmingham	38
10	Sunderland	37
11	Middlesbro	36
12	Blackburn	35
13	Sheff Wed	35
14	Preston	35
15	Liverpool	33
16	Bury	32
17	Man City	32
18	Notts Co	31
19	Derby	27
20	Stoke	26

DIVISION 2

1	Nottm For	60
2	Chelsea	57
3	Leicester	48
4	West Brom	47
5	Bradford	47
6	Wolves	41
7	Burnley	40
8	Barnsley	38
9	Hull	37
10	Leeds City	36
11	Grimsby	35
12	Stockport	35
13	Blackpool	33
14	Gainsboro T	33
15	Glossop NE	32
16	Port Vale	31
17	L.Orient	30
18	Chesterfield	29
19	Lincoln	28
20	Burton Utd	23

Ton-derful

In 1895-96 Liverpool were Division Two Champions with 106 goals in 30 matches. That's still their best-ever total for a League season

CHAMPIONS
Liverpool 1893/94

The League was extended and a Second Division of 12 clubs was formed before the 1892/93 season. During the following campaign, newcomers Liverpool sounded a warning of what was to come. Their team, composed almost entirely of Scottish professionals, went unbeaten to win the 28-match Championship, with 22 victories and six draws to their credit. The Reds went on to win the test match for promotion, and then drew their first two games of the following term, to compile a run of 31 matches without defeat, a run that was not bettered until after the Second World War.

WHAT A STAR ⭐ JOHN GOODALL

They called him John All Good and he had many friends, though his ranking as the first soccer superstar must have aroused considerable envy. Goodall, son of a soldier, was born in London of Scottish parents, was qualified to play for England, and did so 14 times over ten years, a surprisingly long international career for those days. He helped Preston to the double in 1889, scheming and scoring, one of the first 'scientific' players rather than a kicker and rusher. He later played for Derby with his brother Archie, who was born in Belfast and capped by Ireland before becoming a strongman in a circus.

Strange but true!

Arsenal and Blackburn finished equal 14th in 1907-08, with identical records - 12 wins, 12 draws, 14 defeats, 51 goals for and 63 against.

1907-08

DIVISION 1

1	Man Utd	52
2	Aston Villa	43
3	Man City	43
4	Newcastle	42
5	Sheff Utd	42
6	Middlesbro	41
7	Bury	39
8	Liverpool	38
9	Nottm For	37
10	Bristol City	36
11	Everton	36
12	Preston	36
13	Chelsea	36
14	Arsenal	36
14	Blackburn	36
16	Sunderland	35
17	Sheff Utd	35
18	Notts Co	34
19	Bolton	33
20	Birmingham	30

DIVISION 2

1	Bradford	54
2	Leicester	52
3	Oldham	50
4	Fulham	49
5	West Brom	47
6	Derby	46
7	Burnley	46
8	Hull	46
9	Wolves	37
10	Stoke	37
11	Gainsboro T	35
12	Leeds City	32
13	Stockport	32
14	L.Orient	32
15	Blackpool	31
16	Barnsley	30
17	Glossop NE	30
18	3Grimsby	30
19	Chesterfield	23
20	Lincoln	21

1908-09

DIVISION 1

1	Newcastle	53
2	Everton	46
3	Sunderland	44
4	Blackburn	41
5	Sheff Wed	40
6	Arsenal	38
7	Aston Villa	38
8	Bristol City	38
9	Middlesbro	37
10	Preston	37
11	Chelsea	37
12	Sheff Utd	37
13	Man Utd	37
14	Nottm For	36
15	Notts Co	36
16	Liverpool	36
17	Bury	36
18	Bradford	34
19	Man City	34
20	Leicester	25

DIVISION 2

1	Bolton	52
2	Tottenham	51
3	West Brom	51
4	Hull	44
5	Derby	43
6	Oldham	40
7	Wolves	39
8	Glossop NE	38
9	Gainsboro T	38
10	Fulham	37
11	Birmingham	37
12	Leeds City	35
13	Grimsby	35
14	Burnley	33
15	L.Orient	33
16	Bradford PA	32
17	Barnsley	32
18	Stockport	31
19	Chesterfield	30
20	Blackpool	29

1909-10

DIVISION 1

1	Aston Villa	53
2	Liverpool	48
3	Blackburn	45
4	Newcastle	45
5	Man Utd	45
6	Sheff Utd	42
7	Bradford	42
8	Sunderland	41
9	Notts Co	40
10	Everton	40
11	Sheff Wed	39
12	Preston	35
13	Bury	33
14	Nottm For	33
15	Tottenham	32
16	Bristol City	32
17	Middlesbro	31
18	Arsenal	31
19	Chelsea	29
20	Bolton	24

DIVISION 2

1	Man City	54
2	Oldham	53
3	Hull	53
4	Derby	53
5	Leicester	44
6	Glossop NE	43
7	Fulham	41
8	Wolves	40
9	Barnsley	39
10	Bradford PA	38
11	West Brom	37
12	Blackpool	36
13	Stockport	34
14	Burnley	34
15	Lincoln	31
16	L.Orient	30
17	Leeds City	27
18	Gainsboro T	26
19	Grimsby	24
20	Birmingham	23

CHAMPIONS
Aston Villa 1896-97

William McGregor's club, Aston Villa, eventually took over from Preston as the dominant force in the League's first 20 years, with five titles finding their way to Villa Park. Players such as Archie Hunter, John Devey and John Reynolds were major figures as professional organisation took over from amateur enthusiasm. Villa even emulated Preston by doing the double, winning the League by nine points from Sheffield United. By now there were two divisions of 16 clubs each in the game.

1910-1929

DIXIE DEAN THE DESTROYER

The years before World War I saw a period of total dominance for clubs from the north of England. Manchester United, Blackburn (twice), Sunderland and Everton were the Champions in the five seasons before the war interrupted the Football League for five years.

> ## Yo-yo Joe
>
> Joe Williams won two Championship medals and was relegated twice during five seasons in the 20s. He was relegated with Rotherham, won a title with Huddersfield, and did both with Stoke.

On its resumption after the war, football wasted no time in changing things and further expanding the League. The First and Second Divisions were increased in size to 22 clubs, and within two years there were two Third Divisions, first South, then North. The 1920s began with Liverpool winning back-to-back Championships, but by 1923 there was a new, all-conquering power about to enter the fray - Huddersfield Town. Under the management of Herbert Chapman, Huddersfield won three successive League titles, in 1923-24, 1924-25 and 1925-26, although by the time the hat-trick was completed Chapman had moved on to Arsenal. He would later repeat the feat of triple Championship triumphs with The Gunners, although for a very different reason he wouldn't see that through either, a remarkable achievement when you consider that only Liverpool have managed it in the modern game.

But while Huddersfield were the dominant team of that era, Everton's William Ralph Dean - Dixie - was the dominant personality. In the 1927-28 season, Dean scored 60 League goals for Everton, a record that without question will stand for all time.

It is said that Chapman offered Everton anything they wanted to let Dean join Arsenal, but Dixie preferred to spend his prime years at Goodison Park, not surprisingly helping them to win the title in that 1927-28 season. He completed his tally of 60 - to beat the record of 59 Second Division goals scored by Middlesbrough's George Camsell - in amazing fashion. Needing nine goals from Everton's last three games, he scored twice against Aston Villa, scored four at Burnley and then grabbed a hat-trick in the last game, ironically against Arsenal. Dean scored 473 goals in 502 competitive games, and it was fitting that when he died, on March 1, 1980, he was at Goodison Park, watching Everton.

LEAGUE TABLES 1910-11 to 1929-30

1910-11
DIVISION 1

1	Man Utd	52
2	Aston Villa	51
3	Sunderland	45
4	Everton	45
5	Bradford	45
6	Sheff Wed	42
7	Oldham	41
8	Newcastle	40
9	Sheff Utd	38
10	Arsenal	38
11	Notts Co	38
12	Blackburn	37
13	Liverpool	37
14	Preston	35
15	Tottenham	32
16	Middlesbro	32
17	Man City	31
18	Bury	29
19	Bristol City	27
20	Nottm For	25

DIVISION 2

1	West Brom	53
2	Bolton	51
3	Chelsea	49
4	L.Orient	45
5	Hull	44
6	Derby	42
7	Blackpool	42
8	Burnley	41
9	Wolves	38
10	Fulham	37
11	Leeds City	37
12	Bradford PA	37
13	Huddersfield	34
14	Glossop NE	34
15	Leicester	33
16	Birmingham	32
17	Stockport	30
18	Gainsboro T	29
19	Barnsley	28
20	Lincoln	24

1911-12
DIVISION 1

1	Blackburn	49
2	Everton	46
3	Newcastle	44
4	Bolton	43
5	Sheff Wed	41
6	Aston Villa	41
7	Middlesbro	40
8	Sunderland	39
9	West Brom	39
10	Arsenal	38
11	Bradford	38
12	Tottenham	37
13	Man Utd	37
14	Sheff Utd	36
15	Man City	35
16	Notts Co	35
17	Liverpool	34
18	Oldham	34
19	Preston	33
20	Bury	21

DIVISION 2

1	Derby	54
2	Chelsea	54
3	Burnley	52
4	L.Orient	45
5	Wolves	42
6	Barnsley	42
7	Hull	42
8	Fulham	39
9	Grimsby	39
10	Leicester	37
11	Bradford PA	35
12	Birmingham	34
13	Bristol City	34
14	Blackpool	34
15	Nottm For	33
16	Stockport	33
17	Huddersfield	32
18	Glossop NE	28
19	Leeds City	28
20	Gainsboro T	23

1912-13
DIVISION 1

1	Sunderland	54
2	Aston Villa	50
3	Sheff Wed	49
4	Man Utd	46
5	Blackburn	45
6	Man City	44
7	Derby	42
8	Bolton	42
9	Oldham	42
10	West Brom	38
11	Everton	37
12	Liverpool	37
13	Bradford	35
14	Newcastle	34
15	Sheff Utd	34
16	Middlesbro	32
17	Tottenham	30
18	Chelsea	28
19	Notts Co	23
20	Arsenal	18

DIVISION 2

1	Preston	53
2	Burnley	50
3	Birmingham	46
4	Barnsley	45
5	Huddersfield	43
6	Leeds City	40
7	Grimsby	40
8	Lincoln	40
9	Fulham	39
10	Wolves	38
11	Bury	38
12	Hull	36
13	Bradford PA	36
14	L.Orient	34
15	Leicester	33
16	Bristol City	33
17	Nottm For	32
18	Glossop NE	32
19	Stockport	26
20	Blackpool	26

1913-14
DIVISION 1

1	Blackburn	51
2	Aston Villa	44
3	Middlesbro	43
4	Oldham	43
5	West Brom	43
6	Bolton	42
7	Sunderland	40
8	Chelsea	39
9	Bradford	38
10	Sheff Utd	37
11	Newcastle	37
12	Burnley	36
13	Man City	36
14	Man Utd	36
15	Everton	35
16	Liverpool	35
17	Tottenham	34
18	Sheff Wed	34
19	Preston	30
20	Derby	27

DIVISION 2

1	Notts Co	53
2	Bradford PA	49
3	Arsenal	49
4	Leeds City	47
5	Barnsley	45
6	L.Orient	43
7	Hull	41
8	Bristol City	41
9	Wolves	41
10	Bury	40
11	Fulham	38
12	Stockport	36
13	Huddersfield	34
14	Birmingham	34
15	Grimsby	34
16	Blackpool	32
17	Glossop NE	28
18	Leicester	26
19	Lincoln	26
20	Nottm For	23

CHAMPIONS
Liverpool 1922/23

No single club dominated football for more than two or three years before the 1930s. There was no reason why one should, in a League of equal opportunity not ruled solely by the wealthy. Liverpool, however, won the Championship twice in succession, and in the second of those years they enjoyed a run of 11 wins and two draws. Irishman Elisha Scott was a splendid goalkeeper, recognised as one of the best in the game at the time and Harry Chambers (41 goals over the two seasons) and Ted Forshaw (36) were just the first in a long line of impressive Anfield strike partnerships. Combined, the pair were lethal and played a significant part in helping the men from Anfield take an initial stranglehold on the English game.

WHAT A STAR ⭐ CHARLES BUCHAN

One of the greatest players of his era won only six caps, over 11 years, despite his tremendous reputation as a clever inside-forward with splendid finishing ability. Some said that Buchan was too clever for his colleagues, others that he did not take kindly to authority. But he certainly could play, as he showed time and again with Sunderland and then with Arsenal, as the first of the many major stars to grace Highbury. On retirement he became a journalist and founded the first 'intelligent' soccer magazine. But it was on Wearside that Buchan is still best remembered and he formed part of the Roker triangle, along with Frank Cuggy and Jackie Mordue, that guided the club to the Championship in 1913. A year before that he took a holiday in Canada - and sailed on the next boat out of port after the Titanic!

1914-15

DIVISION 1
1	Everton	46
2	Oldham	45
3	Blackburn	43
4	Burnley	43
5	Man City	43
6	Sheff Utd	43
7	Sheff Wed	43
8	Sunderland	41
9	Bradford PA	41
10	West Brom	40
11	Bradford	40
12	Middlesbro	38
13	Liverpool	37
14	Aston Villa	37
15	Newcastle	32
16	Notts Co	31
17	Bolton	30
18	Man Utd	30
19	Chelsea	29
20	Tottenham	28

DIVISION 2
1	Derby	53
2	Preston	50
3	Barnsley	47
4	Wolves	45
5	Arsenal	43
6	Birmingham	43
7	Hull	43
8	Huddersfield	42
9	L.Orient	41
10	Blackpool	39
11	Bury	38
12	Fulham	37
13	Bristol City	37
14	Stockport	37
15	Leeds City	32
16	Lincoln	31
17	Grimsby	31
18	Nottm For	29
19	Leicester	24
20	Glossop NE	18

League football was suspended during World War One

DIVISION 1
1	West Brom	60
2	Burnley	51
3	Chelsea	49
4	Liverpool	48
5	Sunderland	48
6	Bolton	47
7	Man City	45
8	Newcastle	43
9	Aston Villa	42
10	Arsenal	42
11	Bradford PA	42
12	Man Utd	40
13	Middlesbro	40
14	Sheff Utd	40
15	Bradford	39
16	Everton	38
17	Oldham	38
18	Derby	38
19	Preston	38
20	Blackburn	37
21	Notts Co	36
22	Sheff Wed	23

DIVISION 2
1	Tottenham	70
2	Huddersfield	64
3	Birmingham	56
4	Blackpool	52
5	Bury	48
6	Fulham	47
7	West Ham	47
8	Bristol City	43
9	Gateshead	42
10	Stoke	42
11	Hull	42
12	Barnsley	40
13	Port Vale	40
14	Leicester	40
15	L.Orient	38
16	Stockport	37
17	Rotherham	34
18	Nottm For	34
19	Wolves	30
20	Coventry	29
21	Lincoln	27
22	Grimsby	25

1920-21

DIVISION 1
1	Burnley	59
2	Man City	54
3	Bolton	52
4	Liverpool	51
5	Newcastle	50
6	Tottenham	47
7	Everton	47
8	Middlesbro	46
9	Arsenal	44
10	Aston Villa	43
11	Blackburn	41
12	Sunderland	41
13	Man Utd	40
14	West Brom	40
15	Bradford	39
16	Preston	39
17	Huddersfield	39
18	Chelsea	39
19	Oldham	33
20	Sheff Utd	30
21	Derby	26
22	Bradford PA	24

DIVISION 2
1	Birmingham	58
2	Cardiff	58
3	Bristol City	51
4	Blackpool	50
5	West Ham	48
6	Notts Co	47
7	L.Orient	45
8	Gateshead	44
9	Fulham	42
10	Sheff Wed	41
11	Bury	40
12	Leicester	40
13	Hull	40
14	Leeds	38
15	Wolves	38
16	Barnsley	36
17	Port Vale	36
18	Nottm For	36
19	Rotherham	36
20	Stoke	35
21	Coventry	35
22	Stockport	30

DIVISION 3
1	C.Palace	59
2	Southampton	54
3	QPR	53
4	Swindon	52
5	Swansea	51
6	Watford	48
7	Millwall	47
8	Merthyr Tw	45
9	Luton	44
10	Bristol Rovers	43
11	Plymouth	43
12	Portsmouth	39
13	Grimsby	39
14	Northampton	38
15	Newport	37
16	Norwich	36
17	Southend	36
18	Brighton	36
19	Exeter	35
20	Reading	31
21	Brentford	30
22	Gillingham	28

Don't bet on it!

Enoch 'Knocker' West, who helped Manchester United win the League title in 1911 was later banned from the game for his part in a betting scandal.

1921-22

DIVISION 1

1	Liverpool	57
2	Tottenham	51
3	Burnley	49
4	Cardiff	48
5	Aston Villa	47
6	Bolton	47
7	Newcastle	46
8	Middlesbro	46
9	Chelsea	46
10	Man City	45
11	Sheff Utd	40
12	Sunderland	40
13	West Brom	40
14	Huddersfield	39
15	Blackburn	38
16	Preston	38
17	Arsenal	37
18	Birmingham	37
19	Oldham	37
20	Everton	36
21	Bradford	32
22	Man Utd	28

DIVISION 2

1	Nottm For	56
2	Stoke	52
3	Barnsley	52
4	West Ham	48
5	Hull	48
6	Gateshead	46
7	Fulham	45
8	Leeds	45
9	Leicester	45
10	Sheff Wed	44
11	Bury	40
12	Derby	39
13	Notts Co	39
14	C.Palace	39
15	L.Orient	39
16	Rotherham	39
17	Wolves	37
18	Port Vale	36
19	Blackpool	35
20	Coventry	34
21	Bradford PA	33
22	Bristol City	33

DIVISION 3 (NORTH)

1	Stockport	56
2	Darlington	50
3	Grimsby	50
4	Hartlepool	42
5	Accrington St	41
6	Crewe	41
7	Stalybridge C	41
8	Walsall	39
9	Southport	38
10	Ashington	38
11	Durham City	37
12	Wrexham	37
13	Chesterfield	35
14	Lincoln	34
15	Barrow	33
16	Nelson	33
17	Wigan Boro	31
18	Tranmere	29
19	Halifax	29
20	Rochdale	26

DIVISION 3 (SOUTH)

1	Southampton	61
2	Plymouth	61
3	Portsmouth	53
4	Luton	52
5	QPR	49
6	Swindon	45
7	Watford	44
8	Aberdare Ath	44
9	Brentford	43
10	Swansea	41
11	Merthyr Tw	40
12	Millwall	38
13	Reading	38
14	Bristol Rovers	38
15	Norwich	37
16	Charlton	37
17	Northampton	37
18	Gillingham	36
19	Brighton	35
20	Newport	34
21	Exeter	34
22	Southend	27

1922-23

DIVISION 1

1	Liverpool	60
2	Sunderland	54
3	Huddersfield	53
4	Newcastle	48
5	Everton	47
6	Aston Villa	46
7	West Brom	45
8	Man City	45
9	Cardiff	43
10	Sheff Utd	42
11	Arsenal	42
12	Tottenham	41
13	Bolton	40
14	Blackburn	40
15	Burnley	38
16	Preston	37
17	Birmingham	37
18	Middlesbro	36
19	Chelsea	36
20	Nottm For	34
21	Stoke	30
22	Oldham	30

DIVISION 2

1	Notts Co	53
2	West Ham	51
3	Leicester	51
4	Man Utd	48
5	Blackpool	47
6	Bury	47
7	Leeds	47
8	Sheff Wed	46
9	Barnsley	45
10	Fulham	44
11	Southampton	42
12	Hull	42
13	Gateshead	40
14	Derby	39
15	Bradford	37
16	C.Palace	37
17	Port Vale	37
18	Coventry	37
19	L.Orient	36
20	Stockport	36
21	Rotherham	35
22	Wolves	27

DIVISION 3 (NORTH)

1	Nelson	51
2	Bradford PA	47
3	Walsall	46
4	Chesterfield	45
5	Wigan Boro	44
6	Crewe	43
7	Halifax	41
8	Accrington St	41
9	Darlington	40
10	Wrexham	38
11	Stalybridge C	36
12	Rochdale	36
13	Lincoln	36
14	Grimsby	33
15	Hartlepool	32
16	Tranmere	32
17	Southport	31
18	Barrow	30
19	Ashington	30
20	Durham City	28

DIVISION 3 (SOUTH)

1	Bristol City	59
2	Plymouth	53
3	Swansea	53
4	Brighton	51
5	Luton	49
6	Millwall	46
7	Portsmouth	46
8	Northampton	45
9	Swindon	45
10	Watford	44
11	QPR	42
12	Charlton	42
13	Bristol Rovers	42
14	Brentford	38
15	Southend	37
16	Gillingham	37
17	Merthyr Tw	36
18	Norwich	36
19	Reading	34
20	Exeter	33
21	Aberdare Ath	29
22	Newport	27

CHAMPIONS
Huddersfield 1923-24

Huddersfield's hard-working squad shot from near-bankruptcy to a hat-trick of titles, starting in 1923-24, and were second twice after that. Legendary manager Herbert Chapman was the force behind their successes - although he left for Arsenal before the treble was completed - and the team lost only 21 games out of 126 over those three years. The first title was decided in one of the League's closest finishes - with Town finishing ahead on goal average from Cardiff, who drew their last match 0-0 after missing a penalty. Chapman's success at Huddersfield made him the top manager of the era and a second success the following year really put him in the spotlight. Before Town completed the treble, Chapman had moved to Highbury.

1923-24

DIVISION 1

1	Huddersfield	57
2	Cardiff	57
3	Sunderland	53
4	Bolton	50
5	Sheff Utd	50
6	Aston Villa	49
7	Everton	49
8	Blackburn	45
9	Newcastle	44
10	Notts Co	42
11	Man City	42
12	Liverpool	41
13	West Ham	41
14	Birmingham	39
15	Tottenham	38
16	West Brom	38
17	Burnley	36
18	Preston	34
19	Arsenal	33
20	Nottm For	32
21	Chelsea	32
22	Middlesbro	22

DIVISION 2

1	Leeds	54
2	Bury	51
3	Derby	51
4	Blackpool	49
5	Southampton	48
6	Stoke	46
7	Oldham	45
8	Sheff Wed	44
9	Gateshead	44
10	L.Orient	43
11	Barnsley	43
12	Leicester	42
13	Stockport	42
14	Man Utd	40
15	C.Palace	39
16	Port Vale	38
17	Hull	37
18	Bradford	37
19	Coventry	35
20	Fulham	34
21	Nelson	33
22	Bristol City	29

DIVISION 3 (NORTH)

1	Wolves	63
2	Rochdale	62
3	Chesterfield	54
4	Rotherham	52
5	Bradford PA	52
6	Darlington	48
7	Southport	46
8	Ashington	44
9	Doncaster	42
10	Wigan Boro	42
11	Grimsby	41
12	Tranmere	41
13	Accrington St	40
14	Halifax	40
15	Durham City	39
16	Wrexham	38
17	Walsall	36
18	New Brighton	35
19	Lincoln	32
20	Crewe	27
21	Hartlepool	25
22	Barrow	25

DIVISION 3 (SOUTH)

1	Portsmouth	59
2	Plymouth	55
3	Millwall	54
4	Swansea	52
5	Brighton	51
6	Swindon	47
7	Luton	46
8	Northampton	45
9	Bristol Rovers	43
10	Newport	43
11	Norwich	40
12	Aberdare Ath	38
13	Merthyr Tw	38
14	Charlton	37
15	Gillingham	37
16	Exeter	37
17	Brentford	36
18	Reading	35
19	Southend	34
20	Watford	33
21	Bournemouth	33
22	QPR	31

1924-25

DIVISION 1

1	Huddersfield	58
2	West Brom	56
3	Bolton	55
4	Liverpool	50
5	Bury	49
6	Newcastle	48
7	Sunderland	48
8	Birmingham	46
9	Notts Co	45
10	Man City	43
11	Cardiff	43
12	Tottenham	42
13	West Ham	42
14	Sheff Utd	39
15	Aston Villa	39
16	Blackburn	35
17	Everton	35
18	Leeds	34
19	Burnley	34
20	Arsenal	33
21	Preston	26
22	Nottm For	24

DIVISION 2

1	Leicester	59
2	Man Utd	57
3	Derby	55
4	Portsmouth	48
5	Chelsea	47
6	Wolves	46
7	Southampton	44
8	Port Vale	42
9	Gateshead	41
10	Hull	41
11	L.Orient	40
12	Fulham	40
13	Middlesbro	39
14	Sheff Wed	38
15	Barnsley	38
16	Bradford	38
17	Blackpool	37
18	Oldham	37
19	Stockport	37
20	Stoke	35
21	C.Palace	34
22	Coventry	31

DIVISION 3 (NORTH)

1	Darlington	58
2	Nelson	53
3	New Brighton	53
4	Southport	51
5	Bradford PA	50
6	Rochdale	49
7	Chesterfield	45
8	Lincoln	44
9	Halifax	43
10	Ashington	42
11	Wigan Boro	41
12	Grimsby	39
13	Durham City	39
14	Barrow	39
15	Crewe	39
16	Wrexham	38
17	Accrington St	38
18	Doncaster	38
19	Walsall	37
20	Hartlepool	35
21	Tranmere	32
22	Rotherham	21

DIVISION 3 (SOUTH)

1	Swansea	57
2	Plymouth	56
3	Bristol City	53
4	Swindon	51
5	Millwall	49
6	Newport	49
7	Exeter	47
8	Brighton	46
9	Northampton	46
10	Southend	43
11	Watford	43
12	Norwich	41
13	Gillingham	40
14	Reading	38
15	Charlton	38
16	Luton	37
17	Bristol Rovers	37
18	Aberdare Ath	37
19	QPR	36
20	Bournemouth	34
21	Brentford	25
22	Merthyr Tw	21

Broad Mean

Jimmy Broad of Millwall was top scorer in the Third Division South in the 1919-20 season, with 32 goals out of his club's 52. The remaining 20 were shared by eight other players.

1925-26

DIVISION 1			DIVISION 2	
1 Huddersfield	57		1 Sheff Wed	60
2 Arsenal	52		2 Derby	57
3 Sunderland	48		3 Chelsea	52
4 Bury	47		4 Wolves	49
5 Sheff Utd	46		5 Swansea	49
6 Aston Villa	44		6 Blackpool	45
7 Liverpool	44		7 Oldham	44
8 Bolton	44		8 Portsmouth	44
9 Man Utd	44		9 Gateshead	44
10 Newcastle	42		10 Middlesbro	44
11 Everton	42		11 Port Vale	44
12 Blackburn	41		12 Preston	43
13 West Brom	40		13 Hull	41
14 Birmingham	40		14 Southampton	38
15 Tottenham	39		15 Darlington	38
16 Cardiff	39		16 Bradford	36
17 Leicester	38		17 Nottm For	36
18 West Ham	37		18 Barnsley	36
19 Leeds	36		19 Fulham	34
20 Burnley	36		20 L.Orient	33
21 Man City	35		21 Stoke	32
22 Notts Co	33		22 Stockport	25

Luton Down

In the 1927-28 season Luton scored eight goals in two games over Christmas and did not get a point. They lost 2-4 at Charlton and then, after leading by four goals at half-time away to Northampton, they lost 5-6. Not the best Christmas present for The Hatters!

1925-26   cont

DIVISION 3 (NORTH)	
1 Grimsby	61
2 Bradford PA	60
3 Rochdale	59
4 Chesterfield	55
5 Halifax	45
6 Hartlepool	44
7 Tranmere	44
8 Nelson	43
9 Ashington	43
10 Doncaster	43
11 Crewe	43
12 New Brighton	42
13 DUurham City	42
14 Rotherham	41
15 Lincoln	39
16 Coventry	38
17 Wigan Boro	37
18 Accrington St	37
19 Wrexham	32
20 Southport	32
21 Walsall	26
22 Barrow	18

DIVISION 3 (SOUTH)	
1 Reading	57
2 Plymouth	56
3 Millwall	53
4 Bristol City	51
5 Brighton	47
6 Swindon	46
7 Luton	44
8 Bournemouth	43
9 Aberdare Ath	42
10 Gillingham	42
11 Southend	42
12 Northampton	41
13 C.Palace	41
14 Merthyr Tw	39
15 Watford	39
16 Norwich	39
17 Newport	38
18 Brentford	38
19 Bristol Rovers	36
20 Exeter	35
21 Charlton	35
22 QPR	21

1926-27

DIVISION 1	
1 Newcastle	56
2 Huddersfield	51
3 Sunderland	49
4 Bolton	48
5 Burnley	47
6 West Ham	46
7 Leicester	46
8 Sheff Utd	44
9 Liverpool	43
10 Aston Villa	43
11 Arsenal	43
12 Derby	41
13 Tottenham	41
14 Cardiff	41
15 Man Utd	40
16 Sheff Wed	39
17 Birmingham	38
18 Blackburn	38
19 Bury	36
20 Everton	34
21 Leeds	30
22 West Brom	30

DIVISION 2	
1 Middlesbro	62
2 Portsmouth	54
3 Man City	54
4 Chelsea	52
5 Nottm For	50
6 Preston	49
7 Hull	47
8 Port Vale	45
9 Blackpool	44
10 Oldham	44
11 Barnsley	43
12 Swansea	43
13 Southampton	42
14 Reading	40
15 Wolves	35
16 Notts Co	35
17 Grimsby	34
18 Fulham	34
19 Gateshead	33
20 L.Orient	31
21 Darlington	30
22 Bradford	23

WHAT A STAR ⭐ BOB CROMPTON

Not particularly big, but very powerful - thanks in part to playing water polo as a hobby - and well able to take advantage of the less-stringent rules of those days. "When Bob charged you, you went over," said a team-mate. Right-back Crompton won the remarkable total of 42 caps at international level for England, only five against continental opponents, in 12 years, and was on the losing side a mere six times. World War I ended his run, but his total was not surpassed until the Fifties. He helped Blackburn Rovers, his only club, to two Championship triumphs, and was said to be the first footballer to own a car.

WHAT A STAR ⭐ BILLY MEREDITH

He has been dead for 40 years, but remains perhaps the most famous Welsh footballer ever. A physical freak who weighed the same at 60 as he did at 20, played mostly for the two Manchester clubs as a quick, free-scoring winger until he was almost 50, claimed to have appeared in more than 1,400 matches of all sorts, and won the last of his 48 caps (all in the Home Championship) when 46. Once a miner and always a rebel, he was suspended for alleged match-fixing and he was useless at business, as he confessed when declared bankrupt. Later he became a teetotal publican. A one-off, if ever there was one.

1926-27 cont

DIVISION 3 (NORTH)

1	Stoke	63
2	Rochdale	58
3	Bradford PA	55
4	Halifax	53
5	Nelson	51
6	Stockport*	49
7	Chesterfield	47
8	Doncaster	47
9	Tranmere	46
10	New Brighton	46
11	Lincoln	42
12	Southport	39
13	Wrexham	38
14	Walsall	38
15	Crewe	37
16	Ashington	36
17	Hartlepool	34
18	Wigan Boro	32
19	Rotherham	32
20	Durham City	30
21	Accrington St	27
22	Barrow	22

* Stockport had two points deducted for fielding an illegible player

Poor Draw

Middlesbrough drew only two of their 42 Second Division games in the 1925-26 season. The Ayresome Park club won 21, lost 19 and finished ninth in the table.

DIVISION 3 (SOUTH)

1	Bristol City	62
2	Plymouth	60
3	Millwall	56
4	Brighton	53
5	Swindon	51
6	C.Palace	45
7	Bournemouth	44
8	Luton	44
9	Newport	44
10	Bristol Rovers	41
11	Brentford	40
12	Exeter	40
13	Charlton	40
14	QPR	39
15	Coventry	37
16	Norwich	35
17	Merthyr Tw	35
18	Northampton	35
19	Southend	34
20	Gillingham	32
21	Watford	32
22	Aberdare Ath	25

1927-28

DIVISION 1

1	Everton	53
2	Huddersfield	51
3	Leicester	48
4	Derby	44
5	Bury	44
6	Cardiff	44
7	Bolton	43
8	Aston Villa	43
9	Newcastle	43
10	Arsenal	41
11	Birmingham	41
12	Blackburn	41
13	Sheff Utd	40
14	Sheff Wed	39
15	Sunderland	39
16	Liverpool	39
17	West Ham	39
18	Man Utd	39
19	Burnley	39
20	Portsmouth	39
21	Tottenham	38
22	Middlesbro	37

Manchester Pity

Manchester City scored in 35 of their 42 First Division matches during 1925-26, totalling 89 goals, but finished 21st out of 22 and were relegated. They won one match 8-3 and lost the next 3-8 in the space of three days.

DIVISION 2

1	Man City	59
2	Leeds	57
3	Chelsea	54
4	Preston	53
5	Stoke	52
6	Swansea	48
7	Oldham	46
8	West Brom	46
9	Port Vale	44
10	Nottm For	40
11	Grimsby	40
12	Bristol City	39
13	Barnsley	39
14	Hull	39
15	Notts Co	38
16	Wolves	36
17	Southampton	35
18	Reading	35
19	Blackpool	34
20	L.Orient	34
21	Fulham	33
22	Gateshead	23

DIVISION 3 (NORTH)

1	Bradford PA	63
2	Lincoln	55
3	Stockport	54
4	Doncaster	53
5	Tranmere	53
6	Bradford	48
7	Darlington	47
8	Southport	45
9	Accrington St	44
10	New Brighton	42
11	Wrexham	42
12	Halifax	41
13	Rochdale	41
14	Rotherham	39
15	Hartlepool	38
16	Chesterfield	36
17	Crewe	34
18	Ashington	33
19	Barrow	31
20	Wigan Boro	30
21	Durham City	29
22	Nelson	26

Strange but true!

Sheffield United won only six matches in the Second Division in 1920-21, but avoided relegation with four points to spare after drawing 18 and losing 18. Their sole away win was 6-2 against Arsenal.

Strange but true!

The Third Division South came into being in 1921-22 and after the first 12 matches Brighton had 12 goals. But only one player had scored - Irish international Jack Doran had got the lot. He ended the season with 23 out of a total of 45.

Treble Tom

Scottish forward Tom Jennings scored 34 goals for Leeds in 1926-27, including hat-tricks in three successive games, but his club were relegated.

1927-28 cont
DIVISION 3 (SOUTH)

1	Millwall	65
2	Northampton	55
3	Plymouth	53
4	Brighton	48
5	C.Palace	48
6	Swindon	47
7	Southend	46
8	Exeter	46
9	Newport	45
10	QPR	43
11	Charlton	43
12	Brentford	40
13	Luton	39
14	Bournemouth	38
15	Watford	38
16	Gillingham	37
17	Norwich	36
18	Walsall	33
19	Bristol Rovers	32
20	Coventry	31
21	Merthyr Tw	31
22	Torquay	30

1928-29
DIVISION 1

1	Sheff Wed	52
2	Leicester	51
3	Aston Villa	50
4	Sunderland	47
5	Liverpool	46
6	Derby	46
7	Blackburn	45
8	Man City	45
9	Arsenal	45
10	Newcastle	44
11	Sheff Utd	41
12	Man Utd	41
13	Leeds	41
14	Bolton	40
15	Birmingham	40
16	Huddersfield	39
17	West Ham	39
18	Everton	38
19	Burnley	38
20	Portsmouth	36
21	Bury	31
22	Cardiff	29

1928-29 cont
DIVISION 2

1	Middlesbro	55
2	Grimsby	53
3	Bradford PA	48
4	Southampton	48
5	Notts Co	47
6	Stoke	46
7	West Brom	46
8	Blackpool	45
9	Chelsea	44
10	Tottenham	43
11	Nottm For	42
12	Hull	40
13	Preston	39
14	Millwall	39
15	Reading	39
16	Barnsley	38
17	Wolves	37
18	Oldham	37
19	Swansea	36
20	Bristol City	36
21	Port Vale	34
22	L.Orient	32

DIVISION 3 (NORTH)

1	Bradford	63
2	Stockport	62
3	Wrexham	52
4	Wigan Boro	51
5	Doncaster	50
6	Lincoln	48
7	Tranmere	47
8	Carlisle	46
9	Crewe	44
10	Gateshead	44
11	Chesterfield	41
12	Southport	40
13	Halifax	39
14	New Brighton	39
15	Nelson	39
16	Rotherham	39
17	Rochdale	36
18	Accrington St	34
19	Darlington	33
20	Barrow	28
21	Hartlepool	26
22	Ashington	23

DIVISION 3 (SOUTH)

1	Charlton	54
2	C.Palace	54
3	Northampton	52
4	Plymouth	52
5	Fulham	52
6	QPR	52
7	Luton	49
8	Watford	48
9	Bournemouth	47
10	Swindon	43
11	Coventry	42
12	Southend	41
13	Brentford	38
14	Walsall	38
15	Brighton	38
16	Newport	35
17	Norwich	34
18	Torquay	34
19	Bristol Rovers	33
20	Merthyr Tw	30
21	Exeter	29
22	Gillingham	29

1929-30
DIVISION 1

1	Sheff Wed	60
2	Derby	50
3	Man City	47
4	Aston Villa	47
5	Leeds	46
6	Blackburn	45
7	West Ham	43
8	Leicester	43
9	Sunderland	43
10	Huddersfield	43
11	Birmingham	41
12	Liverpool	41
13	Portsmouth	40
14	Arsenal	39
15	Bolton	39
16	Middlesbro	38
17	Man Utd	38
18	Grimsby	37
19	Newcastle	37
20	Sheff Utd	36
21	Burnley	36
22	Everton	35

DIVISION 2

1	Blackpool	58
2	Chelsea	55
3	Oldham	53
4	Bradford PA	50
5	Bury	49
6	West Brom	47
7	Southampton	45
8	Cardiff	44
9	Wolves	41
10	Nottm For	41
11	Stoke	40
12	Tottenham	39
13	Charlton	39
14	Millwall	39
15	Swansea	37
16	Preston	37
17	Barnsley	36
18	Bradford	36
19	Reading	35
20	Bristol City	35
21	Hull	35
22	Notts Co	33

CHAMPIONS
Middlesbrough 1926-27

Dixie Dean's feat of scoring 60 League goals for Everton in 1927-28 took a lot of the glory away from George Camsell, but in the previous year the Boro front-man had shot his club to the Second Division title almost single-handed, with 59 goals out of his club's 122. Boro were top with six points to spare and Camsell's record - achieved after he had been unable to get into the team for the first three games - seemed likely to stand for ever. The amazing Dean ensured that it did not, but Camsell went on to score 325 goals in a fine career.

CHAMPIONS
Sheffield Wednesday 1928-29

Wednesday, Second Division winners in 1926, were twice Champions of the First Division, three times third and Cup-winners once in the next nine years. Not until Don Revie's Leeds emerged in the Sixties did a Yorkshire team achieve such consistent success. Wednesday's win in 1929, inspired by inside-forward Jimmy Seed, was a close affair, but they edged it with 52 points to 51 by Leicester and 50 by Aston Villa. Throughout this successful period Wednesday had the same manager, Bob Brown - not a famous name, but a good advertisement for stability. And in Ernie Blenkinsop they had an outstanding defender who gave the club 12 excellent years' service and won all his 26 England caps while at Hillsborough.

1929-30 cont

DIVISION 3 (NORTH)			DIVISION 3 (SOUTH)	
1	Port Vale	67	1 Plymouth	68
2	Stockport	63	2 Brentford	61
3	Darlington	50	3 QPR	51
4	Chesterfield	50	4 Northampton	50
5	Lincoln	48	5 Brighton	50
6	York	46	6 Coventry	47
7	Gateshead	46	7 Fulham	47
8	Hartlepool	45	8 Norwich	46
9	Southport	43	9 C.Palace	46
10	Rochdale	43	10 Bournemouth	43
11	Crewe	42	11 Southend	43
12	Tranmere	41	12 L.Orient	41
13	New Brighton	40	13 Luton	40
14	Doncaster	39	14 Swindon	38
15	Carlisle	39	15 Watford	38
16	Acc Stanley	37	16 Exeter	35
17	Wrexham	34	17 Walsall	34
18	Wigan Boro	33	18 Newport	34
19	Nelson	33	19 Torquay	31
20	Rotherham	30	20 Bristol Rovers	30
21	Halifax	28	21 Gillingham	30
22	Barrow	27	22 Merthyr Tw	21

Strange but true!

In December and January of the 1926-27 season, Middlesbrough played eight home League games and only one away - on Christmas Day.

Good start

Ronnie Dix became the youngest scorer in League history when he notched for Bristol Rovers against Norwich in March 1928, at the age of 15. He made his debut the week before.

Merrie-Go-Round

Between 1925 and 1935, Alex Merrie was transferred seven times between Scotland and England. He played in turn for St. Mirren, Portsmouth, Ayr, Hull, Clyde, Crewe, Brechin and Aldershot.

Did you know that...

George Allison became BBC Radio's first football commentator during this era.

Did you know that...

The new offside law was introduced in 1925.

Did you know that...

Dixie Dean scored 379 League goals in his career, spanning stays at Tranmere, Everton and Notts County between 1923-1939.

Did you know that...

Fiery Scot, Hughie Gallacher, scored 387 League goals in 541 games in his time at Newcastle, Chelsea, Derby, Notts County, Grimsby and Gateshead. He also hit an amazing 22 goals in 20 games for Scotland.

1930-1949

TOP GUNNERS

The 1930s dawned with Herbert Chapman, now of course at Arsenal, still accumulating trophies at an alarming rate. The Championship ended up at Highbury in 1932-33, 1933-34 and 1934-35, repeating his achievement with Huddersfield ten years earlier. But not only did Chapman emulate his deeds with Huddersfield, he also ended a period of complete northern dominance. In fact, when Arsenal took the crown in 1932-33, it was the first time a 'southern' side had done so, with the previous 38 titles being shared out between the north and the midlands.

But although Chapman is always given credit for Arsenal's Championship hat-trick, he actually won only one, the first. Sadly, mid-way through the 1933-34 season, he died suddenly after catching a chill, following 90 minutes watching Arsenal's third team in action.

Pneumonia had set in and three days after that game, he was gone. He was succeeded as Arsenal manager by one of the club's directors George Allison - an experienced journalist with no career as a player - but by sticking to Chapman's principles, The Gunners kept on winning.

April 1936 also saw a record set which is unlikely to be broken when Luton's Joe Payne - a wing-half filling in at centre-forward - scored 10 goals against Bristol Rovers.

But just three years later World War II broke out and the Football League was once again suspended. On its resumption in the 1946-47 season, crowds were huge and over the four campaigns before the 50s, the aggregate attendance at grounds was a tasty 157 million.

The first Championship after the war was won by Liverpool, which meant the trophy had to make just a short journey across Stanley Park from Everton, who had won the last pre-war title. Merseyside were the kings of English football again.

Boxing Slay

Tranmere beat Oldham 13-4 on Boxing Day 1935, the highest-scoring Football League match in history, and lost 3-9 to Manchester City on Boxing Day two years later.

Lions Mauled

Manchester United won 2-0 away to Millwall on the last day of the 1933-34 season, and avoided relegation by a point. Millwall, nicknamed The Lions, went down instead, along with Lincoln.

Strange but true!

There were 16 instances of clubs scoring ten or more goals in a game during the 1930s, a record for any decade. Four happened in 1933-34 season - Luton 10 Torquay 2; Middlesbrough 10 Sheffield United 3; Stockport 13 Halifax 0; Barrow 12 Gateshead 1.

WHAT A STAR ⭐ DIXIE DEAN

Dixie Dean's record 60 League goals in 1927-28 remains unchallenged - the highest top-division total in a season since then is 49. He was only 21 at the time, but he was no one-season wonder. In a 12-year career he scored 379 League goals, a figure surpassed only by Arthur Rowley, and his 349 for Everton remains the most ever scored by one player for one club. He also got 18 for England in only 16 games. All this after surviving a fractured skull in a road crash, and a variety of operations made necessary by his robust style and unscrupulous opponents.

LEAGUE TABLES 1930-31 to 1948-49

1930-31

DIVISION 1

1	Arsenal	66
2	Aston Villa	59
3	Sheff Wed	52
4	Portsmouth	49
5	Huddersfield	48
6	Derby	46
7	Middlesbro	46
8	Man City	46
9	Liverpool	42
10	Blackburn	42
11	Sunderland	41
12	Chelsea	40
13	Grimsby	39
14	Bolton	39
15	Sheff Utd	38
16	Leicester	38
17	Newcastle	36
18	West Ham	36
19	Birmingham	36
20	Blackpool	32
21	Leeds	31
22	Man Utd	22

DIVISION 2

1	Everton	61
2	West Brom	54
3	Tottenham	51
4	Wolves	47
5	Port Vale	47
6	Bradford PA	46
7	Preston	45
8	Burnley	45
9	Southampton	44
10	Bradford	44
11	Stoke	44
12	Oldham	42
13	Bury	41
14	Millwall	39
15	Charlton	39
16	Bristol City	38
17	Nottm For	37
18	Plymouth	36
19	Barnsley	35
20	Swansea	34
21	Reading	30
22	Cardiff	25

DIVISION 3 (NORTH)

1	Chesterfield	58
2	Lincoln	57
3	Wrexham	54
4	Tranmere	54
5	Southport	53
6	Hull	50
7	Stockport	49
8	Carlisle	45
9	Gateshead	45
10	Wigan Boro	43
11	Darlington	42
12	York	42
13	Accrington St	39
14	Rotherham	38
15	Doncaster	37
16	Barrow	37
17	Halifax	35
18	Crewe	34
19	New Brighton	33
20	Hartlepool	30
21	Rochdale	30
22	Nelson	19

DIVISION 3 (SOUTH)

1	Notts Co	59
2	C.Palace	51
3	Brentford	50
4	Brighton	49
5	Southend	49
6	Northampton	48
7	Luton	46
8	QPR	43
9	Fulham	43
10	Bournemouth	43
11	Torquay	43
12	Swindon	42
13	Exeter	42
14	Coventry	41
15	Bristol Rovers	40
16	Gillingham	38
17	Walsall	37
18	Watford	35
19	L.Orient	35
20	Thames	34
21	Newport	28
22	Norwich	28

1931-32

DIVISION 1

1	Everton	56
2	Arsenal	54
3	Sheff Wed	50
4	Huddersfield	48
5	Aston Villa	46
6	West Brom	46
7	Sheff Utd	46
8	Portsmouth	45
9	Birmingham	44
10	Liverpool	44
11	Newcastle	42
12	Chelsea	40
13	Sunderland	40
14	Man City	38
15	Derby	38
16	Blackburn	38
17	Bolton	38
18	Middlesbro	38
19	Leicester	37
20	Blackpool	33
21	Grimsby	32
22	West Ham	31

DIVISION 2

1	Wolves	56
2	Leeds	54
3	Stoke	52
4	Plymouth	49
5	Bury	49
6	Bradford PA	49
7	Bradford	45
8	Tottenham	43
9	Millwall	43
10	Charlton	43
11	Nottm For	42
12	Man Utd	42
13	Preston	42
14	Southampton	41
15	Swansea	39
16	Notts Co	38
17	Chesterfield	37
18	Oldham	38
19	Burnley	38
20	Port Vale	33
21	Barnsley	33
22	Bristol City	23

DIVISION 3 (NORTH)

1	Lincoln	57
2	Gateshead	57
3	Chester	50
4	Tranmere	49
5	Barrow	49
6	Crewe	48
7	Southport	46
8	Hull	45
9	York	43
10	Wrexham	43
11	Darlington	38
12	Stockport	37
13	Hartlepool	37
14	Accrington St	36
15	Doncaster	36
16	Walsall	35
17	Halifax	34
18	Carlisle	33
19	Rotherham	32
20	New Brighton	24
21	Rochdale	11
22	* see footnote	

DIVISION 3 (SOUTH)

1	Fulham	57
2	Reading	55
3	Southend	53
4	C.Palace	51
5	Brentford	48
6	Luton	47
7	Exeter	47
8	Brighton	46
9	Cardiff	46
10	Norwich	46
11	Watford	46
12	Coventry	44
13	QPR	42
14	Northampton	39
15	Bournemouth	38
16	L.Orient	35
17	Swindon	34
18	Bristol Rovers	34
19	Torquay	33
20	Mansfield	32
21	Gillingham	28
22	Thames	23

Wigan Borough resigned from the League after 12 games

1932-33

DIVISION 1

1	Arsenal	58
2	Aston Villa	54
3	Sheff Wed	51
4	West Brom	49
5	Newcastle	49
6	Huddersfield	47
7	Derby	44
8	Leeds	44
9	Portsmouth	43
10	Sheff Utd	43
11	Everton	41
12	Sunderland	40
13	Birmingham	39
14	Liverpool	39
15	Blackburn	38
16	Man City	37
17	Middlesbro	37
18	Chelsea	35
19	Leicester	35
20	Wolves	35
21	Bolton	33
22	Blackpool	33

DIVISION 2

1	Stoke	56
2	Tottenham	55
3	Fulham	50
4	Bury	49
5	Nottm For	49
6	Man Utd	43
7	Millwall	43
8	Bradford PA	42
9	Preston	42
10	Swansea	42
11	Bradford	41
12	Southampton	41
13	Grimsby	41
14	Plymouth	41
15	Notts Co	40
16	Oldham	38
17	Port Vale	38
18	Lincoln	37
19	Burnley	36
20	West Ham	35
21	Chesterfield	34
22	Charlton	31

DIVISION 3 (NORTH)

1	Hull	59
2	Wrexham	57
3	Stockport	54
4	Chester	52
5	Walsall	48
6	Doncaster	48
7	Gateshead	47
8	Barnsley	46
9	Barrow	43
10	Crewe	43
11	Tranmere	42
12	Southport	41
13	Accrington St	40
14	Hartlepool	39
15	Halifax	38
16	Mansfield	35
17	Rotherham	34
18	Rochdale	33
19	Carlisle	33
20	York	32
21	New Brighton	32
22	Darlington	28

DIVISION 3 (SOUTH)

1	Brentford	62
2	Exeter	58
3	Norwich	57
4	Reading	51
5	C.Palace	46
6	Coventry	44
7	Gillingham	44
8	Northampton	44
9	Bristol Rovers	44
10	Torquay	44
11	Watford	44
12	Brighton	42
13	Southend	41
14	Luton	39
15	Bristol City	37
16	QPR	37
17	Aldershot	36
18	Bournemouth	36
19	Cardiff	31
20	L.Orient	29
21	Newport	29
22	Swindon	29

Strange but true!

What odds against two clubs from the same city drawing 4-4 on the same day? Everton were 0-3 down at Middlesbrough on March 11, 1933, and Liverpool were 4-1 up at home to Portsmouth, but both games ended 4-4.

1933-34

DIVISION 1

1	Arsenal	59
2	Huddersfield	56
3	Tottenham	49
4	Derby	45
5	Man City	45
6	Sunderland	44
7	West Brom	44
8	Blackburn	43
9	Leeds	42
10	Portsmouth	42
11	Sheff Wed	41
12	Stoke	41
13	Aston Villa	40
14	Everton	40
15	Wolves	40
16	Middlesbro	39
17	Leicester	39
18	Liverpool	38
19	Chelsea	36
20	Birmingham	36
21	Newcastle	34
22	Sheff Utd	31

DIVISION 2

1	Grimsby	59
2	Preston	52
3	Bolton	51
4	Brentford	51
5	Bradford PA	49
6	Bradford	46
7	West Ham	45
8	Port Vale	45
9	Oldham	44
10	Plymouth	43
11	Blackpool	43
12	Bury	43
13	Burnley	42
14	Southampton	38
15	Hull	38
16	Fulham	37
17	Nottm For	35
18	Notts Co	35
19	Swansea	35
20	Man Utd	34
21	Millwall	33
22	Lincoln	26

Joy & Payne

Joe Payne of Luton did not get a goal until the 37th match of 1935-36, but finished as his club's top scorer with 13 strikes, which included a record ten against Bristol Rovers.

CHAMPIONS
Plymouth Argyle 1929-1930

Argyle's success in topping the Third Division South could be put down to the old saying that "if at first you don't succeed, try, try again". From 1921-22, in the days when only Champions gained promotion, they finished second six times in succession, missing out once on goal average and twice by a single point. Then, after dropping to third and fourth, they at last made up for previous misfortunes by topping the table with 68 points in the 1929-30 season - finishing seven clear of their nearest rivals - with 98 goals, and only four defeats. The manager during this period was Bob Jack, father of transfer record-holder David and in the following term, 1930-31, Argyle managed to stay afloat in the Second Division.

1933-34 cont

DIVISION 3 (NORTH)

1	Barnsley	62
2	Chesterfield	61
3	Stockport	59
4	Walsall	53
5	Doncaster	53
6	Wrexham	51
7	Tranmere	47
8	Barrow	47
9	Halifax	44
10	Chester	40
11	Hartlepool	39
12	York	38
13	Carlisle	38
14	Crewe	36
15	New Brighton	36
16	Darlington	35
17	Mansfield	34
18	Southport	33
19	Gateshead	33
20	Accrington St	33
21	Rotherham	28
22	Rochdale	24

DIVISION 3 (SOUTH)

1	Norwich	61
2	Coventry	54
3	Reading	54
4	QPR	54
5	Charlton	52
6	Luton	52
7	Bristol Rovers	51
8	Swindon	45
9	Exeter	43
10	Brighton	43
11	L.Orient	42
12	C.Palace	41
13	Northampton	40
14	Aldershot	38
15	Watford	37
16	Southend	34
17	Gillingham	33
18	Newport	33
19	Bristol City	33
20	Torquay	33
21	Bournemouth	27
22	Cardiff	24

1934-35

DIVISION 1

1	Arsenal	58
2	Sunderland	54
3	Sheff Wed	49
4	Man City	48
5	Grimsby	45
6	Derby	45
7	Liverpool	45
8	Everton	44
9	West Brom	44
10	Stoke	42
11	Preston	42
12	Chelsea	41
13	Aston Villa	41
14	Portsmouth	40
15	Blackburn	39
16	Huddersfield	38
17	Wolves	38
18	Leeds	38
19	Birmingham	36
20	Middlesbro	34
21	Leicester	33
22	Tottenham	30

DIVISION 2

1	Brentford	61
2	Bolton	56
3	West Ham	56
4	Blackpool	53
5	Man Utd	50
6	Newcastle	48
7	Fulham	46
8	Plymouth	46
9	Nottm For	42
10	Bury	42
11	Sheff Utd	41
12	Burnley	41
13	Hull	41
14	Norwich	39
15	Bradford PA	38
16	Barnsley	38
17	Swansea	36
18	Port Vale	34
19	Southampton	34
20	Bradford	32
21	Oldham	26
22	Notts Co	25

DIVISION 3 (NORTH)

1	Doncaster	57
2	Halifax	55
3	Chester	54
4	Lincoln	51
5	Darlington	51
6	Tranmere	51
7	Stockport	47
8	Mansfield	47
9	Rotherham	45
10	Chesterfield	44
11	Wrexham	43
12	Hartlepool	41
13	Crewe	39
14	Walsall	36
15	York	36
16	New Brighton	36
17	Barrow	35
18	Accrington St	34
19	Gateshead	34
20	Rochdale	33
21	Southport	32
22	Carlisle	23

DIVISION 3 (SOUTH)

1	Charlton	61
2	Reading	53
3	Coventry	51
4	Luton	50
5	C.Palace	48
6	Watford	47
7	Northampton	46
8	Bristol Rovers	44
9	Brighton	43
10	Torquay	42
11	Exeter	41
12	Millwall	41
13	QPR	41
14	L.Orient	40
15	Bristol City	39
16	Swindon	38
17	Bournemouth	37
18	Aldershot	36
19	Cardiff	35
20	Gillingham	35
21	Southend	31
22	Newport	25

Strange but true!

Centre-forward Jack Palethorpe won promotion with Stoke in 1933 and Preston in 1934, won the FA Cup with Sheffield Wednesday in 1935, and was relegated with Aston Villa in 1936.

Score Blimey

Everton and Sunderland met four times in a month in 1933-34 and scored 27 goals between them. Everton won 6-2 and lost 0-7 in League games over Christmas, and won 6-4 in the FA Cup after a 1-1 draw.

CHAMPIONS
Arsenal 1930-31

Arsenal dominated the 1930s as no club had dominated before, finishing 14, 1, 2, 1, 1, 1, 6, 3, 1 and 5, and winning the Cup twice, despite manager Herbert Chapman's early death during the second of the hat-trick seasons. Although often derided as being defensive, they scored more goals than any other club over those ten years, in which they had 18 players capped. Ironically in 1930-31, when Alex James and the teenage sensation Cliff Bastin first led them to greatness, their 127 goals - they netted in all but one League game - did not make them top scorers: runners-up Aston Villa scored 128. But there was no denying that Arsenal were Top Gunners over that 10 year period in the thirties.

1935-36

DIVISION 1

1	Sunderland	56
2	Derby	48
3	Huddersfield	48
4	Stoke	47
5	Brentford	46
6	Arsenal	45
7	Preston	44
8	Chelsea	43
9	Man City	42
10	Portsmouth	42
11	Leeds	41
12	Birmingham	41
13	Bolton	41
14	Middlesbro	40
15	Wolves	40
16	Everton	39
17	Grimsby	39
18	West Brom	38
19	Liverpool	38
20	Sheff Wed	38
21	Aston Villa	35
22	Blackburn	33

DIVISION 2

1	Man Utd	56
2	Charlton	55
3	Sheff Utd	52
4	West Ham	52
5	Tottenham	49
6	Leicester	48
7	Plymouth	48
8	Newcastle	46
9	Fulham	44
10	Blackpool	43
11	Norwich	43
12	Bradford	43
13	Swansea	39
14	Bury	38
15	Burnley	37
16	Bradford PA	37
17	Southampton	37
18	Doncaster	37
19	Nottm For	35
20	Barnsley	33
21	Port Vale	32
22	Hull	20

DIVISION 3 (NORTH)

1	Chesterfield	60
2	Chester	55
3	Tranmere	55
4	Lincoln	53
5	Stockport	48
6	Crewe	47
7	Oldham	45
8	Hartlepool	42
9	Accrington St	42
10	Walsall	41
11	Rotherham	41
12	Darlington	40
13	Carlisle	40
14	Gateshead	40
15	Barrow	38
16	York	38
17	Halifax	37
18	Wrexham	37
19	Mansfield	37
20	Rochdale	33
21	Southport	31
22	New Brighton	24

DIVISION 3 (SOUTH)

1	Coventry	57
2	Luton	56
3	Reading	54
4	QPR	53
5	Watford	49
6	C.Palace	49
7	Brighton	44
8	Bournemouth	43
9	Notts Co	42
10	Torquay	41
11	Aldershot	40
12	Millwall	40
13	Bristol City	40
14	L.Orient	38
15	Northampton	38
16	Gillingham	37
17	Bristol Rovers	36
18	Southend	36
19	Swindon	36
20	Cardiff	36
21	Newport	31
22	Exeter	27

Count Everiss

A long-service record ended in 1948 when Bill Everiss retired as West Brom's secretary-manager, after 42 years with the club.

1936-37

DIVISION 1

1	Man City	57
2	Charlton	54
3	Arsenal	52
4	Derby	49
5	Wolves	47
6	Brentford	46
7	Middlesbro	46
8	Sunderland	44
9	Portsmouth	44
10	Stoke	42
11	Birmingham	41
12	Grimsby	41
13	Chelsea	41
14	Preston	41
15	Huddersfield	39
16	West Brom	38
17	Everton	37
18	Liverpool	35
19	Leeds	34
20	Bolton	34
21	Man Utd	32
22	Sheff Wed	30

DIVISION 2

1	Leicester	56
2	Blackpool	55
3	Bury	52
4	Newcastle	49
5	Plymouth	49
6	West Ham	49
7	Sheff Utd	46
8	Coventry	45
9	Aston Villa	44
10	Tottenham	43
11	Fulham	43
12	Blackburn	42
13	Burnley	42
14	Barnsley	41
15	Chesterfield	40
16	Swansea	37
17	Norwich	36
18	Nottm For	34
19	Southampton	34
20	Bradford PA	33
21	Bradford	30
22	Doncaster	24

Strange but true!

Carlisle were bottom of the Third Division North in 1934-35, conceding 102 goals and winning only eight games. They also lost 1-6 at home to non-League Wigan in the FA Cup.

WHAT A STAR ⭐ TOMMY LAWTON

"You'll never be as good as Dixie," said the tram conductor as the teenage Lawton, signed from Burnley, made his first-day journey to Everton. Maybe so, but Lawton was still a great player on either side of Hitler's War. He began his League career at Burnley at the age of 16, too young to sign professional forms, but four days after his 17th birthday, he smashed a hat-trick past Tottenham. He was the First Division's top scorer twice in a row, and a fine servant of his country with 23 'proper' goals to go with 25 in wartime. He later played for Chelsea, Notts County (where the gates quadrupled) and Brentford, where he had a spell as player manager, and even had an Indian summer with Arsenal when deep into his thirties.

WHAT A STAR ⭐ ALEX JAMES

He was an abrasive Scot who scored plenty of goals for Raith and Preston, despite being short and dumpy, but Arsenal manager Herbert Chapman converted him into a deep-lying inside-left...and a legend was born. James, baggy shorts below his knees, created countless goals for the flying Gunners with his passes, perfectly timed and weighted no matter how heavy the old leather ball became, no matter what the underfoot conditions. He had a shortish career, but few players of his era made more impression. And James was certainly a massive hero with the Arsenal faithful with his famous trademark of button down sleeves and baggy shorts weaving a magic wand around his opponents. His career wasn't the longest - but it was certainly one of the best.

Blackpool Shock

In 1930-31 Blackpool conceded 125 goals, including a ten and three sevens, but avoided relegation. They had a point to spare over Leeds, and TEN to spare over Manchester United.

1936-37 cont

DIVISION 3 (NORTH)		DIVISION 3 (SOUTH)	
1 Stockport	60	1 Luton	58
2 Lincoln	57	2 Notts Co	56
3 Chester	53	3 Brighton	53
4 Oldham	51	4 Watford	49
5 Hull	46	5 Reading	49
6 Hartlepool	45	6 Bournemouth	49
7 Halifax	45	7 Northampton	46
8 Wrexham	44	8 Millwall	44
9 Mansfield	44	9 QPR	45
10 Carlisle	44	10 Southend	45
11 Port Vale	44	11 Gillingham	44
12 York	43	12 L.Orient	43
13 Accrington St	41	13 Swindon	39
14 Southport	37	14 C.Palace	38
15 New Brighton	37	15 Bristol Rovers	36
16 Barrow	36	16 Bristol City	36
17 Rotherham	35	17 Walsall	36
18 Rochdale	35	18 Cardiff	35
19 Tranmere	33	19 Newport	34
20 Crewe	32	20 Torquay	32
21 Gateshead	32	21 Exeter	32
22 Darlington	30	22 Aldershot	23

Strange but true!

In 1947-48 Liverpool were beaten in four successive matches, all in the same county and all by the same score, 3-0. They lost away to Burnley, Manchester United and Bolton, and at home to Portsmouth.

1937-38

DIVISION 1		DIVISION 3 (NORTH)	
1 Arsenal	52	1 Tranmere	56
2 Wolves	51	2 Doncaster	54
3 Preston	49	3 Hull	53
4 Charlton	46	4 Oldham	51
5 Middlesbro	46	5 Gateshead	51
6 Brentford	45	6 Rotherham	50
7 Bolton	45	7 Lincoln	46
8 Sunderland	45	8 Crewe	45
9 Leeds	43	9 Chester	44
10 Chelsea	41	10 Wrexham	43
11 Liverpool	41	11 York	42
12 Blackpool	40	12 Carlisle	39
13 Derby	40	13 New Brighton	38
14 Everton	39	14 Bradford	38
15 Huddersfield	39	15 Port Vale	38
16 Leicester	39	16 Southport	38
17 Stoke	38	17 Rochdale	37
18 Birmingham	38	18 Halifax	36
19 Portsmouth	38	19 Darlington	32
20 Grimsby	38	20 Hartlepool	32
21 Man City	36	21 Barrow	32
22 West Brom	36	22 Accrington St	29

DIVISION 2		DIVISION 3 (SOUTH)	
1 Aston Villa	57	1 Millwall	56
2 Man Utd	53	2 Bristol City	55
3 Sheff Utd	53	3 QPR	53
4 Coventry	52	4 Watford	53
5 Tottenham	44	5 Brighton	51
6 Burnley	44	6 Reading	51
7 Bradford PA	43	7 C.Palace	48
8 Fulham	43	8 Swindon	44
9 West Ham	42	9 Northampton	43
10 Bury	41	10 Cardiff	42
11 Chesterfield	41	11 Notts Co	41
12 Luton	40	12 Southend	40
13 Plymouth	40	13 Bournemouth	40
14 Norwich	39	14 Mansfield	39
15 Southampton	39	15 Bristol Rovers	39
16 Blackburn	38	16 Newport	38
17 Sheff Wed	38	17 Exeter	38
18 Swansea	38	18 Aldershot	35
19 Newcastle	36	19 L.Orient	33
20 Nottm For	36	20 Torquay	30
21 Barnsley	36	21 Walsall	29
22 Stockport	31	22 Gillingham	26

1938-39

DIVISION 1

1	Everton	59
2	Wolves	55
3	Charlton	50
4	Middlesbro	49
5	Arsenal	47
6	Derby	46
7	Stoke	46
8	Bolton	45
9	Preston	44
10	Grimsby	43
11	Liverpool	42
12	Aston Villa	41
13	Leeds	41
14	Man Utd	38
15	Blackpool	38
16	Sunderland	38
17	Portsmouth	37
18	Brentford	36
19	Huddersfield	35
20	Chelsea	33
21	Birmingham	32
22	Leicester	29

DIVISION 2

1	Blackburn	55
2	Sheff Utd	54
3	Sheff Wed	53
4	Coventry	50
5	Man City	49
6	Chesterfield	49
7	Luton	49
8	Tottenham	47
9	Newcastle	46
10	West Brom	45
11	West Ham	44
12	Fulham	44
13	Millwall	42
14	Burnley	39
15	Plymouth	38
16	Bury	37
17	Bradford PA	35
18	Southampton	35
19	Swansea	34
20	Nottm For	31
21	Norwich	31
22	Tranmere	17

DIVISION 3 (NORTH)

1	Barnsley	67
2	Doncaster	56
3	Bradford	52
4	Southport	50
5	Oldham	49
6	Chester	49
7	Hull	46
8	Crewe	44
9	Stockport	43
10	Gateshead	42
11	Rotherham	42
12	Halifax	42
13	Barrow	41
14	Wrexham	41
15	Rochdale	39
16	New Brighton	39
17	Lincoln	33
18	Darlington	33
19	Carlisle	33
20	York	32
21	Hartlepool	31
22	Accrington St	20

DIVISION 3 (SOUTH)

1	Newport	55
2	C.Palace	52
3	Brighton	49
4	Watford	46
5	Reading	46
6	QPR	44
7	Ipswich	44
8	Bristol City	44
9	Swindon	44
10	Aldershot	44
11	Notts Co	43
12	Southend	41
13	Cardiff	41
14	Exeter	40
15	Bournemouth	39
16	Mansfield	39
17	Northampton	38
18	Port Vale	37
19	Torquay	37
20	L.Orient	35
21	Walsall	33
22	Bristol Rovers	33

Billy Liddellpool

Billy Liddell scored 216 goals in 492 League games for Liverpool and won 28 caps for Scotland. Such was his impact on The Reds that they were dubbed 'Liddellpool'

1939-40 (aban)

DIVISION 1

1	Blackpool	6
2	Sheff Utd	5
3	Arsenal	5
4	Liverpool	4
5	Bolton	4
6	Derby	4
7	Charlton	4
8	Stoke	3
9	Man Utd	3
10	Aston Villa	3
11	Brentford	3
12	Chelsea	3
13	Everton	3
14	Grimsby	3
15	Sunderland	3
16	Wolves	2
17	Huddersfield	2
18	Portsmouth	2
19	Preston	2
20	Blackburn	1
21	Middlesbro	1
22	Leeds	1

(abandoned)

DIVISION 2

1	Luton	5
2	Birmingham	5
3	Leicester	4
4	Coventry	4
5	Plymouth	4
6	West Ham	4
7	Tottenham	4
8	Nottm For	4
9	Millwall	3
10	Newport	3
11	West Brom	3
12	Bury	3
13	Man City	3
14	Newcastle	2
15	Chesterfield	2
16	Barnsley	2
17	Southampton	2
18	Sheff Wed	2
19	Swansea	2
20	Fulham	1
21	Burnley	1
22	Bradford PA	1

Boys Don Good

Doncaster Rovers won promotion from the Third Division North in 1947 with the remarkable total of 72 points out of a possible 84. Four years later they won the same Championship again, this time with 55 points.

CHAMPIONS
Everton 1931-32

This was the middle year in a fine Everton treble, with the Second Division title, First Division title and FA Cup being won in three successive seasons. It also contained the most remarkable scoring spell in English football history, when - incredible though it may appear - Goodison fans saw successive home victories by 9-3, 8-1, 7-2, 9-2, 5-1 and 5-0. Dixie Dean and company scored 84 goals at home, although they lost three matches, plus 32 away: Dean's 38 appearances brought him 45 goals, including two fives, a four and seven threes and made him THE biggest star ever to grace Goodison Park. The Blues were managed by Thomas McIntosh, who was in charge at the club for 16 years.

CHAMPIONS
Portsmouth 1948-49

Among the outstanding feats of the early post-war years were Portsmouth's two successive Championships, the first of them being achieved in style by a squad without a single international - although Jimmy Dickinson, Peter Harris, Len Phillips and Jack Froggatt were later capped by England and Jimmy Scoular by Scotland. The double looked likely until Second Division Leicester surprisingly won a Highbury Semi-Final to stop the Fratton Park men reaching the FA Cup Final, but Pompey did not allow the blow to affect them, and finished five points ahead of the highly-rated Manchester United to pick up the Championship trophy. The South Coast hasn't seen a party like it since!

Your number's up!

The compulsory numbering on shirts was brought into place in 1939, one year after the laws of the game were re-written

1939-40 cont
DIVISION 3 (NORTH)

1	Accrington St	6
2	Halifax	5
3	Chester	5
4	Darlington	5
5	New Brighton	4
6	Rochdale	4
7	Wrexham	4
8	Tranmere	3
9	Lincoln	3
10	Rotherham	3
11	Crewe	2
12	Carlisle	2
13	Hull	2
14	Gateshead	2
15	Barrow	2
16	Doncaster	2
17	Southport	2
18	Oldham	2
19	Hartlepool	2
20	York	1
21	Bradford	1
22	Stockport	0

(Div 3s abandoned)
DIVISION 3 (SOUTH)

1	Reading	5
2	C.Palace	5
3	Notts Co	4
4	Exeter	4
5	Brighton	4
6	Cardiff	4
7	L.Orient	4
8	Bournemouth	3
9	Bristol City	3
10	Ipswich	3
11	Mansfield	3
12	Norwich	3
13	Southend	3
14	Torquay	3
15	Walsall	3
16	QPR	2
17	Watford	2
18	Northampton	2
19	Aldershot	1
20	Swindon	1
21	Bristol Rovers	1
22	Port Vale	1

Tied in Notts

Tommy Lawton became the first player to break the £20,000 transfer mark when he moved from Chelsea to Notts County in 1947

1946-47
LEAGUE DIVISION 1

1	Liverpool	57
2	Man Utd	56
3	Wolves	56
4	Stoke	55
5	Blackpool	50
6	Sheff Utd	49
7	Preston	47
8	Aston Villa	45
9	Sunderland	44
10	Everton	43
11	Middlesbro	42
12	Portsmouth	41
13	Arsenal	41
14	Derby	41
15	Chelsea	39
16	Grimsby	38
17	Blackburn	36
18	Bolton	34
19	Charlton	34
20	Huddersfield	33
21	Brentford	25
22	Leeds	18

LEAGUE DIVISION 2

1	Man City	62
2	Burnley	58
3	Birmingham	55
4	Chesterfield	50
5	Newcastle	48
6	Tottenham	48
7	West Brom	48
8	Coventry	45
9	Leicester	43
10	Barnsley	42
11	Nottm For	40
12	West Ham	40
13	Luton	39
14	Southampton	39
15	Fulham	39
16	Bradford PA	39
17	Bury	36
18	Millwall	36
19	Plymouth	33
20	Sheff Wed	32
21	Swansea	29
22	Newport	23

DIVISION 3 (NORTH)

1	Doncaster	72
2	Rotherham	64
3	Chester	56
4	Stockport	50
5	Bradford	50
6	Rochdale	48
7	Wrexham	46
8	Crewe	43
9	Barrow	41
10	Tranmere	41
11	Hull	40
12	Lincoln	39
13	Hartlepool	39
14	Gateshead	38
15	York	37
16	Carlisle	37
17	Darlington	36
18	New Brighton	36
19	Oldham	32
20	Accrington St	32
21	Southport	25
22	Halifax	22

DIVISION 3 (SOUTH)

1	Cardiff	66
2	QPR	57
3	Bristol City	51
4	Swindon	49
5	Walsall	46
6	Ipswich	46
7	Bournemouth	44
8	Southend	44
9	Reading	43
10	Port Vale	43
11	Torquay	42
12	Notts Co	40
13	Northampton	40
14	Bristol Rovers	40
15	Exeter	39
16	Watford	39
17	Brighton	38
18	C.Palace	37
19	L.Orient	32
20	Aldershot	32
21	Norwich	28
22	Mansfield	28

1947-48

DIVISION 1

1	Arsenal	59
2	Man Utd	52
3	Burnley	52
4	Derby	50
5	Wolves	47
6	Aston Villa	47
7	Preston	47
8	Portsmouth	45
9	Blackpool	44
10	Man City	42
11	Liverpool	42
12	Sheff Utd	42
13	Charlton	40
14	Everton	40
15	Stoke	38
16	Middlesbro	37
17	Bolton	37
18	Chelsea	37
19	Huddersfield	36
20	Sunderland	36
21	Blackburn	32
22	Grimsby	22

DIVISION 2

1	Birmingham	59
2	Newcastle	56
3	Southampton	52
4	Sheff Wed	51
5	Cardiff	47
6	West Ham	46
7	West Brom	45
8	Tottenham	44
9	Leicester	43
10	Coventry	41
11	Fulham	40
12	Barnsley	40
13	Luton	40
14	Bradford PA	40
15	Brentford	40
16	Chesterfield	39
17	Plymouth	38
18	Leeds	36
19	Nottm For	35
20	Bury	34
21	Doncaster	29
22	Millwall	29

DIVISION 3 (NORTH)

1	Lincoln	60
2	Rotherham	59
3	Wrexham	50
4	Gateshead	49
5	Hull	47
6	Accrington St	46
7	Barrow	45
8	Mansfield	45
9	Carlisle	43
10	Crewe	43
11	Oldham	41
12	Rochdale	41
13	York	40
14	Bradford	40
15	Southport	39
16	Darlington	39
17	Stockport	38
18	Tranmere	36
19	Hartlepool	36
20	Chester	35
21	Halifax	27
22	New Brighton	25

DIVISION 3 (SOUTH)

1	QPR	61
2	Bournemouth	57
3	Walsall	51
4	Ipswich	49
5	Swansea	48
6	Notts Co	46
7	Bristol City	43
8	Port Vale	43
9	Southend	43
10	Reading	41
11	Exeter	41
12	Newport	41
13	C.Palace	39
14	Northampton	39
15	Watford	38
16	Swindon	36
17	L.Orient	36
18	Torquay	35
19	Aldershot	35
20	Bristol Rovers	34
21	Norwich	34
22	Brighton	34

Strange but true!

Nat Lofthouse was a miner before he became one of football's top centre-forwards with Bolton. He would start work at 4.00am on Saturdays and do an eight hour shift down the pits before playing.

Ton of Talent

Arsenal star Dennis Compton scored 123 centuries in his time as one of England's greatest cricketers. His brother Leslie won one cap for his country at football.

1948-49

DIVISION 1

1	Portsmouth	58
2	Man Utd	53
3	Derby	53
4	Newcastle	52
5	Arsenal	49
6	Wolves	46
7	Man City	45
8	Sunderland	43
9	Charlton	42
10	Aston Villa	42
11	Stoke	41
12	Liverpool	40
13	Chelsea	38
14	Bolton	38
15	Burnley	38
16	Blackpool	38
17	Birmingham	37
18	Everton	37
19	Middlesbro	34
20	Huddersfield	34
21	Preston	33
22	Sheff Utd	33

DIVISION 2

1	Fulham	57
2	West Brom	56
3	Southampton	55
4	Cardiff	51
5	Tottenham	50
6	Chesterfield	47
7	West Ham	46
8	Sheff Wed	43
9	Barnsley	40
10	Luton	40
11	Grimsby	40
12	Bury	40
13	QPR	39
14	Blackburn	38
15	Leeds	37
16	Coventry	37
17	Bradford PA	37
18	Brentford	36
19	Leicester	36
20	Plymouth	36
21	Nottm For	35
22	Lincoln	28

DIVISION 3 (NORTH)

1	Hull	65
2	Rotherham	62
3	Doncaster	50
4	Darlington	46
5	Gateshead	45
6	Oldham	45
7	Rochdale	45
8	Stockport	43
9	Wrexham	43
10	Mansfield	43
11	Tranmere	41
12	Crewe	41
13	Barrow	40
14	York	39
15	Carlisle	39
16	Hartlepool	38
17	New Brighton	36
18	Chester	35
19	Halifax	35
20	Accrington St	34
21	Southport	31
22	Bradford	29

DIVISION 3 (SOUTH)

1	Swansea	62
2	Reading	55
3	Bournemouth	52
4	Swindon	51
5	Bristol Rovers	48
6	Brighton	48
7	Ipswich	45
8	Millwall	45
9	Torquay	45
10	Norwich	44
11	Notts Co	43
12	Exeter	40
13	Port Vale	39
14	Walsall	38
15	Newport	37
16	Bristol City	36
17	Watford	35
18	Southend	34
19	L.Orient	34
20	Northampton	33
21	Aldershot	33
22	C.Palace	27

Swift action

One of the greatest goalkeepers in English football history, Frank Swift, was a special constable in Manchester in the early part of World War II - but his beat wasn't always a happy one. "On my very first day on traffic duty," he recalled. "I got everything so muddled that, on the advice of a colleague, I walked away leaving the traffic to sort itself out. I felt at that moment how many full-backs must have felt when they tried to stop Stanley Matthews in his tracks!"

1950-1959

LEGENDS ARE LOST

Manchester United and Wolves dominated the 50s, winning three Championships apiece, but with very different styles. United were the purists and under the management of Matt Busby - later to become Sir Matt - they were a joy to watch. Wolves, on the other hand, were more direct under Stan Cullis' stewardship and some critics labelled their style 'kick and rush'.

Cullis, though, was unrepentant. "Our forwards are not encouraged to parade their ability in ostentatious fashion," he said, preferring instead for the ball to be played as quickly as possible into the opponents' penalty area and to be kept there. But although Wolves won few friends with their no-nonsense style, there was no arguing with their success rate and titles in 1953-54, 1957-58 and 1958-59 bear testimony to that.

However, whether they would have enjoyed so much success were it not for a fateful afternoon in Germany in February 1958 no-one will ever know. Manchester United had already won the Championship in 1951-52, 1955-56 and 1956-57 and by now were beginning to make a real impression in Europe. But it was on the way back from one of their European adventures - a Champions' Cup match against Red Star Belgrade - that tragedy struck the team known as the Busby Babes.

The plane carrying the team home was forced to land at Munich airport because of the bad flying conditions, but the aircraft crashed in the ice on the runway with heartbreaking consequences.

Among the 23 people who lost their lives were eight players - Roger Byrne, Geoff Bent, Eddie Colman, Mark Jones, Bill Whelan, Tommy Taylor, David Pegg and Duncan Edwards - the latter having been an England international by the time he was 17 and who would surely have become one of football's true great players.

And had that team survived, who knows what they would have achieved and how history would have been altered? Football was a big loser for that fateful day in Munich.

Few Blues

Chelsea's one and only League Championship, in 1954-55, was achieved with 52 points - the lowest total by a title-winning team in a 42-match season, but enough to give them a four-point margin. They won 20 games, drew 12 and lost 10.

By Royals Command

Two successive home games in 1946 contained four hat-tricks by Reading players. Magnus McPhee scored four and three goals and Maurice Edelston two triples in emphatic wins for The Royals over Crystal Palace, 10-2, and Southend, 7-2.

LEAGUE TABLES 1949-50 to 1959-60

1949-50

DIVISION 1		DIVISION 3 (NORTH)	
1 Portsmouth	53	1 Doncaster	55
2 Wolves	53	2 Gateshead	53
3 Sunderland	52	3 Rochdale	51
4 Man Utd	50	4 Lincoln	51
5 Newcastle	50	5 Tranmere	49
6 Arsenal	49	6 Rotherham	48
7 Blackpool	49	7 Crewe	48
8 Liverpool	48	8 Mansfield	48
9 Middlesbro	47	9 Carlisle	47
10 Burnley	45	10 Stockport	45
11 Derby	44	11 Oldham	43
12 Aston Villa	42	12 Chester	40
13 Chelsea	40	13 Accrington St	39
14 West Brom	40	14 New Brighton	38
15 Huddersfield	37	15 Barrow	37
16 Bolton	34	16 Southport	37
17 Fulham	34	17 Darlington	35
18 Everton	34	18 Hartlepool	33
19 Stoke	34	19 Bradford	32
20 Charlton	32	20 Wrexham	32
21 Man City	29	21 Halifax	32
22 Birmingham	28	22 York	31

DIVISION 2		DIVISION 3 (SOUTH)	
1 Tottenham	61	1 Notts Co	58
2 Sheff Wed	52	2 Northampton	51
3 Sheff Utd	52	3 Southend	51
4 Southampton	52	4 Nottm For	49
5 Leeds	47	5 Torquay	48
6 Preston	45	6 Watford	45
7 Hull	45	7 C.Palace	44
8 Swansea	43	8 Brighton	44
9 Brentford	43	9 Bristol Rovers	43
10 Cardiff	42	10 Reading	42
11 Grimsby	40	11 Norwich	42
12 Coventry	39	12 Bournemouth	42
13 Barnsley	39	13 Port Vale	41
14 Chesterfield	39	14 Swindon	41
15 Leicester	39	15 Bristol City	40
16 Blackburn	38	16 Exeter	39
17 Luton	38	17 Ipswich	35
18 Bury	37	18 L.Orient	35
19 West Ham	36	19 Walsall	34
20 QPR	34	20 Aldershot	34
21 Plymouth	32	21 Newport	34
22 Bradford PA	31	22 Millwall	32

1950-51

DIVISION 1		DIVISION 2	
1 Tottenham	60	1 Preston	57
2 Man Utd	56	2 Man City	52
3 Blackpool	50	3 Cardiff	50
4 Newcastle	49	4 Birmingham	49
5 Arsenal	47	5 Leeds	48
6 Middlesbro	47	6 Blackburn	46
7 Portsmouth	47	7 Coventry	45
8 Bolton	45	8 Sheff Utd	44
9 Liverpool	43	9 Brentford	44
10 Burnley	42	10 Hull	43
11 Derby	40	11 Doncaster	43
12 Sunderland	40	12 Southampton	43
13 Stoke	40	13 West Ham	42
14 Wolves	38	14 Leicester	41
15 Aston Villa	37	15 Barnsley	40
16 West Brom	37	16 QPR	40
17 Charlton	37	17 Notts Co	39
18 Fulham	37	18 Swansea	36
19 Huddersfield	36	19 Luton	32
20 Chelsea	32	20 Bury	32
21 Sheff Wed	32	21 Chesterfield	30
22 Everton	32	22 Grimsby	28

CHAMPIONS
Tottenham 1950-51

Spurs achieved the rare feat of topping the Second and First Divisions in successive seasons, with a virtually unchanged staff. Manager Arthur Rowe knew that his men were good enough to succeed, with their brand of 'push and run' teamwork allied to a lot of individual skill from the likes of Ted Ditchburn, Alf Ramsey, Bill Nicholson, Ron Burgess and Eddie Baily. Blackpool's 4-1 win on the opening day was one of only two home defeats, there was one run of eight consecutive wins, and the average gate at a grateful White Hart Lane was more than 55,000.

WHAT A STAR ⭐ JOE MERCER

His career with Everton and Arsenal lasted almost 20 years, in which he switched from an attacking wing-half to something like a second central defender, always using the ball well and winning it surprisingly often for a man whose legs "wouldn't last a postman his morning round', as Dixie Dean said. Above all, he was an inspirational captain, never better than in adversity. 'Uncle Joe' later became an equally inspirational manager and had a caretaker spell in charge of England as well as a successful time at Manchester City with Malcolm Allison. Sadly, he died on his 76th birthday but he will always be remembered around the world as one of football's gentlemen.

1950-51 cont

DIVISION 3 (NORTH)

1	Rotherham	71
2	Mansfield	64
3	Carlisle	62
4	Tranmere	59
5	Lincoln	58
6	Bradford PA	54
7	Bradford	52
8	Gateshead	50
9	Crewe	48
10	Stockport	48
11	Rochdale	45
12	Scunthorpe	44
13	Chester	43
14	Wrexham	42
15	Oldham	40
16	Hartlepool	39
17	York	39
18	Darlington	39
19	Barrow	38
20	Shrewsbury	37
21	Southport	36
22	Halifax	34
23	Accrington St	32
24	New Brighton	30

DIVISION 3 (SOUTH)

1	Nottm For	70
2	Norwich	64
3	Reading	57
4	Plymouth	57
5	Millwall	56
6	Bristol Rovers	55
7	Southend	52
8	Ipswich	52
9	Bournemouth	51
10	Bristol City	51
11	Newport	47
12	Port Vale	45
13	Brighton	43
14	Exeter	42
15	Walsall	40
16	Colchester	40
17	Swindon	40
18	Aldershot	40
19	L.Orient	38
20	Torquay	37
21	Northampton	36
22	Gillingham	35
23	Watford	29
24	C.Palace	27

1951-52

DIVISION 1

1	Man Utd	57
2	Tottenham	53
3	Arsenal	53
4	Portsmouth	48
5	Bolton	48
6	Aston Villa	49
7	Preston	46
8	Newcastle	45
9	Blackpool	45
10	Charlton	44
11	Liverpool	43
12	Sunderland	42
13	West Brom	41
14	Burnley	40
15	Man City	39
16	Wolves	38
17	Derby	37
18	Middlesbro	36
19	Chelsea	36
20	Stoke	31
21	Huddersfield	28
22	Fulham	27

DIVISION 2

1	Sheff Wed	53
2	Cardiff	51
3	Birmingham	51
4	Nottm For	49
5	Leicester	47
6	Leeds	47
7	Everton	44
8	Luton	44
9	Rotherham	42
10	Brentford	42
11	Sheff Utd	41
12	West Ham	41
13	Southampton	41
14	Blackburn	40
15	Notts Co	39
16	Doncaster	38
17	Bury	37
18	Hull	37
19	Swansea	36
20	Barnsley	36
21	Coventry	34
22	QPR	34

DIVISION 3 (NORTH)

1	Lincoln	69
2	Grimsby	66
3	Stockport	59
4	Oldham	57
5	Gateshead	53
6	Mansfield	52
7	Carlisle	51
8	Bradford PA	50
9	Hartlepool	50
10	York	49
11	Tranmere	48
12	Barrow	46
13	Chesterfield	45
14	Scunthorpe	44
15	Bradford	42
16	Crewe	42
17	Southport	41
18	Wrexham	39
19	Chester	39
20	Halifax	35
21	Rochdale	35
22	Accrington St	32
23	Darlington	31
24	Workington	29

DIVISION 3 (SOUTH)

1	Plymouth	66
2	Reading	61
3	Norwich	61
4	Millwall	58
5	Brighton	58
6	Newport	54
7	Bristol Rovers	52
8	Northampton	49
9	Southend	48
10	Colchester	46
11	Torquay	44
12	Aldershot	44
13	Port Vale	43
14	Bournemouth	42
15	Bristol City	42
16	Swindon	42
17	Ipswich	41
18	L.Orient	41
19	C.Palace	39
20	Shrewsbury	36
21	Watford	36
22	Gillingham	35
23	Exeter	35
24	Walsall	31

Strange but true!

Liverpool achieved a remarkable 'feat' by conceding ten penalties in the course of eight successive games during 1954-55. Nine led to goals, one was saved.

Sheffield Steal

Sheffield Wednesday were second to Spurs in Division Two in 1950, and promoted, but neighbours United were third and stayed behind, although they had the same points and goal difference - 19. Goals average was used in those days, and Wednesday had 1.3958 to United's 1.3877.

WHAT A STAR ⭐ NAT LOFTHOUSE

He earned the title 'Lion of Vienna' for his exploits in an England shirt, and scored 30 goals in 33 games for his country, but Lofthouse was even more influential at club level. His 255 League goals for his beloved Bolton is a figure surpassed by only seven other players, and he was very much a one-man forward line for some of his long career. A strong, brave and talented centre-forward of the old type, Lofthouse was Footballer of the Year in 1953, when he was a Cup Final loser, but got his reward with two goals in the 1958 Final, in which Bolton beat Manchester United 2-0.

That's Taylor-made

Frank Taylor became manager of Wolves and his brother Jack became manager of Queens Park Rangers in the same month - June 1952.

1952-53

DIVISION 1		DIVISION 2	
1 Arsenal	54	1 Sheff Utd	60
2 Preston	54	2 Huddersfield	58
3 Wolves	51	3 Luton	52
4 West Brom	50	4 Plymouth	49
5 Charlton	49	5 Leicester	48
6 Burnley	48	6 Birmingham	48
7 Blackpool	47	7 Nottm For	44
8 Man Utd	46	8 Fulham	44
9 Sunderland	43	9 Blackburn	44
10 Tottenham	41	10 Leeds	43
11 Aston Villa	41	11 Swansea	42
12 Cardiff	40	12 Rotherham	41
13 Middlesbro	39	13 Doncaster	40
14 Bolton	39	14 West Ham	39
15 Portsmouth	38	15 Lincoln	39
16 Newcastle	37	16 Everton	38
17 Liverpool	36	17 Brentford	37
18 Sheff Wed	35	18 Hull	36
19 Chelsea	35	19 Notts Co	36
20 Man City	35	20 Bury	35
21 Stoke	34	21 Southampton	33
22 Derby	32	22 Barnsley	18

Brighton Rocked

New Brighton won their first four matches in 1950-51, all 1-0, and were top of the Third Division North. They finished bottom, failed to gain re-election, and have never got back.

1952-53   cont
DIVISION 3 (NORTH)

1 Oldham	59
2 Port Vale	58
3 Wrexham	56
4 York	53
5 Grimsby	52
6 Southport	51
7 Bradford PA	50
8 Gateshead	49
9 Carlisle	49
10 Crewe	48
11 Stockport	47
12 Chesterfield	47
13 Tranmere	47
14 Halifax	47
15 Scunthorpe	46
16 Bradford	46
17 Hartlepool	46
18 Mansfield	46
19 Barrow	44
20 Chester	37
21 Darlington	34
22 Rochdale	33
23 Workington	32
24 Accrington St	27

DIVISION 3 (SOUTH)

1 Bristol Rovers	64
2 Millwall	62
3 Northampton	62
4 Norwich	60
5 Bristol City	59
6 Coventry	50
7 Brighton	50
8 Southend	49
9 Bournemouth	47
10 Watford	47
11 Reading	46
12 Torquay	45
13 C.Palace	43
14 L.Orient	42
15 Newport	42
16 Ipswich	41
17 Exeter	40
18 Swindon	40
19 Aldershot	39
20 QPR	39
21 Gillingham	39
22 Colchester	38
23 Shrewsbury	36
24 Walsall	24

1953-54
DIVISION 1

1 Wolves	57
2 West Brom	53
3 Huddersfield	51
4 Man Utd	48
5 Bolton	48
6 Blackpool	48
7 Burnley	46
8 Chelsea	44
9 Charlton	44
10 Cardiff	44
11 Preston	43
12 Arsenal	43
13 Aston Villa	41
14 Portsmouth	39
15 Newcastle	38
16 Tottenham	37
17 Man City	37
18 Sunderland	36
19 Sheff Wed	36
20 Sheff Utd	33
21 Middlesbro	30
22 Liverpool	28

DIVISION 2

1 Leicester	56
2 Everton	56
3 Blackburn	55
4 Nottm For	52
5 Rotherham	49
6 Luton	48
7 Birmingham	47
8 Fulham	44
9 Bristol Rovers	44
10 Leeds	43
11 Stoke	41
12 Doncaster	41
13 West Ham	39
14 Notts Co	39
15 Hull	38
16 Lincoln	37
17 Bury	36
18 Derby	35
19 Plymouth	34
20 Swansea	34
21 Brentford	31
22 Oldham	25

That's home

The Football League's headquarters in Lytham St Annes, Lancashire was formerly a private hotel and was purchased in 1959 for £11,000 with improvements costing a further £40,000.

1953-54 cont

DIVISION 3 (NORTH)		DIVISION 3 (SOUTH)	
1 Port Vale	69	1 Ipswich	64
2 Barnsley	58	2 Brighton	61
3 Scunthorpe	57	3 Bristol City	56
4 Gateshead	55	4 Watford	52
5 Bradford	53	5 Northampton	51
6 Chesterfield	52	6 Southampton	51
7 Mansfield	51	7 Norwich	51
8 Wrexham	51	8 Reading	49
9 Bradford PA	50	9 Exeter	48
10 Stockport	47	10 Gillingham	48
11 Southport	46	11 L.Orient	47
12 Barrow	44	12 Millwall	47
13 Carlisle	43	13 Torquay	46
14 Tranmere	43	14 Coventry	45
15 Accrington St	42	15 Newport	44
16 Crewe	41	16 Southend	43
17 Grimsby	41	17 Aldershot	43
18 Hartlepool	40	18 QPR	42
19 Rochdale	40	19 Bournemouth	40
20 Workington	40	20 Swindon	40
21 Darlington	38	21 Shrewsbury	40
22 York	37	22 C.Palace	40
23 Halifax	34	23 Colchester	30
24 Chester	32	24 Walsall	26

Seventh Heaven

Wolves, title-winners in 1953-54, scored 96 goals but had only seven scorers - Wilshaw 26, Hancocks 24, Swinbourne 24, Broadbent 12, Mullen 7, Slater 2 and Smith 1.

1954-55

DIVISION 1		DIVISION 3 (NORTH)	
1 Chelsea	52	1 Barnsley	65
2 Wolves	48	2 Accrington St	61
3 Portsmouth	48	3 Scunthorpe	58
4 Sunderland	48	4 York	58
5 Man Utd	47	5 Hartlepool	55
6 Aston Villa	47	6 Chesterfield	54
7 Man City	46	7 Gateshead	52
8 Newcastle	43	8 Workington	50
9 Arsenal	43	9 Stockport	48
10 Burnley	43	10 Oldham	48
11 Everton	42	11 Southport	48
12 Huddersfield	41	12 Rochdale	48
13 Sheff Utd	41	13 Mansfield	45
14 Preston	40	14 Halifax	43
15 Charlton	40	15 Darlington	42
16 Tottenham	40	16 Bradford PA	41
17 West Brom	40	17 Barrow	40
18 Bolton	39	18 Wrexham	38
19 Blackpool	38	19 Tranmere	37
20 Cardiff	37	20 Carlisle	36
21 Leicester	35	21 Bradford	36
22 Sheff Wed	26	22 Crewe	34
		23 Grimsby	34
		24 Chester	33

DIVISION 2		DIVISION 3 (SOUTH)	
1 Birmingham	54	1 Bristol City	70
2 Luton	54	2 L.Orient	61
3 Rotherham	54	3 Southampton	59
4 Leeds	53	4 Gillingham	55
5 Stoke	52	5 Millwall	51
6 Blackburn	50	6 Brighton	50
7 Notts Co	48	7 Watford	50
8 West Ham	46	8 Torquay	48
9 Bristol Rovers	45	9 Coventry	47
10 Swansea	43	10 Southend	46
11 Liverpool	42	11 Brentford	46
12 Middlesbro	42	12 Norwich	46
13 Bury	41	13 Northampton	46
14 Fulham	39	14 Aldershot	45
15 Nottm For	39	15 QPR	44
16 Lincoln	36	16 Shrewsbury	42
17 Port Vale	35	17 Bournemouth	42
18 Doncaster	35	18 Reading	41
19 Hull	34	19 Newport	38
20 Plymouth	31	20 C.Palace	38
21 Ipswich	28	21 Swindon	37
22 Derby	23	22 Exeter	37
		23 Walsall	34
		24 Colchester	31

CHAMPIONS
Manchester United 1951-52

The legendary Matt Busby, appointed manager with no experience of management at any level, was born to the job. In the first five post-war seasons he took United to second place four times and fourth once, before getting them to the top at last with a mixture of veterans and youngsters. Johnny Carey still organised the defence, Jack 'Bomber' Rowley hit a club record 30 League goals, and the whole unit ran like clockwork. This was United's third Championship, but their first for 40 years and in some ways the most satisfying, even today.

1955-56

DIVISION 1

1	Man Utd	60
2	Blackpool	49
3	Wolves	49
4	Man City	46
5	Arsenal	46
6	Birmingham	45
7	Burnley	44
8	Bolton	43
9	Sunderland	43
10	Luton	42
11	Newcastle	41
12	Portsmouth	41
13	West Brom	41
14	Charlton	40
15	Everton	40
16	Chelsea	39
17	Cardiff	39
18	Tottenham	37
19	Preston	36
20	Aston Villa	35
21	Huddersfield	35
22	Sheff Utd	33

DIVISION 2

1	Sheff Wed	55
2	Leeds	52
3	Liverpool	48
4	Blackburn	48
5	Leicester	48
6	Bristol Rovers	48
7	Nottm For	47
8	Lincoln	46
9	Fulham	46
10	Swansea	46
11	Bristol City	45
12	Port Vale	45
13	Stoke	44
14	Middlesbro	40
15	Bury	40
16	West Ham	39
17	Doncaster	35
18	Barnsley	34
19	Rotherham	33
20	Notts Co	31
21	Plymouth	28
22	Hull	26

DIVISION 3 (NORTH)

1	Grimsby	68
2	Derby	63
3	Accrington St	59
4	Hartlepool	57
5	Southport	57
6	Chesterfield	54
7	Stockport	51
8	Bradford	49
9	Scunthorpe	48
10	Workington	47
11	York	47
12	Rochdale	47
13	Gateshead	45
14	Wrexham	42
15	Darlington	41
16	Tranmere	41
17	Chester	40
18	Mansfield	39
19	Halifax	39
20	Oldham	38
21	Carlisle	38
22	Barrow	37
23	Bradford PA	33
24	Crewe	28

DIVISION 3 (SOUTH)

1	L.Orient	66
2	Brighton	65
3	Ipswich	64
4	Southend	53
5	Torquay	52
6	Brentford	52
7	Norwich	51
8	Coventry	49
9	Bournemouth	48
10	Gillingham	48
11	Northampton	47
12	Colchester	47
13	Shrewsbury	46
14	Southampton	44
15	Aldershot	40
16	Exeter	40
17	Reading	39
18	QPR	39
19	Newport	39
20	Walsall	38
21	Watford	37
22	Millwall	36
23	C.Palace	34
24	Swindon	30

1956-57

DIVISION 1

1	Man Utd	64
2	Tottenham	56
3	Preston	56
4	Blackpool	53
5	Arsenal	50
6	Wolves	48
7	Burnley	46
8	Leeds	44
9	Bolton	44
10	Aston Villa	43
11	West Brom	42
12	Birmingham	39
13	Chelsea	39
14	Sheff Wed	38
15	Everton	38
16	Luton	37
17	Newcastle	36
18	Man City	35
19	Portsmouth	33
20	Sunderland	32
21	Cardiff	29
22	Charlton	22

DIVISION 2

1	Leicester	61
2	Nottm For	54
3	Liverpool	53
4	Blackburn	52
5	Stoke	48
6	Middlesbro	48
7	Sheff Utd	46
8	West Ham	46
9	Bristol Rovers	45
10	Swansea	45
11	Fulham	42
12	Huddersfield	42
13	Bristol City	41
14	Doncaster	40
15	L.Orient	40
16	Grimsby	39
17	Rotherham	37
18	Lincoln	34
19	Barnsley	34
20	Notts Co	30
21	Bury	25
22	Port Vale	22

WHAT A STAR ⭐ TOM FINNEY

A great player who did not get his due reward from the game in terms of medals or money, although few have had better international careers. He scored 30 goals in 76 games on England's wing, and also possessed superb ball control, pace off the mark and astute passing, with either foot. He was Bill Shankly's favourite player - "Nothing to look at, but just give him a ball!" - and twice Footballer of the Year. Preston, his one and only club, named a stand after him. Few players have had such a tribute and none has deserved it more, although one Second Division Championship was his only title.

WHAT A STAR ⭐ DON REVIE

Long before he was a controversial manager he was a controversial player, and Footballer of the Year in 1955 when Manchester City copied the Hungarian deep-lying centre-forward plan with some success. He ate up the ground with his long stride and was a hard man to better, in a tackle or an argument. Revie began at Second Division Leicester, helping them to a Cup Final he missed because of illness, and provided plenty of entertainment at Sunderland, Leeds and Hull before turning Leeds into one of the world's best teams. He left for Saudi Arabia after an unhappy spell as England boss.

1956-57 cont
DIVISION 3 (NORTH)
1	Derby	63
2	Hartlepool	59
3	Accrington St	58
4	Workington	58
5	Stockport	54
6	Chesterfield	53
7	York	52
8	Hull	52
9	Bradford	52
10	Barrow	51
11	Halifax	49
12	Wrexham	48
13	Rochdale	48
14	Scunthorpe	45
15	Carlisle	45
16	Mansfield	44
17	Gateshead	44
18	Darlington	42
19	Oldham	39
20	Bradford PA	35
21	Chester	33
22	Southport	32
23	Tranmere	27
24	Crewe	21

DIVISION 3 (SOUTH)
1	Ipswich	59
2	Torquay	59
3	Colchester	58
4	Southampton	54
5	Bournemouth	52
6	Brighton	52
7	Southend	48
8	Brentford	48
9	Shrewsbury	48
10	QPR	47
11	Watford	46
12	Newport	45
13	Reading	45
14	Northampton	45
15	Walsall	44
16	Coventry	44
17	Millwall	44
18	Plymouth	43
19	Aldershot	42
20	C.Palace	40
21	Exeter	37
22	Gillingham	37
23	Swindon	36
24	Norwich	31

1957-58
DIVISION 1
1	Wolves	64
2	Preston	59
3	Tottenham	51
4	West Brom	50
5	Man City	49
6	Burnley	47
7	Blackpool	44
8	Luton	44
9	Man Utd	43
10	Nottm For	42
11	Chelsea	42
12	Arsenal	39
13	Birmingham	39
14	Aston Villa	39
15	Bolton	38
16	Everton	37
17	Leeds	37
18	Leicester	33
19	Newcastle	32
20	Portsmouth	32
21	Sunderland	32
22	Sheff Wed	31

DIVISION 2
1	West Ham	57
2	Blackburn	56
3	Charlton	55
4	Liverpool	54
5	Fulham	52
6	Sheff Utd	52
7	Middlesbro	45
8	Ipswich	44
9	Huddersfield	44
10	Bristol Rovers	42
11	Stoke	42
12	L.Orient	41
13	Grimsby	40
14	Barnsley	40
15	Cardiff	37
16	Derby	36
17	Bristol City	35
18	Rotherham	33
19	Swansea	31
20	Lincoln	31
21	Notts Co	30
22	Doncaster	27

DIVISION 3 (NORTH)
1	Scunthorpe	66
2	Accrington St	59
3	Bradford	57
4	Bury	56
5	Hull	53
6	Mansfield	52
7	Halifax	51
8	Chesterfield	51
9	Stockport	47
10	Rochdale	46
11	Tranmere	46
12	Wrexham	46
13	York	46
14	Gateshead	45
15	Oldham	45
16	Carlisle	44
17	Hartlepool	44
18	Barrow	41
19	Workington	41
20	Darlington	41
21	Chester	39
22	Bradford PA	37
23	Southport	28
24	Crewe	23

CHAMPIONS
Sheffield Wednesday 1951-52

Wednesday, relegated in 1950-51 on goal average despite winning their last match 6-0, came rocketing back up again at the first attempt thanks largely to big Derek Dooley. He had been with the club for three years but had played only two senior games when he was given another chance - and became the League's top scorer with 46 goals in 30 appearances. The romance turned into a tragedy the following season, when Dooley broke a leg and had to have it amputated after gangrene set in. But his exploits will never be forgotten in Sheffield and he went on to play a role on their commercial side after his career was ended.

What a finish

In 1957, Charlton staged the greatest fightback in history when they recovered from 5-1 down at home to Huddersfield to score six goals in the last 28 minutes and win 7-6 - and all with only 10 men.

Crowded Out

Football's big boom continued well into the 1950s and the average aggregate attendance for the 10 seasons after the Second World War was 34,702,608.

1957-58 cont
DIVISION 3 (SOUTH)
1	Brighton	60
2	Brentford	58
3	Plymouth	58
4	Swindon	57
5	Reading	55
6	Southampton	54
7	Southend	54
8	Norwich	53
9	Bournemouth	51
10	QPR	50
11	Newport	48
12	Colchester	47
13	Northampton	44
14	C.Palace	43
15	Port Vale	42
16	Watford	42
17	Shrewsbury	40
18	Aldershot	40
19	Coventry	39
20	Walsall	37
21	Torquay	35
22	Gillingham	35
23	Millwall	31
24	Exeter	31

1958-59
DIVISION 1
1	Wolves	61
2	Man Utd	55
3	Arsenal	50
4	Bolton	50
5	West Brom	49
6	West Ham	48
7	Burnley	48
8	Blackpool	47
9	Birmingham	46
10	Blackburn	44
11	Newcastle	41
12	Preston	41
13	Nottm For	40
14	Chelsea	40
15	Leeds	39
16	Everton	38
17	Luton	37
18	Tottenham	36
19	Leicester	32
20	Man City	31
21	Aston Villa	30
22	Portsmouth	21

1958-59 cont
DIVISION 2
1	Sheff Wed	62
2	Fulham	60
3	Sheff Utd	53
4	Liverpool	53
5	Stoke	49
6	Bristol Rovers	48
7	Derby	48
8	Charlton	43
9	Cardiff	43
10	Bristol City	43
11	Swansea	41
12	Brighton	41
13	Middlesbro	40
14	Huddersfield	40
15	Sunderland	40
16	Ipswich	40
17	L.Orient	36
18	Scunthorpe	33
19	Lincoln	29
20	Rotherham	29
21	Grimsby	28
22	Barnsley	27

DIVISION 3
1	Plymouth	62
2	Hull	61
3	Brentford	57
4	Norwich	57
5	Colchester	52
6	Reading	50
7	Tranmere	50
8	Southend	50
9	Halifax	50
10	Bury	48
11	Bradford	47
12	Bournemouth	46
13	QPR	46
14	Southampton	45
15	Swindon	45
16	Chesterfield	44
17	Newport	43
18	Wrexham	42
19	Accrington St	42
20	Mansfield	41
21	Stockport	36
22	Doncaster	33
23	Notts Co	29
24	Rochdale	28

1958-59 cont
DIVISION 4
1	Port Vale	64
2	Coventry	60
3	York	60
4	Shrewsbury	58
5	Exeter	57
6	Walsall	52
7	C.Palace	52
8	Northampton	51
9	Millwall	50
10	Carlisle	50
11	Gillingham	49
12	Torquay	44
13	Chester	44
14	Bradford PA	43
15	Watford	42
16	Darlington	42
17	Workington	40
18	Crewe	40
19	Hartlepool	40
20	Gateshead	40
21	Oldham	36
22	Aldershot	35
23	Barrow	28
24	Southport	26

1959-60
DIVISION 1
1	Burnley	55
2	Wolves	54
3	Tottenham	53
4	West Brom	49
5	Sheff Wed	49
6	Bolton	48
7	Man Utd	45
8	Newcastle	44
9	Preston	44
10	Fulham	44
11	Blackpool	40
12	Leicester	39
13	Arsenal	39
14	West Ham	38
15	Everton	37
16	Man City	37
17	Blackburn	37
18	Chelsea	37
19	Birmingham	36
20	Nottm For	35
21	Leeds	34
22	Luton	30

DIVISION 2
1	Aston Villa	59
2	Cardiff	58
3	Liverpool	50
4	Sheff Utd	50
5	Middlesbro	48
6	Huddersfield	47
7	Charlton	47
8	Rotherham	47
9	Bristol Rovers	47
10	L.Orient	44
11	Ipswich	44
12	Swansea	40
13	Lincoln	39
14	Brighton	38
15	Scunthorpe	36
16	Sunderland	36
17	Stoke	35
18	Derby	35
19	Plymouth	35
20	Portsmouth	32
21	Hull	30
22	Bristol City	27

1959-60 cont
DIVISION 3
1	Southampton	61
2	Norwich	59
3	Shrewsbury	52
4	Grimsby	52
5	Coventry	52
6	Brentford	51
7	Bury	51
8	QPR	49
9	Colchester	47
10	Bournemouth	47
11	Reading	46
12	Southend	46
13	Newport	46
14	Port Vale	46
15	Halifax	46
16	Swindon	46
17	Barnsley	44
18	Chesterfield	43
19	Bradford	42
20	Tranmere	41
21	York	38
22	Mansfield	36
23	Wrexham	36
24	Accrington St	27

DIVISION 4
1	Walsall	65
2	Notts Co	60
3	Torquay	60
4	Watford	57
5	Millwall	53
6	Northampton	53
7	Gillingham	52
8	C.Palace	50
9	Exeter	49
10	Stockport	49
11	Bradford PA	49
12	Rochdale	46
13	Aldershot	45
14	Crewe	45
15	Darlington	45
16	Workington	42
17	Doncaster	42
18	Barrow	41
19	Carlisle	41
20	Chester	40
21	Southport	34
22	Gateshead	33
23	Oldham	28
24	Hartlepool	27

Ice Age

In 1958, Everton became one of the first League clubs to install undersoil heating in an attempt to beat the frost and ice. Their initial system cost in the region of £7,000 but unfortunately was not a success.

1960-1969

SWINGING SIXTIES

Football was booming in the 60s, with England's World Cup triumph just one of the many highlights in a great decade for English football. For the first time our clubs were winning in Europe - Manchester United becoming the first English team to win the Champions' Cup, 10 years after Munich.

And interest in domestic football was still huge. The game was attracting big crowds and football welcomed the swinging sixties as much as any industry.

Goals Galore

The ten First Division matches played on Boxing Day 1963 contained a total of 66 goals - a record. Fulham beat Ipswich 10-1, and Blackburn won 8-2 against West Ham, away.

Tottenham earned their place in the history books in the first season of the new decade when they became the first team in the 20th century to complete the League Championship and FA Cup double.

Ipswich followed Spurs as Champions in 1961-62 - their only League title - under the management of Alf Ramsey, who would have much to celebrate with England four years later. But then the big north-west clubs took centre stage once again, with Everton, Liverpool, Manchester United and Manchester City sharing the next six League Championships, before Leeds snatched the final one of the decade.

Liverpool and United were the only sides to claim the Championship twice and both had great, great sides. The Anfield club won the title in 1963-64 and 1965-66, with United triumphing in 1964-65 and 1966-67. As always, it is impossible to compare teams from different eras but these two would be right up there among the best of any time.

Liverpool had players of the calibre of Ian St John, Roger Hunt and Ian Callaghan, while United boasted arguably the best trio of all time - George Best, Bobby Charlton and Denis Law. There is little doubt that those three, especially if they played together, would walk into any side in the country in any football era.

Strange but true!

George Graham was married in September 1967 with Terry Venables as his best man. Later that day they played against each other at Highbury, with Graham's Arsenal beating Spurs 4-0.

Interestingly, both sides at the time were managed by Scots - Liverpool by Bill Shankly and United by Matt Busby. Now that really was a sign of things to come for both those two soccer giants who have gone on to enjoy plenty of success under men from that country.

LEAGUE TABLES 1960-61 to 1969-70

1960-61

DIVISION 1

1	Tottenham	66
2	Sheff Wed	58
3	Wolves	57
4	Burnley	51
5	Everton	50
6	Leicester	45
7	Man Utd	45
8	Blackburn	43
9	Aston Villa	43
10	West Brom	41
11	Arsenal	41
12	Chelsea	37
13	Man City	37
14	Nottm For	37
15	Cardiff	37
16	West Ham	36
17	Fulham	36
18	Bolton	35
19	Birmingham	34
20	Blackpool	33
21	Newcastle	32
22	Preston	30

DIVISION 2

1	Ipswich	59
2	Sheff Utd	58
3	Liverpool	52
4	Norwich	49
5	Middlesbro	48
6	Sunderland	47
7	Swansea	47
8	Southampton	44
9	Scunthorpe	43
10	Charlton	43
11	Plymouth	42
12	Derby	40
13	Luton	39
14	Leeds	38
15	Rotherham	37
16	Brighton	37
17	Bristol Rovers	37
18	Stoke	36
19	L.Orient	36
20	Huddersfield	35
21	Portsmouth	33
22	Lincoln	24

DIVISION 3

1	Bury	68
2	Walsall	62
3	QPR	60
4	Watford	52
5	Notts Co	51
6	Grimsby	50
7	Port Vale	49
8	Barnsley	49
9	Halifax	49
10	Shrewsbury	46
11	Hull	46
12	Torquay	45
13	Newport	45
14	Bristol City	44
15	Coventry	44
16	Swindon	43
17	Brentford	43
18	Reading	40
19	Bournemouth	40
20	Southend	39
21	Tranmere	38
22	Bradford	36
23	Colchester	33
24	Chesterfield	32

DIVISION 4

1	Peterborough	66
2	C.Palace	64
3	Northampton	60
4	Bradford PA	60
5	York	51
6	Millwall	50
7	Darlington	49
8	Workington	49
9	Crewe	49
10	Aldershot	45
11	Doncaster	45
12	Oldham	45
13	Stockport	45
14	Southport	44
15	Gillingham	43
16	Wrexham	42
17	Rochdale	42
18	Accrington St	40
19	Carlisle	39
20	Mansfield	38
21	Exeter	38
22	Barrow	37
23	Hartlepool	32
24	Chester	31

Strange but true!

Manchester United finished 15th in 1961-62 and had their lowest post-war average attendance - 33,491, which was higher than the average figure attained by more than half the clubs now in the League.

1961-62

DIVISION 1

1	Ipswich	56
2	Burnley	53
3	Tottenham	52
4	Everton	51
5	Sheff Utd	47
6	Sheff Wed	46
7	Aston Villa	44
8	West Ham	44
9	West Brom	43
10	Arsenal	43
11	Bolton	42
12	Man City	41
13	Blackpool	41
14	Leicester	40
15	Man Utd	39
16	Blackburn	39
17	Birmingham	38
18	Wolves	36
19	Nottm For	36
20	Fulham	33
21	Cardiff	32
22	Chelsea	28

DIVISION 2

1	Liverpool	62
2	L.Orient	54
3	Sunderland	53
4	Scunthorpe	49
5	Plymouth	46
6	Southampton	45
7	Huddersfield	44
8	Stoke	42
9	Rotherham	41
10	Preston	40
11	Newcastle	39
12	Middlesbro	39
13	Luton	39
14	Walsall	39
15	Charlton	39
16	Derby	39
17	Norwich	39
18	Bury	39
19	Leeds	36
20	Swansea	36
21	Bristol Rovers	33
22	Brighton	31

Owls about that!

Between Boxing Day 1964 and October 1966 Sheffield Wednesday played 82 matches in the League, FA Cup and League Cup, without having a single penalty awarded to The Owls.

WHAT A STAR ⭐ GEORGE BEST

A legend. The greatest ever. Simply the Best. All the cliches applied to Best hardly do justice to the man's many gifts, but in addition to his talent with the ball he was mentally and physically strong, and rarely out of the team until the treadmill of fame and fortune began to turn too quickly for him to keep himself under control. Sadly a great career with Manchester United (two League titles, European Cup, Footballer of the Year, European Player of the Year) descended into the near-farce of retirements and comebacks with lesser teams.

WHAT A STAR ⭐ JIMMY GREAVES

He scored 357 League goals, all in the First Division, several of them justifying the 'impossible' tag. Until his then-secret-now-famous defeat by the bottle, he ranked among the greatest finishers in history, with Chelsea (and, briefly, AC Milan), then Spurs, even in decline with West Ham, and England. He could pass and sometimes tackle, too, but it is as a goalscorer, an instinctive, consistent scorer, that he will be remembered. That, and as a man who eventually got himself straight and found the strength to keep drink at bay. He became a TV star in the 1990s with his pal Ian St John under the Saint and Greavsie guise and is still in demand in the media.

1961-62 cont

DIVISION 3

1	Portsmouth	65
2	Grimsby	62
3	Bournemouth	59
4	QPR	59
5	Peterborough	58
6	Bristol City	54
7	Reading	53
8	Northampton	51
9	Swindon	49
10	Hull	48
11	Bradford PA	47
12	Port Vale	45
13	Notts Co	43
14	Coventry	43
15	C.Palace	42
16	Southend	42
17	Watford	41
18	Halifax	40
19	Shrewsbury	38
20	Barnsley	38
21	Torquay	36
22	Lincoln	35
23	Brentford	34
24	Newport	22

DIVISION 4

1	Millwall	56
2	Colchester	55
3	Wrexham	53
4	Carlisle	52
5	Bradford	51
6	York	50
7	Aldershot	49
8	Workington	49
9	Barrow	48
10	Crewe	46
11	Oldham	46
12	Rochdale	45
13	Darlington	45
14	Mansfield	44
15	Tranmere	44
16	Stockport	43
17	Southport	43
18	Exeter	37
19	Chesterfield	37
20	Gillingham	37
21	Doncaster	29
22	Hartlepool	27
23	Chester	26
24	Accrington	

1962-63

DIVISION 1

1	Everton	61
2	Tottenham	55
3	Burnley	54
4	Leicester	52
5	Wolves	50
6	Sheff Wed	48
7	Arsenal	46
8	Liverpool	44
9	Nottm For	44
10	Sheff Utd	44
11	Blackburn	42
12	West Ham	40
13	Blackpool	40
14	West Brom	39
15	Aston Villa	38
16	Fulham	38
17	Ipswich	35
18	Bolton	35
19	Man Utd	34
20	Birmingham	33
21	Man City	31
22	L.Orient	21

DIVISION 2

1	Stoke	53
2	Chelsea	52
3	Sunderland	52
4	Middlesbro	49
5	Leeds	48
6	Huddersfield	48
7	Newcastle	47
8	Bury	47
9	Scunthorpe	44
10	Cardiff	43
11	Southampton	42
12	Plymouth	42
13	Norwich	42
14	Rotherham	40
15	Swansea	39
16	Portsmouth	37
17	Preston	37
18	Derby	36
19	Grimsby	35
20	Charlton	31
21	Walsall	31
22	Luton	29

DIVISION 3

1	Northampton	62
2	Swindon	58
3	Port Vale	54
4	Coventry	53
5	Bournemouth	52
6	Peterborough	51
7	Notts Co	51
8	Southend	50
9	Wrexham	49
10	Hull	48
11	C.Palace	47
12	Colchester	47
13	QPR	45
14	Bristol City	45
15	Shrewsbury	44
16	Millwall	43
17	Watford	42
18	Barnsley	41
19	Bristol Rovers	41
20	Reading	40
21	Bradford PA	40
22	Brighton	36
23	Carlisle	35
24	Halifax	30

DIVISION 4

1	Brentford	62
2	Oldham	59
3	Crewe	59
4	Mansfield	57
5	Gillingham	57
6	Torquay	56
7	Rochdale	51
8	Tranmere	50
9	Barrow	50
10	Workington	47
11	Aldershot	47
12	Darlington	44
13	Southport	44
14	York	43
15	Chesterfield	42
16	Doncaster	42
17	Exeter	42
18	Oxford	41
19	Stockport	41
20	Newport	39
21	Chester	39
22	Lincoln	35
23	Bradford	32
24	Hartlepool	25

Buy Buy Allan!

Allan 'Sniffer' Clarke was transferred from Fulham to Leicester in June 1968 and from Leicester to Leeds in June 1969, both times for a record fee - £150,000 and £165,000. Both Fulham and Leicester were relegated during his time with them.

Bye Bye Stanley

Accrington Stanley resigned from the League in the 1961-62 season. They were playing in the Fourth Division at the time.

WHAT A STAR ⭐ BOBBY MOORE

An inspirational captain and a player who made the most of his gifts. That was Bobby Moore, who may well remain the only England captain ever to lift the World Cup. In a career of exactly 900 senior games with West Ham (642), Fulham (150) and England (108), Mooro was never mastered, keeping all but the finest of opponents under control, even though he was not particularly quick, nor outstanding in the air. But he could see several moves ahead, and react to the sight. His death from cancer at 52 saddened the nation. But he will never be forgotten in football - least of all by the great Brazilian Pele, who labelled Moore his toughest ever opponent.

1963-64

DIVISION 1		DIVISION 2	
1 Liverpool	57	1 Leeds	63
2 Man Utd	53	2 Sunderland	61
3 Everton	52	3 Preston	56
4 Tottenham	51	4 Charlton	48
5 Chelsea	50	5 Southampton	47
6 Sheff Wed	49	6 Man City	46
7 Blackburn	46	7 Rotherham	45
8 Arsenal	45	8 Newcastle	45
9 Burnley	44	9 Portsmouth	43
10 West Brom	43	10 Middlesbro	41
11 Leicester	43	11 Northampton	41
12 Sheff Utd	43	12 Huddersfield	40
13 Nottm For	41	13 Derby	39
14 West Ham	40	14 Swindon	38
15 Fulham	39	15 Cardiff	38
16 Wolves	39	16 L.Orient	36
17 Stoke	38	17 Norwich	35
18 Blackpool	35	18 Bury	35
19 Aston Villa	34	19 Swansea	33
20 Birmingham	29	20 Plymouth	32
21 Bolton	28	21 Grimsby	32
22 Ipswich	25	22 Scunthorpe	30

Strange but true!

The Arsenal v Leeds game in May 1966 drew a crowd of 4,554. The European Cup-Winners' Cup Final, Liverpool v Borussia Dortmund, was live on TV that evening.

DIVISION 3		DIVISION 4	
1 Coventry	60	1 Gillingham	60
2 C.Palace	60	2 Carlisle	60
3 Watford	58	3 Workington	59
4 Bournemouth	56	4 Exeter	58
5 Bristol City	55	5 Bradford	56
6 Reading	52	6 Torquay	51
7 Mansfield	51	7 Tranmere	51
8 Hull	49	8 Brighton	50
9 Oldham	48	9 Aldershot	48
10 Peterborough	47	10 Halifax	48
11 Shrewsbury	47	11 Lincoln	47
12 Bristol Rovers	46	12 Chester	46
13 Port Vale	46	13 Bradford PA	45
14 Southend	45	14 Doncaster	42
15 QPR	45	15 Newport	42
16 Brentford	44	16 Chesterfield	42
17 Colchester	43	17 Stockport	42
18 Luton	42	18 Oxford	41
19 Walsall	40	19 Darlington	40
20 Barnsley	39	20 Rochdale	39
21 Millwall	38	21 Southport	39
22 Crewe	34	22 York	35
23 Wrexham	32	23 Hartlepool	33
24 Notts Co	27	24 Barrow	30

Denis Law - a Man United legend

Thousand Island

At one period in the 1960s, Crystal Palace had nine players on their books who had scored more than 1000 League goals between them. The nine were Allen, Burridge, Dowsett, Heckman, Holton, Imlach, McNichol, Summersby and Uphill.

1964-65

DIVISION 1

1	Man Utd	61
2	Leeds	61
3	Chelsea	56
4	Everton	49
5	Nottm For	47
6	Tottenham	45
7	Liverpool	44
8	Sheff Wed	43
9	West Ham	42
10	Blackburn	42
11	Stoke	42
12	Burnley	42
13	Arsenal	41
14	West Brom	39
15	Sunderland	37
16	Aston Villa	37
17	Blackpool	35
18	Leicester	35
19	Sheff Utd	35
20	Fulham	34
21	Wolves	30
22	Birmingham	27

DIVISION 2

1	Newcastle	57
2	Northampton	56
3	Bolton	50
4	Southampton	48
5	Ipswich	47
6	Norwich	47
7	C.Palace	45
8	Huddersfield	44
9	Derby	43
10	Coventry	43
11	Man City	41
12	Preston	41
13	Cardiff	40
14	Rotherham	40
15	Plymouth	40
16	Bury	38
17	Middlesbro	35
18	Charlton	35
19	L.Orient	35
20	Portsmouth	34
21	Swindon	32
22	Swansea	32

1964-65 cont

DIVISION 3

1	Carlisle	60
2	Bristol City	59
3	Mansfield	59
4	Hull	58
5	Brentford	57
6	Bristol Rovers	55
7	Gillingham	55
8	Peterborough	51
9	Watford	50
10	Grimsby	49
11	Bournemouth	47
12	Southend	46
13	Reading	46
14	QPR	46
15	Workington	46
16	Shrewsbury	42
17	Exeter	41
18	Scunthorpe	40
19	Walsall	37
20	Oldham	36
21	Luton	33
22	Port Vale	32
23	Colchester	30
24	Barnsley	29

DIVISION 4

1	Brighton	63
2	Millwall	62
3	York	62
4	Oxford	61
5	Tranmere	60
6	Rochdale	58
7	Bradford PA	57
8	Chester	56
9	Doncaster	51
10	Crewe	49
11	Torquay	49
12	Chesterfield	48
13	Notts Co	44
14	Wrexham	43
15	Hartlepool	43
16	Newport	42
17	Darlington	42
18	Aldershot	37
19	Bradford	32
20	Southport	32
21	Barrow	30
22	Lincoln	28
23	Halifax	28
24	Stockport	27

Helping Hand

Reading goalkeeper Arthur Wilkie scored twice in a 4-2 win over Halifax in August 1962. He had moved into the attack after injuring a hand.

Strange but true!

Bristol City pipped Mansfield to promotion from the Third Division in 1965 by a goal average of 0.11. Popular City star John Atyeo was the hero scoring the decisive second goal seven minutes from time in their last match win over Oldham.

1965-66

DIVISION 1

1	Liverpool	61
2	Leeds	55
3	Burnley	55
4	Man Utd	51
5	Chelsea	51
6	West Brom	50
7	Leicester	49
8	Tottenham	44
9	Sheff Utd	43
10	Stoke	42
11	Everton	41
12	West Ham	39
13	Blackpool	37
14	Arsenal	37
15	Newcastle	37
16	Aston Villa	36
17	Sheff Wed	36
18	Nottm For	36
19	Sunderland	36
20	Fulham	35
21	Northampton	33
22	Blackburn	20

DIVISION 2

1	Man City	59
2	Southampton	54
3	Coventry	53
4	Huddersfield	51
5	Bristol City	51
6	Wolves	50
7	Rotherham	46
8	Derby	43
9	Bolton	41
10	Birmingham	41
11	C.Palace	41
12	Portsmouth	40
13	Norwich	39
14	Carlisle	39
15	Ipswich	39
16	Charlton	38
17	Preston	37
18	Plymouth	37
19	Bury	35
20	Cardiff	34
21	Middlesbro	33
22	L.Orient	23

CHAMPIONS
Tottenham 1960-61

Exactly ten years after one great Spurs team had been Champions, an even better White Hart Lane outfit did the first League and Cup double of the century, with a record-equalling total of 66 points (33 home, 33 away), and a goal difference of plus 60. They won a record 31 of their 42 League games, including the first 11 in succession, and although things fell apart after Danny Blanchflower retired, John White was killed by lightning and Dave Mackay twice broke his leg, the memories of that superb side will not fade.

Pro-File: BOBBY CHARLTON

Bobby Charlton was, quite simply, one of the greatest footballers who ever lived.

Even now, some 25 years after he retired, his name is still known the whole world over and wherever he goes he is welcomed with open arms.

But the reason for his popularity isn't purely because of his ability. With Charlton, it wasn't only that he could play the game, it was the way he played the game that mattered.

He is one of the best ambassadors English football has had, both during and after his long and distinguished playing career, a career spent almost entirely at Manchester United.

A survivor of the 1958 Munich air disaster, he went on to carve an indelible place in the Old Trafford club's history, playing more than 600 League games for them.

And he also played in two of the greatest games English football has witnessed.

He helped Matt Busby achieve his holy grail when United won the European Cup in 1968, and two years earlier he had played a major role in England's first, and so far only, World Cup triumph.

A great passer of the ball with a thunderous shot in either foot, Bobby Charlton would have been a star in any era.

And now as a director of Manchester United, he has seen the club return to the forefront of English football, a position they enjoyed in his time as a player.

Charlton still takes part in the odd training session and has revelled in United's domination of the Premiership as much as any other member of the Old Trafford staff. They now have a team he can be proud of.

Career details
● **Represented:** England, Manchester United, Preston North End.
● **Position:** Inside forward ● **Born:** Ashington, 11.10.37. ● **Height:** 5ft 10in
● **Weight:** 12st ● **Club Honours:** ● League Championship 1956-57, 1964-65, 1967-68; FA Cup 1963; European Cup 1968; Football Writers' Footballer of the Year 1966 ● **International Honours:** England 6 U23, 106 full caps, Football League Representative XI; World Cup winner 1966

Club League Record

Era	Club	Games	Goals
1956-72	Manchester United	606	199
1974-75	Preston North End	38	8

League Highlights

May 1957: Charlton, aged just 19, helps United win their second successive League Championship.

May 1965: He has to wait eight years to win it again but now, with Best and Law alongside him, Charlton plays his part in United's golden era.

May 1967: The League Championship trophy is safely back at Old Trafford, as a prequel to United's greatest ever triumph, the 1968 European Cup win with Charlton scoring twice in that Final.

On Charlton:

● The Prince of Wales's visit is big news here, but Mr Charlton was even bigger. **British Embassy Spokesman in Morocco in 1995.**

DID YOU KNOW THAT...

● Charlton won 106 caps for England, the second most capped outfield player. Only Bobby Moore, with 108, won more.

● His trademark was a rocket shot, with either foot, from outside the penalty area.

● His greatest moment with England came when he helped them win the 1966 World Cup against West Germany. His brother, Jack, also played in that game.

● Bobby and Jack Charlton were the last set of brothers to line up for England until, ironically, Manchester United pair Gary and Phil Neville.

● Bobby runs his own coaching school for young soccer enthusiasts.

● He tried his hand at management with Preston but, like so many great players, he failed to make the grade as a boss.

● Sir Alf Ramsey was blamed for England's exit from the 1970 World Cup finals for taking Charlton off in the Quarter-Final against West Germany with England 2-0 up. They lost 3-2.

● Charlton is England's record goalscorer with 49 goals from his 106 internationals.

1965-66 cont
DIVISION 3
1	Hull	69
2	Millwall	65
3	QPR	57
4	Scunthorpe	53
5	Workington	52
6	Gillingham	52
7	Swindon	51
8	Reading	51
9	Walsall	50
10	Shrewsbury	49
11	Grimsby	47
12	Watford	47
13	Peterborough	46
14	Oxford	46
15	Brighton	43
16	Bristol Rovers	42
17	Swansea	41
18	Bournemouth	38
19	Mansfield	38
20	Oldham	37
21	Southend	36
22	Exeter	35
23	Brentford	32
24	York	27

DIVISION 4
1	Doncaster	59
2	Darlington	59
3	Torquay	58
4	Colchester	56
5	Tranmere	56
6	Luton	56
7	Chester	52
8	Notts Co	50
9	Newport	48
10	Southport	48
11	Bradford PA	47
12	Barrow	47
13	Stockport	42
14	Crewe	41
15	Halifax	41
16	Barnsley	40
17	Aldershot	40
18	Hartlepool	40
19	Port Vale	39
20	Chesterfield	39
21	Rochdale	37
22	Lincoln	37
23	Bradford	37
24	Wrexham	35

1966-67
DIVISION 1
1	Man Utd	60
2	Nottm For	56
3	Tottenham	56
4	Leeds	55
5	Liverpool	51
6	Everton	48
7	Arsenal	46
8	Leicester	44
9	Chelsea	44
10	Sheff Utd	42
11	Sheff Wed	41
12	Stoke	41
13	West Brom	39
14	Burnley	39
15	Man City	39
16	West Ham	36
17	Sunderland	36
18	Fulham	34
19	Southampton	34
20	Newcastle	33
21	Aston Villa	29
22	Blackpool	21

DIVISION 2
1	Coventry	59
2	Wolves	58
3	Carlisle	52
4	Blackburn	51
5	Ipswich	50
6	Huddersfield	49
7	C.Palace	48
8	Millwall	45
9	Bolton	42
10	Birmingham	40
11	Norwich	40
12	Hull	39
13	Preston	39
14	Portsmouth	39
15	Bristol City	38
16	Plymouth	37
17	Derby	36
18	Rotherham	36
19	Charlton	35
20	Cardiff	33
21	Northampton	30
22	Bury	28

Hot Spurs

Spurs scored 111 goals in 1962-63, but finished second to Everton. No club has scored a century of goals in the top division since then.

Strange but true!

Substitutes were allowed for the first time in the League during the 1965-66 season. Players were only allowed to be replaced in that term if they were injured but the following season, substitutions were allowed to be made for any reason.

DIVISION 3
1	QPR	67
2	Middlesbro	55
3	Watford	54
4	Reading	53
5	Bristol Rovers	53
6	Shrewsbury	52
7	Torquay	51
8	Swindon	50
9	Mansfield	49
10	Oldham	48
11	Gillingham	46
12	Walsall	46
13	Colchester	44
14	L.Orient	44
15	Peterborough	43
16	Oxford	43
17	Grimsby	43
18	Scunthorpe	42
19	Brighton	41
20	Bournemouth	41
21	Swansea	39
22	Darlington	37
23	Doncaster	32
24	Workington	31

DIVISION 4
1	Stockport	64
2	Southport	59
3	Barrow	59
4	Tranmere	58
5	Crewe	54
6	Southend	53
7	Wrexham	52
8	Hartlepool	51
9	Brentford	49
10	Aldershot	48
11	Bradford	48
12	Halifax	44
13	Port Vale	44
14	Exeter	43
15	Chesterfield	42
16	Barnsley	41
17	Luton	41
18	Newport	40
19	Chester	40
20	Notts Co	37
21	Rochdale	37
22	York	35
23	Bradford PA	35
24	Lincoln	31

CHAMPIONS
Peterborough 1960-61

So it was only the Fourth Division, hardly the top of the soccer tree, but Peterborough's exploits in their first season of League membership are worth recording. They came from the Midlands League wondering if they could cope...and scored 134 goals, a record that still stands, not just for the division but for the entire League. Terry Bly netted 52, one of the highest individual totals ever, and the team lost only eight of their 46 matches. They only beat Crystal Palace by two points, but nobody could claim that they did not deserve their success.

Leeds' Johnny Giles

1967-68

DIVISION 1

1	Man City	58
2	Man Utd	56
3	Liverpool	55
4	Leeds	53
5	Everton	52
6	Chelsea	48
7	Tottenham	47
8	West Brom	46
9	Arsenal	44
10	Newcastle	41
11	Nottm For	39
12	West Ham	38
13	Leicester	38
14	Burnley	38
15	Sunderland	37
16	Southampton	37
17	Wolves	36
18	Stoke	35
19	Sheff Wed	34
20	Coventry	33
21	Sheff Utd	32
22	Fulham	27

DIVISION 2

1	Ipswich	59
2	QPR	58
3	Blackpool	58
4	Birmingham	52
5	Portsmouth	49
6	Middlesbro	43
7	Millwall	45
8	Blackburn	43
9	Norwich	43
10	Carlisle	41
11	C.Palace	39
12	Bolton	39
13	Cardiff	38
14	Huddersfield	38
15	Charlton	37
16	Aston Villa	37
17	Hull	37
18	Derby	36
19	Bristol City	36
20	Preston	35
21	Rotherham	31
22	Plymouth	27

DIVISION 3

1	Oxford	57
2	Bury	56
3	Shrewsbury	55
4	Torquay	53
5	Reading	51
6	Watford	50
7	Walsall	50
8	Barrow	50
9	Swindon	49
10	Brighton	48
11	Gillingham	48
12	Bournemouth	47
13	Stockport	47
14	Southport	46
15	Bristol Rovers	43
16	Oldham	43
17	Northampton	41
18	L.Orient	41
19	Tranmere	40
20	Mansfield	37
21	Grimsby	37
22	Colchester	33
23	Scunthorpe	32
24	Peterboro*	31

DIVISION 4

1	Luton	66
2	Barnsley	61
3	Hartlepool	60
4	Crewe	58
5	Bradford	57
6	Southend	54
7	Chesterfield	53
8	Wrexham	53
9	Aldershot	53
10	Doncaster	51
11	Halifax	46
12	Newport	45
13	Lincoln	43
14	Brentford	43
15	Swansea	42
16	Darlington	41
17	Notts Co	41
18	Port Vale	39
19	Rochdale	38
20	Exeter	38
21	York	36
22	Chester	32
23	Workington	31
24	Bradford PA	23

1968-69

DIVISION 1

1	Leeds	67
2	Liverpool	61
3	Everton	57
4	Arsenal	56
5	Chelsea	50
6	Tottenham	45
7	Southampton	45
8	West Ham	44
9	Newcastle	44
10	West Brom	43
11	Man Utd	42
12	Ipswich	41
13	Man City	40
14	Burnley	39
15	Sheff Wed	36
16	Wolves	35
17	Sunderland	34
18	Nottm For	33
19	Stoke	33
20	Coventry	31
21	Leicester	30
22	QPR	18

DIVISION 2

1	Derby	63
2	C.Palace	56
3	Charlton	50
4	Middlesbro	49
5	Cardiff	47
6	Huddersfield	46
7	Birmingham	44
8	Blackpool	43
9	Sheff Utd	43
10	Millwall	43
11	Hull	42
12	Carlisle	42
13	Norwich	40
14	Preston	39
15	Portsmouth	38
16	Bristol City	38
17	Bolton	38
18	Aston Villa	38
19	Blackburn	37
20	Oxford	33
21	Bury	30
22	Fulham	25

DIVISION 3

1	Watford	64
2	Swindon	64
3	Luton	61
4	Bournemouth	51
5	Plymouth	49
6	Torquay	48
7	Tranmere	48
8	Southport	47
9	Stockport	46
10	Barnsley	46
11	Rotherham	45
12	Brighton	45
13	Walsall	44
14	Reading	43
15	Mansfield	43
16	Bristol Rovers	43
17	Shrewsbury	43
18	L.Orient	42
19	Barrow	42
20	Gillingham	41
21	Northampton	40
22	Hartlepool	39
23	Crewe	35
24	Oldham	35

DIVISION 4

1	Doncaster	59
2	Halifax	57
3	Rochdale	56
4	Bradford	56
5	Darlington	52
6	Colchester	52
7	Southend	51
8	Lincoln	51
9	Wrexham	50
10	Swansea	49
11	Brentford	48
12	Workington	47
13	Port Vale	46
14	Chester	45
15	Aldershot	45
16	Scunthorpe	44
17	Exeter	43
18	Peterborough	42
19	Notts Co	42
20	Chesterfield	41
21	York	39
22	Newport	36
23	Grimsby	33
24	Bradford PA	20

Bad Break

Scottish international Dave Mackay broke his left leg twice in nine months during his career at Tottenham. The tough tackling midfielder was playing his first comeback match, after the initial injury, in September 1964 against Shrewsbury in a reserve match at White Hart Lane when the second break occured.

* Peterborough had 19 points deducted and were relegated as punishment for offering irregular bonuses to their players.

CHAMPIONS
Leeds United 1968-69

Leeds had to wait a long time for their first Championship, but they certainly got there in style, with a then-record total of 67 points, six clear of second placed Liverpool. This was a great team, astutely managed by Don Revie, prompted by Johnny Giles and Billy Bremner, cemented together by Jack Charlton and Norman Hunter, kept on target by Allan Clarke and Mick Jones. If only they had kept on playing their football, instead of trying to referee as well, they would have been remembered with even more respect. 1975 should have provided their finest hour when they dominated the European Cup Final against Bayern Munich but ended up losing 2-0 in Paris.

Les is More

Les Allen set a record with Queens Park Rangers in 1968-69 by becoming the First Division's first player-manager. He is part of the famous Allen football family with sons Clive and Bradley and nephews Paul and Martin making a living out of the game

1969-70

DIVISION 1		DIVISION 2	
1 Everton	66	1 Huddersfield	60
2 Leeds	57	2 Blackpool	53
3 Chelsea	55	3 Leicester	51
4 Derby	53	4 Middlesbro	50
5 Liverpool	51	5 Swindon	50
6 Coventry	49	6 Sheff Utd	49
7 Newcastle	47	7 Cardiff	49
8 Man Utd	45	8 Blackburn	47
9 Stoke	45	9 QPR	45
10 Man City	43	10 Millwall	44
11 Tottenham	43	11 Norwich	43
12 Arsenal	42	12 Carlisle	41
13 Wolves	40	13 Hull	41
14 Burnley	39	14 Bristol City	39
15 Nottm For	38	15 Oxford	39
16 West Brom	37	16 Bolton	36
17 West Ham	36	17 Portsmouth	35
18 Ipswich	31	18 Birmingham	33
19 Southampton	29	19 Watford	31
20 C.Palace	27	20 Charlton	31
21 Sunderland	26	21 Aston Villa	29
22 Sheff Wed	25	22 Preston	28

DIVISION 3		DIVISION 4	
1 L.Orient	62	1 Chesterfield	64
2 Luton	60	2 Wrexham	61
3 Bristol Rovers	56	3 Swansea	60
4 Fulham	55	4 Port Vale	59
5 Brighton	55	5 Brentford	56
6 Mansfield	53	6 Aldershot	53
7 Barnsley	53	7 Notts Co	52
8 Reading	53	8 Lincoln	50
9 Rochdale	46	9 Peterborough	48
10 Bradford	46	10 Colchester	48
11 Doncaster	46	11 Chester	48
12 Walsall	46	12 Scunthorpe	46
13 Torquay	45	13 York	46
14 Rotherham	44	14 Northampton	44
15 Shrewsbury	44	15 Crewe	44
16 Tranmere	44	16 Grimsby	43
17 Plymouth	43	17 Southend	40
18 Halifax	43	18 Exeter	39
19 Bury	41	19 Oldham	39
20 Gillingham	39	20 Workington	38
21 Bournemouth	39	21 Newport	37
22 Southport	38	22 Darlington	36
23 Barrow	30	23 Hartlepool	30
24 Stockport	23	24 Bradford PA	23

Snow joke!

More than 400 League and Cup games were called off over a six week period in 1963 as snow and ice gripped the country. QPR even left their Loftus Road ground to play at the aptly named White City during the year but returned shortly afterwards.

Kid gloves

Derek Foster became the youngest player to appear in the First Division when he played in goal for Sunderland against Leicester in August 1964. The young number one was aged only 15 years, 185 days at the time but went on to play only 30 League games in a 10 year career with the Rokermen, Charlton and finally Brighton. He also represented England at schoolboy international level but his football career never reached those international heights again.

1970-1979

OLD BIG 'EAD

Arsenal kicked off the 70s by emulating Tottenham's achievement of ten years earlier by winning the double, but that was the start of a dark period for The Gunners and they would have to wait 18 years for another title.

Derby, under Brian Clough, won the League in 1971-72 and again in 1974-75, although by now Dave Mackay was in charge. Leeds also claimed the crown on one occasion - in 1973-74 - but for much of the 70s the League Championship trophy had a permanent home - Anfield.

Liverpool took the title five times, including three out of the last four, as

Brian Clough

they began a period of complete dominance of the English League scene. Bob Paisley had built a fantastic side and it appeared as though one brilliant team just merged into another.

They said Kevin Keegan could not be replaced when he left for Hamburg in 1977. Instead, Paisley went north to Glasgow to sign Kenny Dalglish, who turned out be even better than his famous predecessor.

Liverpool were virtually untouchable and the Red machine just rolled over everything in its path, both at home and abroad, where they won the European Cup two years in succession - 1977 and 1978.

The only time their dominance was challenged was in 1977-78, when Nottingham Forest upset the apple-cart and Liverpool had to

Forest Fire

Nottingham Forest scraped into the third promotion place in Division Two in 1976-77, by one point. In the next three years they won the Championship once, the European Cup twice and the League Cup twice.

settle for second place. And the man who masterminded Forest's takeover was none other than Brian Clough, repeating his achievement with Derby in 1971-72.

And that triumph cannot be underestimated as Old Big 'Ead, as he dubbed himself, took two unfashionable clubs to the heights of the English game in his own, inimitable style, with teams playing with great flair to win them a place in the nation's favours.

LEAGUE TABLES 1970-71 to 1979-80

1970-71

DIVISION 1

1	Arsenal	65
2	Leeds	64
3	Tottenham	52
4	Wolves	52
5	Liverpool	51
6	Chelsea	51
7	Southampton	46
8	Man Utd	43
9	Derby	42
10	Coventry	42
11	Man City	41
12	Newcastle	41
13	Stoke	37
14	Everton	37
15	Huddersfield	36
16	Nottm For	36
17	West Brom	35
18	C.Palace	35
19	Ipswich	34
20	West Ham	34
21	Burnley	27
22	Blackpool	23

DIVISION 2

1	Leicester	59
2	Sheff Utd	56
3	Cardiff	53
4	Carlisle	53
5	Hull	51
6	Luton	49
7	Middlesbro	48
8	Millwall	47
9	Birmingham	46
10	Norwich	44
11	QPR	43
12	Swindon	42
13	Sunderland	42
14	Oxford	42
15	Sheff Wed	36
16	Portsmouth	34
17	L.Orient	34
18	Watford	33
19	Bristol City	31
20	Charlton	30
21	Blackburn	27
22	Bolton	24

DIVISION 3

1	Preston	61
2	Fulham	60
3	Halifax	56
4	Aston Villa	53
5	Chesterfield	51
6	Bristol Rovers	51
7	Mansfield	51
8	Rotherham	50
9	Wrexham	49
10	Torquay	49
11	Swansea	46
12	Barnsley	45
13	Shrewsbury	45
14	Brighton	44
15	Plymouth	43
16	Rochdale	43
17	Port Vale	42
18	Tranmere	42
19	Bradford	40
20	Walsall	39
21	Reading	39
22	Bury	37
23	Doncaster	35
24	Gillingham	33

DIVISION 4

1	Notts Co	69
2	Bournemouth	60
3	Oldham	59
4	York	56
5	Chester	55
6	Colchester	54
7	Northampton	51
8	Southport	48
9	Exeter	48
10	Workington	48
11	Stockport	46
12	Darlington	45
13	Aldershot	45
14	Brentford	44
15	Crewe	44
16	Peterborough	43
17	Scunthorpe	43
18	Southend	43
19	Grimsby	43
20	Cambridge	43
21	Lincoln	39
22	Newport	28
23	Hartlepool	28
24	Barrow	22

Strange but true!

Three-up-three-down was introduced in 1973-74 and Carlisle won promotion from Division Two with 48 points - the lowest total by a third-placed club for 18 years.

1971-72

DIVISION 1

1	Derby	58
2	Leeds	57
3	Liverpool	57
4	Man City	57
5	Arsenal	52
6	Tottenham	51
7	Chelsea	48
8	Man Utd	48
9	Wolves	47
10	Sheff Utd	46
11	Newcastle	41
12	Leicester	39
13	Ipswich	38
14	West Ham	36
15	Everton	36
16	West Brom	35
17	Stoke	35
18	Coventry	33
19	Southampton	31
20	C.Palace	29
21	Nottm For	25
22	Huddersfield	25

DIVISION 2

1	Norwich	57
2	Birmingham	56
3	Millwall	55
4	QPR	54
5	Sunderland	50
6	Blackpool	47
7	Burnley	46
8	Bristol City	46
9	Middlesbro	46
10	Carlisle	43
11	Swindon	42
12	Hull	38
13	Luton	38
14	Sheff Wed	38
15	Oxford	38
16	Portsmouth	37
17	L.Orient	37
18	Preston	36
19	Cardiff	34
20	Fulham	34
21	Charlton	33
22	Watford	19

Strange but true!

Little Willie Carlin completed a nap hand in 1973, by being with a promoted club for the FIFTH time. During a 500-match career he was with Liverpool (Second), Carlisle (Third), Derby (Second), Leicester (Second) and Notts County (Third).

WHAT A STAR ⭐ JOHNNY GILES

Of the many internationals Leeds employed in their greatest years, Johnny Giles was perhaps the one who stood out most. Although short and none too fast, he was a marvellous passer, long or short, in any direction. Giles made Leeds tick and, unlike some midfielders, he was strong in the tackle and sometimes surprised everybody by hitting a fierce shot, although he scored only five goals in 59 games for the Republic of Ireland. He began with Manchester United and later played for West Brom and Shamrock Rovers.

CHAMPIONS
Arsenal 1970-71

The Gunners duly copied neighbours Spurs by doing the double, although only the Highbury die-hards could claim that their team matched Blanchflower and co. for attractive football. Bertie Mee's squad were functional whereas Bill Nicholson's had been romantics. However, both worked very well. Arsenal, led by inspirational skipper Frank McLintock, clinched the League in the dying moments of their final game against great rivals Spurs at White Hart Lane - as they were to do in even more dramatic circumstances at Anfield in 1989 - then came from behind to win the Cup Final at Wembley against Liverpool.

1971-72 cont

DIVISION 3
1	Aston Villa	70
2	Brighton	65
3	Bournemouth	62
4	Notts Co	62
5	Rotherham	55
6	Bristol Rovers	54
7	Bolton	50
8	Plymouth	50
9	Walsall	48
10	Blackburn	47
11	Oldham	45
12	Shrewsbury	44
13	Chesterfield	44
14	Swansea	44
15	Port Vale	41
16	Wrexham	40
17	Halifax	38
18	Rochdale	37
19	York	36
20	Tranmere	36
21	Mansfield	36
22	Barnsley	36
23	Torquay	32
24	Bradford	32

DIVISION 4
1	Grimsby	63
2	Southend	60
3	Brentford	59
4	Scunthorpe	57
5	Lincoln	56
6	Workington	51
7	Southport	50
8	Peterborough	50
9	Bury	50
10	Cambridge	48
11	Colchester	48
12	Doncaster	46
13	Gillingham	45
14	Newport	44
15	Exeter	43
16	Reading	42
17	Aldershot	40
18	Hartlepool	40
19	Darlington	39
20	Chester	38
21	Northampton	37
22	Barrow	37
23	Stockport	32
24	Crewe	29

Bob-a-Job

Bob Latchford scored 30 League goals for Everton during 1977-78, and won a £10,000 prize offered by a national newspaper (Daily Express) to the first player to achieve the feat. Latchford got his last two goals in his final game, a 6-0 win over Chelsea.

1972-73

DIVISION 1
1	Liverpool	60
2	Arsenal	57
3	Leeds	53
4	Ipswich	48
5	Wolves	47
6	West Ham	46
7	Derby	46
8	Tottenham	45
9	Newcastle	45
10	Birmingham	42
11	Man City	41
12	Chelsea	40
13	Southampton	40
14	Sheff Utd	40
15	Stoke	38
16	Leicester	37
17	Everton	37
18	Man Utd	37
19	Coventry	35
20	Norwich	32
21	C.Palace	30
22	West Brom	28

DIVISION 2
1	Burnley	62
2	QPR	61
3	Aston Villa	50
4	Middlesbro	47
5	Bristol City	46
6	Sunderland	46
7	Blackpool	46
8	Oxford	45
9	Fulham	44
10	Sheff Wed	44
11	Millwall	42
12	Luton	41
13	Hull	40
14	Nottm For	40
15	L.Orient	36
16	Swindon	36
17	Portsmouth	35
18	Carlisle	34
19	Preston	34
20	Cardiff	33
21	Huddersfield	33
22	Brighton	29

1972-73 cont

DIVISION 3
1	Bolton	61
2	Notts Co	57
3	Blackburn	55
4	Oldham	54
5	Bristol Rovers	53
6	Port Vale	53
7	Bournemouth	50
8	Plymouth	50
9	Grimsby	48
10	Tranmere	46
11	Charlton	45
12	Wrexham	45
13	Rochdale	45
14	Southend	44
15	Shrewsbury	43
16	Chesterfield	43
17	Walsall	43
18	York	41
19	Watford	41
20	Halifax	41
21	Rotherham	41
22	Brentford	37
23	Swansea	37
24	Scunthorpe	30

DIVISION 4
1	Southport	62
2	Hereford	58
3	Cambridge	57
4	Aldershot	56
5	Newport	56
6	Mansfield	54
7	Reading	52
8	Exeter	50
9	Gillingham	49
10	Lincoln	48
11	Stockport	48
12	Bury	46
13	Workington	46
14	Barnsley	44
15	Chester	43
16	Bradford	43
17	Doncaster	42
18	Torquay	41
19	Peterborough	41
20	Hartlepool	41
21	Crewe	36
22	Colchester	31
23	Northampton	31
24	Darlington	29

Strange but true!

Norwich avoided relegation to the Second Division in 1972-73 with two points to spare, despite scoring the fewest goals in the First Division, 36, and conceding the most, 63.

CHAMPIONS
Middlesbrough 1973-74

New manager Jack Charlton applied the lessons he had learned during his long and successful career, and a Middlesbrough team virtually unchanged all season won the Second Division with 65 points, the highest total for 54 years, and by an astonishing 15-point margin. There was a nine-match winning streak towards the end of the season, and players such as Graeme Souness and David Mills - who were both eventually sold for record fees - Willie Maddren and David Armstrong went on to establish themselves as top-quality performers at the very highest level.

1973-74

DIVISION 1

1	Leeds	62
2	Liverpool	57
3	Derby	48
4	Ipswich	47
5	Stoke	46
6	Burnley	46
7	Everton	44
8	QPR	43
9	Leicester	42
10	Arsenal	42
11	Tottenham	42
12	Wolves	41
13	Sheff Utd	40
14	Man City	40
15	Newcastle	38
16	Coventry	38
17	Chelsea	37
18	West Ham	37
19	Birmingham	37
20	Southampton	36
21	Man Utd	32
22	Norwich	29

DIVISION 2

1	Middlesbro	65
2	Luton	50
3	Carlisle	49
4	L.Orient	48
5	Blackpool	47
6	Sunderland	47
7	Nottm For	45
8	West Brom	44
9	Hull	43
10	Notts Co	43
11	Bolton	42
12	Millwall	42
13	Fulham	42
14	Aston Villa	41
15	Portsmouth	40
16	Bristol City	38
17	Cardiff	36
18	Oxford	36
19	Sheff Wed	35
20	C.Palace	34
21	Preston NE*	31
22	Swindon	25

* Preston had one point deducted for fielding an ineligible player.

DIVISION 3

1	Oldham	62
2	Bristol Rovers	61
3	York	61
4	Wrexham	56
5	Chesterfield	56
6	Grimsby	51
7	Watford	50
8	Aldershot	49
9	Halifax	49
10	Huddersfield	47
11	Bournemouth	47
12	Southend	46
13	Blackburn	46
14	Charlton	46
15	Walsall	45
16	Tranmere	45
17	Plymouth	44
18	Hereford	43
19	Brighton	43
20	Port Vale	42
21	Cambridge	35
22	Shrewsbury	31
23	Southport	28
24	Rochdale	21

DIVISION 4

1	Peterborough	65
2	Gillingham	62
3	Colchester	60
4	Bury	59
5	Northampton	53
6	Reading	51
7	Chester	49
8	Bradford	48
9	Newport**	45
10	Exeter+	44
11	Hartlepool	44
12	Lincoln	44
13	Barnsley	44
14	Swansea	43
15	Rotherham	43
16	Torquay	43
17	Mansfield	43
18	Scunthorpe+	42
19	Brentford	40
20	Darlington	39
21	Crewe	38
22	Doncaster	35
23	Workington	35
24	Stockport	34

** Newport had one point deducted for fielding an ineligible player.

+The Scunthorpe v Exeter game was never played, Scunthorpe were awarded the points after Exeter failed to turn up.

Penalty Pain

Peterborough's Alan Slough scored a hat-trick of penalties in an AWAY game in April 1978, but was on the losing side. Chester won 4-3.

1974-75

DIVISION 1

1	Derby	53
2	Liverpool	51
3	Ipswich	51
4	Everton	50
5	Stoke	49
6	Sheff Utd	49
7	Middlesbro	48
8	Man City	46
9	Leeds	45
10	Burnley	45
11	QPR	42
12	Wolves	39
13	West Ham	39
14	Coventry	39
15	Newcastle	39
16	Arsenal	37
17	Birmingham	37
18	Leicester	36
19	Tottenham	34
20	Luton	33
21	Chelsea	33
22	Carlisle	29

DIVISION 2

1	Man Utd	61
2	Aston Villa	58
3	Norwich	53
4	Sunderland	51
5	Bristol City	50
6	West Brom	45
7	Blackpool	45
8	Hull	44
9	Fulham	42
10	Bolton	42
11	Oxford	42
12	L.Orient	42
13	Southampton	41
14	Notts Co	40
15	York	38
16	Nottm For	38
17	Portsmouth	37
18	Oldham	35
19	Bristol Rovers	35
20	Millwall	32
21	Cardiff	32
22	Sheff Wed	21

Strange but true!

Jack Charlton became manager of Middlesbrough on May 7, 1973 - three days after brother Bobby had become manager of Preston.

1974-75 cont

DIVISION 3

1	Blackburn	60
2	Plymouth	59
3	Charlton	55
4	Swindon	53
5	C.Palace	51
6	Port Vale	51
7	Peterborough	50
8	Walsall	49
9	Preston	49
10	Gillingham	48
11	Colchester	47
12	Hereford	46
13	Wrexham	45
14	Bury	44
15	Chesterfield	44
16	Grimsby	43
17	Halifax	43
18	Southend	42
19	Brighton	42
20	Aldershot	38
21	Bournemouth	38
22	Tranmere	37
23	Watford	37
24	Huddersfield	32

DIVISION 4

1	Mansfield	68
2	Shrewsbury	62
3	Rotherham	59
4	Chester	57
5	Lincoln	57
6	Cambridge	54
7	Reading	52
8	Brentford	49
9	Exeter	49
10	Bradford	47
11	Southport	47
12	Newport	47
13	Hartlepool	43
14	Torquay	42
15	Barnsley	41
16	Northampton	41
17	Doncaster	40
18	Crewe	40
19	Rochdale	39
20	Stockport	38
21	Darlington	36
22	Swansea	36
23	Workington	31
24	Scunthorpe	29

Strange but true!

Mansfield did not score a single home goal until their tenth match in 1971-72, when in Division Three. Their results were 0-0, 0-3, 0-2, 0-1, 0-0, 0-0, 0-5, 0-1, 0-0 and - on December 18 - 2-1. They were relegated, when two more goals would have kept them safe.

1975-76

DIVISION 1

1	Liverpool	60
2	QPR	59
3	Man Utd	56
4	Derby	53
5	Leeds	51
6	Ipswich	46
7	Leicester	45
8	Man City	43
9	Tottenham	43
10	Norwich	42
11	Everton	42
12	Stoke	41
13	Middlesbro	40
14	Coventry	40
15	Newcastle	39
16	Aston Villa	39
17	Arsenal	36
18	West Ham	36
19	Birmingham	33
20	Wolves	30
21	Burnley	28
22	Sheff Utd	22

DIVISION 2

1	Sunderland	56
2	Bristol City	53
3	West Brom	53
4	Bolton	52
5	Notts Co	49
6	Southampton	49
7	Luton	48
8	Nottm For	46
9	Charlton	42
10	Blackpool	42
11	Chelsea	40
12	Fulham	40
13	L.Orient	40
14	Hull	39
15	Blackburn	38
16	Plymouth	38
17	Oldham	38
18	Bristol Rovers	38
19	Carlisle	37
20	Oxford	33
21	York	28
22	Portsmouth	25

Everton's Alan Ball

Strange but true!

Liverpool's 42 First Division matches in 1970-71 contained a record low total of only 66 goals. They scored 42, conceded 24, finished fifth, and had the League's best average gate, 45,606.

WHAT A STAR ⭐ ALAN BALL

Little Alan Ball had been England's outstanding player in the 1966 World Cup Final, when only 21. As he matured, he became more consistent and even more effective, as a winger-cum-inside-forward, combining non-stop running with considerable passing skill and ball control. He went from Blackpool to Everton to Arsenal, for a then record £220,000, and on to Southampton, but with surprisingly little to show in the way of club honours. He also became a strangely unsuccessful manager with a series of clubs, including Exeter, Southampton and Manchester City.

Pro-File: PETER SHILTON

Arguably the finest English goalkeeper of all time, Shilton enjoyed a career that anyone in the history of the game would probably have willingly swapped for.

Although not the biggest of 'keepers, he more than made up for his lack of inches with agility and positioning that was simply second to none.

Add that to the fact that, at the first two clubs of his glittering career - Leicester and Stoke - he followed in the footsteps of the legendary Gordon Banks and you get some idea of how highly he was rated.

His best days came during the late 70s and early 80s when he helped turn Nottingham Forest into one of Europe's best sides, twice winning the Champions' Cup.

But although his club career was nothing less than a success, it was on the international scene that Shilton truly made his mark.

An English record 125 appearances stands testimony to his ability, particularly when you consider that his main rival for the England No.1 jersey during that period, Ray Clemence, won 63 caps.

The two often alternated and had Shilton played in even half of those games he surely would have created a record no-one could ever have touched.

Career details

● **Represented:** England, Leicester, Stoke, Nottingham Forest, Southampton, Derby, Plymouth, Wimbledon, Bolton, Leyton Orient ● **Position:** Goalkeeper ● **Born:** Leicester, 18.09.49 ● **Height:** 6ft 1in ● **Weight:** 14st ● **Club Honours:** League Championship 1977-78; European Cup 1979, 1980; League Cup 1979; PFA Player of the Year 1978; PFA Merit Award 1990 ● **International Honours:** England 12Youth, 13 U23, 4 B, 125 full caps

Club League Record

Era	Club	Games	Goals
1966-74	Leicester	286	1
1974-77	Stoke	110	0
1977-82	Nottm Forest	202	0
1982-87	Southampton	188	0
1987-92	Derby	175	0
1992-95	Plymouth	34	0
1995-96	Wimbledon	0	0
1995-96	Bolton	1	0
1996-97	L.Orient	9	0

League Highlights

May 1978: Shilton helps Nottingham Forest win the First Division Championship, just a year after being promoted. Forest conceded only 24 goals in their 42 games.

Dec 22 1996: Shilton makes his 1,000th League appearance, the first man ever to reach that milestone, for Leyton Orient against Brighton. Fittingly, he keeps a clean sheet

SHILTON ON:

● As an apprentice earning £8 a week my only ambition was to get into the first team. What has happened since has been beyond my wildest dreams. **Shilton on his glorious career.**

● If I have one regret it's that I didn't make my 1,000th appearance in the Premiership, but the reception I got at Brisbane Road was fantastic. **Shilton on reaching his famous milestone.**

DID YOU KNOW THAT...

● Shilton made his League debut against Everton on May 4, 1966, six weeks before England won the World Cup.

● He is one of the few goalkeepers to have scored a goal. He did so for Leicester at Southampton on October 14, 1967.

● Shilton retired from international football at the age of 40 after the 1990 World Cup Finals. At the time, his tally of 125 caps was a world record.

● Shilton was part of the Nottingham Forest side which set a record of 42 matches unbeaten between November 1977 and December 1978. The run consisted of 21 wins and 21 draws.

● He became the first player to play 1,000 League matches when he turned out for Leyton Orient against Brighton in December 1996 and received a standing ovation.

● His nickname was Shilts.

● Shilton has made 86 appearances in the FA Cup. Only two players have made more - former Liverpool star Ian Callaghan and Stanley Matthews.

● Shilton never actually won an FA Cup winners' medal. The closest he came was finishing runners-up with Leicester in 1969.

CHAMPIONS
Lincoln 1975-76

Graham Taylor took a lot of stick while England manager, but he did a magnificent job at club level. His Lincoln City team made a virtue of attack, and raced to the Fourth Division title with records for most points (74), most wins (32) and fewest defeats (4). They had one sequence of 12 wins and two draws, followed by another of 10 wins and four draws, and seven of their players scored eight goals or more. Peter Grotier, the 'keeper who had cost City's record fee (£16,666 from West Ham) conceded a mere 39 goals in their 46 games.

Regular Rovers

Tranmere did not make a single team change in 1977-78 until their 29th League match, fielding the same line-up in all those games, and 11 players made 40 or more appearances during the season.

1976-77

DIVISION 1		DIVISION 2	
1 Liverpool	57	1 Wolves	57
2 Man City	56	2 Chelsea	55
3 Ipswich	52	3 Nottm For	52
4 Aston Villa	51	4 Bolton	51
5 Newcastle	49	5 Blackpool	51
6 Man Utd	47	6 Luton	48
7 West Brom	45	7 Charlton	48
8 Arsenal	43	8 Notts Co	48
9 Everton	42	9 Southampton	44
10 Leeds	42	10 Millwall	43
11 Leicester	42	11 Sheff Utd	40
12 Middlesbro	41	12 Blackburn	39
13 Birmingham	38	13 Oldham	38
14 QPR	38	14 Hull	37
15 Derby	37	15 Bristol Rovers	36
16 Norwich	37	16 Burnley	36
17 West Ham	36	17 Fulham	35
18 Bristol City	35	18 Cardiff	34
19 Coventry	35	19 L.Orient	34
20 Sunderland	34	20 Carlisle	34
21 Stoke	34	21 Plymouth	32
22 Tottenham	33	22 Hereford	31

1975-76	cont		
DIVISION 3		**DIVISION 4**	
1 Hereford	63	1 Lincoln	74
2 Cardiff	57	2 Northampton	68
3 Millwall	56	3 Reading	60
4 Brighton	53	4 Tranmere	58
5 C.Palace	53	5 Huddersfield	56
6 Wrexham	52	6 Bournemouth	52
7 Walsall	50	7 Exeter	50
8 Preston	48	8 Watford	50
9 Shrewsbury	48	9 Torquay	50
10 Peterborough	48	10 Doncaster	49
11 Mansfield	47	11 Swansea	47
12 Port Vale	46	12 Barnsley	44
13 Bury	44	13 Cambridge	43
14 Chesterfield	43	14 Hartlepool	42
15 Gillingham	43	15 Rochdale	42
16 Rotherham	42	16 Crewe	41
17 Chester	42	17 Bradford	41
18 Grimsby	40	18 Brentford	41
19 Swindon	40	19 Scunthorpe	38
20 Sheff Wed	40	20 Darlington	38
21 Aldershot	39	21 Stockport	38
22 Colchester	38	22 Newport	35
23 Southend	37	23 Southport	26
24 Halifax	35	24 Workington	21

Good Friday

A player named Robin Friday was transferred from Reading to Cardiff on a Thursday in December 1976, spent Friday adjusting to his new surroundings and scored two goals on the Saturday, in his first match for his new club.

WHAT A STAR ⭐ TREVOR FRANCIS

A boy wonder with Birmingham, he grew up to have a ten-year career with England and a longer one at club level, but was never particularly lucky. If he had not been so prone to injuries, he might perhaps have been a truly great player instead of a very good one. He was quick and usually deadly when taking chances, and won the European Cup for Forest not long after becoming the first £1 million British player. Later he had spells with Manchester City, and with Sampdoria and Atalanta in Italy.

1976-77 cont
DIVISION 3
1	Mansfield	64
2	Brighton	61
3	C.Palace	59
4	Rotherham	59
5	Wrexham	58
6	Preston	54
7	Bury	54
8	Sheff Wed	53
9	Lincoln	52
10	Shrewsbury	47
11	Swindon	45
12	Gillingham	44
13	Chester	44
14	Tranmere	43
15	Walsall	41
16	Peterborough	41
17	Oxford	39
18	Chesterfield	38
19	Port Vale	38
20	Portsmouth	38
21	Reading	35
22	Northampton	34
23	Grimsby	33
24	York	32

DIVISION 4
1	Cambridge	65
2	Exeter	62
3	Colchester	59
4	Bradford	59
5	Swansea	58
6	Barnsley	55
7	Watford	51
8	Doncaster	51
9	Huddersfield	50
10	Southend	49
11	Darlington	49
12	Crewe	49
13	Bournemouth	48
14	Stockport	45
15	Brentford	43
16	Torquay	43
17	Aldershot	43
18	Rochdale	38
19	Newport	38
20	Scunthorpe	37
21	Halifax	36
22	Hartlepool	32
23	Southport	25
24	Workington	19

That's Nott Very Likely

In 1976 Nottingham Forest won 5-1 and Notts County lost 5-1 on the same day. Two weeks later, again on the same day, Forest won 6-1 and County lost 6-1.

1977-78
DIVISION 1
1	Nottm For	64
2	Liverpool	57
3	Everton	55
4	Man City	52
5	Arsenal	52
6	West Brom	50
7	Coventry	48
8	Aston Villa	46
9	Leeds	46
10	Man Utd	42
11	Birmingham	41
12	Derby	41
13	Norwich	40
14	Middlesbro	39
15	Wolves	36
16	Chelsea	36
17	Bristol City	35
18	Ipswich	35
19	QPR	33
20	West Ham	32
21	Newcastle	22
22	Leicester	22

DIVISION 2
1	Bolton	58
2	Southampton	57
3	Tottenham	56
4	Brighton	56
5	Blackburn	45
6	Sunderland	44
7	Stoke	42
8	Oldham	42
9	C.Palace	41
10	Fulham	41
11	Burnley	40
12	Sheff Utd	40
13	Luton	38
14	L.Orient	38
15	Notts Co	38
16	Millwall	38
17	Charlton	38
18	Bristol Rovers	38
19	Cardiff	38
20	Blackpool	37
21	Mansfield	31
22	Hull	28

Strange but true!

Derby won the League title in 1971-72 while in Majorca. Neither Leeds nor Liverpool got the results they needed to steal the crown in their last matches, so The Rams claimed their first Championship trophy while already away on an end-of-season trip.

1977-78 cont
DIVISION 3
1	Wrexham	61
2	Cambridge	58
3	Preston	56
4	Peterborough	56
5	Chester	54
6	Walsall	53
7	Gillingham	50
8	Colchester	48
9	Chesterfield	48
10	Swindon	48
11	Shrewsbury	47
12	Tranmere	47
13	Carlisle	47
14	Sheff Wed	46
15	Bury	45
16	Lincoln	45
17	Exeter	44
18	Oxford	40
19	Plymouth	39
20	Rotherham	39
21	Port Vale	36
22	Bradford	34
23	Hereford	32
24	Portsmouth	31

DIVISION 4
1	Watford	71
2	Southend	60
3	Swansea	56
4	Brentford	56
5	Aldershot	54
6	Grimsby	53
7	Barnsley	50
8	Reading	50
9	Torquay	47
10	Northampton	47
11	Huddersfield	45
12	Doncaster	45
13	Wimbledon	44
14	Scunthorpe	44
15	Crewe	44
16	Newport	43
17	Bournemouth	43
18	Stockport	42
19	Darlington	41
20	Halifax	41
21	Hartlepool	37
22	York	36
23	Southport	31
24	Rochdale	24

WHAT A STAR ⭐ GORDON BANKS

Perhaps England's finest goalkeeper. He was 32 when he made THE save, from Pele in the 1970 World Cup, but many good judges thought he was better than ever in the latter stages of a long career with Leicester and Stoke. His withdrawal, sick, from the Quarter-Final in that 1970 tournament was decidedly costly as England lost 3-2 to their great rivals West Germany. One League Cup medal was his only club trophy, but he still had several years at the top left in him when he lost an eye in a car crash and had to retire from 'proper' football, though he still played occasional matches in the USA and elsewhere, as he was always in demand.

CHAMPIONS
Nottingham Forest 1977-78

Brian Clough, the manager who had taken Derby to the Championship in 1971-72, now repeated the feat with nearby Forest, who had been promoted the previous season. Clough helped to create a great side out of apparently average players. The signing of England 'keeper Peter Shilton made the vital difference, and Forest had the title sewn up with four games to go, during an unbeaten run which carried over into the following season and eventually stretched to a record 42 League games.

1978-79

DIVISION 1			DIVISION 2	
1 Liverpool	68		1 C.Palace	57
2 Nottm For	60		2 Brighton	56
3 West Brom	59		3 Stoke	56
4 Everton	51		4 Sunderland	55
5 Leeds	50		5 West Ham	50
6 Ipswich	49		6 Notts Co	44
7 Arsenal	48		7 Preston	42
8 Aston Villa	46		8 Newcastle	42
9 Man Utd	45		9 Cardiff	42
10 Coventry	44		10 Fulham	41
11 Tottenham	41		11 L.Orient	40
12 Middlesbro	40		12 Cambridge	40
13 Bristol City	40		13 Burnley	40
14 Southampton	40		14 Oldham	39
15 Man City	39		15 Wrexham	38
16 Norwich	37		16 Bristol Rovers	38
17 Bolton	35		17 Leicester	37
18 Wolves	34		18 Luton	36
19 Derby	31		19 Charlton	35
20 QPR	25		20 Sheff Utd	34
21 Birmingham	22		21 Millwall	32
22 Chelsea	20		22 Blackburn	30

Millionaire's Row

Trevor Francis became British football's first £1 million player when he joined Nottingham Forest from Birmingham in February 1979.

1978-79

DIVISION 3			DIVISION 4	
1 Shrewsbury	61		1 Reading	65
2 Watford	60		2 Grimsby	61
3 Swansea	60		3 Wimbledon	61
4 Gillingham	59		4 Barnsley	61
5 Swindon	57		5 Aldershot	57
6 Carlisle	52		6 Wigan	55
7 Colchester	51		7 Portsmouth	52
8 Hull	49		8 Newport	52
9 Exeter	49		9 Huddersfield	47
10 Brentford	47		10 York	47
11 Oxford	46		11 Torquay	46
12 Blackpool	45		12 Scunthorpe	45
13 Southend	45		13 Hartlepool	44
14 Sheff Wed	45		14 Hereford	43
15 Plymouth	44		15 Bradford	43
16 Chester	44		16 Port Vale	42
17 Rotherham	44		17 Stockport	40
18 Mansfield	43		18 Bournemouth	39
19 Bury	42		19 Northampton	39
20 Chesterfield	40		20 Rochdale	39
21 Peterborough	36		21 Darlington	37
22 Walsall	32		22 Doncaster	37
23 Tranmere	28		23 Halifax	26
24 Lincoln	25		24 Crewe	26

Double Delight

Only three men have led two different clubs to Championship wins - Brian Clough (Derby and Forest), Herbert Chapman (Huddersfield and Arsenal) and Kenny Dalglish (Liverpool and Blackburn).

WHAT A STAR ⭐ KEVIN KEEGAN

If ever a man made the most of himself, Keegan did. Although he was not especially gifted by nature, he turned himself into a great player by sheer hard work and self-discipline. After three years scuffling around with Scunthorpe, watched but ignored by dozens of clubs, he was signed by Liverpool and, almost overnight, turned into a star. At Anfield and in Hamburg, at Southampton and Newcastle, he always gave value for the large sums of money he made, with his work-rate and sharp finishing, and was twice European Player of the Year.

1979-80
DIVISION 1

1	Liverpool	60
2	Man Utd	58
3	Ipswich	53
4	Arsenal	52
5	Nottm For	48
6	Wolves	47
7	Aston Villa	46
8	Southampton	45
9	Middlesbro	44
10	West Brom	41
11	Leeds	40
12	Norwich	40
13	C.Palace	40
14	Tottenham	40
15	Coventry	39
16	Brighton	37
17	Man City	37
18	Stoke	36
19	Everton	35
20	Bristol City	31
21	Derby	30
22	Bolton	25

Liverpool 1979

Bye Bye

English football's most famous brothers - Bobby and Jack Charlton - both retired on the same day, April 28, 1973. Bobby played his 606th game for Manchester United at Chelsea, while Jack bowed out after his 629th appearance for Leeds, at Southampton.

DIVISION 2

1	Leicester	55
2	Sunderland	54
3	Birmingham	53
4	Chelsea	53
5	QPR	49
6	Luton	49
7	West Ham	47
8	Cambridge	44
9	Newcastle	44
10	Preston	43
11	Oldham	43
12	Swansea	43
13	Shrewsbury	41
14	L.Orient	41
15	Cardiff	40
16	Wrexham	38
17	Notts Co	37
18	Watford	37
19	Bristol Rovers	35
20	Fulham	29
21	Burnley	27
22	Charlton	22

DIVISION 3

1	Grimsby	62
2	Blackburn	59
3	Sheff Wed	58
4	Chesterfield	57
5	Colchester	52
6	Carlisle	48
7	Reading	48
8	Exeter	48
9	Chester	47
10	Swindon	46
11	Barnsley	46
12	Sheff Utd	46
13	Rotherham	46
14	Millwall	45
15	Plymouth	44
16	Gillingham	42
17	Oxford	41
18	Blackpool	41
19	Brentford	41
20	Hull	40
21	Bury	39
22	Southend	38
23	Mansfield	36
24	Wimbledon	34

DIVISION 4

1	Huddersfield	66
2	Walsall	64
3	Newport	61
4	Portsmouth	60
5	Bradford	60
6	Wigan	55
7	Lincoln	53
8	Peterborough	52
9	Torquay	47
10	Aldershot	45
11	Bournemouth	44
12	Doncaster	44
13	Northampton	44
14	Scunthorpe	43
15	Tranmere	41
16	Stockport	40
17	York	39
18	Halifax	39
19	Hartlepool	38
20	Port Vale	36
21	Hereford	36
22	Darlington	35
23	Crewe	35
24	Rochdale	27

CHAMPIONS
Liverpool 1978-79

A record-busting season for Bob Paisley, who bettered even Bill Shankly's legendary feats at Anfield. By winning their last five matches - the fourth such sequence during the season - Liverpool reached 68 points, beating the First Division record by one, and just 16 goals against was an all-time record. Dalglish, Clemence, Hansen, Ray Kennedy, McDermott and Souness were all among the country's finest players in their respective positions as the Red machine rolled over all before it.

1980-1989

REDS RULE ROOST

The 80s started as the 70s had ended - with Liverpool in complete control. The Reds had been fantastically successful in the 70s, but somehow they seemed to find another gear and simply turned the screw even tighter. They won the title in 1981-82, 1982-83, 1983-84, 1985-86 and 1987-88 and finished runners-up, ironically to Everton on both occasions, in the years in between.

It was an unbelievable period and seemed then as though it would never be matched, although the Manchester United team of the 90s may have other ideas. But for those years during the early and mid-80s Liverpool had no equals. They were, quite simply, in a League of their own and other clubs could only watch as they sailed towards one Championship after another.

With first Ray Clemence and then Bruce Grobbelaar as mean as ever in goal, Alan Hansen and Mark Lawrenson offering them more than ample protection, Graeme Souness pulling the strings in midfield, and Kenny Dalglish and Ian Rush adding the finishing touches they were indeed a formidable outfit.

Everton, under Howard Kendall, did interrupt the Anfield procession in both 1984-85 and 1986-87, and they too played with real style and panache. The real pity is that, because of the Heysel disaster in 1985 and the subsequent ban on English clubs in Europe, Everton never had the chance to pit their wits against the very best in the Champions' Cup.

Strange but true!

Former England centre-half Dave Watson's second goal for Notts County came 17 years after his first. He got one goal for Notts in October 1967 and his second came in April 1985, when he rejoined the club after playing for eight others and winning 65 caps.

Kerry Fold

Kerry Dixon scored four goals for Reading in an away match in 1982, and finished on the losing side. Doncaster beat them 8-5.

Rolling Moss

Much-travelled Ernie Moss won promotion in 1985 for the fifth time - with Chesterfield, Mansfield, Port Vale, Doncaster and Chesterfield again.

But the 80s saved the best 'til last with the most dramatic finish to a season ever, and one that will surely never be bettered. Arsenal travelled to Anfield needing to win, and score at least two goals, to deny Liverpool the title. And they did so, with the winning goal from Michael Thomas coming in the last minute. Photo-finishes don't come any tighter than that.

LEAGUE TABLES 1980-81 to 1989-90

Aston Villa's Dennis Mortimor toasts their 1981 title success

1980-81 cont
DIVISION 3

1	Rotherham	61
2	Barnsley	59
3	Charlton	59
4	Huddersfield	56
5	Chesterfield	56
6	Portsmouth	53
7	Plymouth	52
8	Burnley	50
9	Brentford	47
10	Reading	46
11	Exeter	45
12	Newport	43
13	Fulham	43
14	Oxford	43
15	Gillingham	42
16	Millwall	42
17	Swindon	41
18	Chester	41
19	Carlisle	41
20	Walsall	41
21	Sheff Utd	40
22	Colchester	39
23	Blackpool	32
24	Hull	32

DIVISION 4

1	Southend	67
2	Lincoln	65
3	Doncaster	56
4	Wimbledon	55
5	Peterborough	52
6	Aldershot	50
7	Mansfield	49
8	Darlington	49
9	Hartlepool	49
10	Northampton	49
11	Wigan	47
12	Bury	45
13	Bournemouth	44
14	Bradford	44
15	Rochdale	43
16	Scunthorpe	42
17	Torquay	41
18	Crewe	40
19	Port Vale	39
20	Stockport	39
21	Tranmere	36
22	Hereford	35
23	Halifax	34
24	York	33

1981-82
DIVISION 1

1	Liverpool	87
2	Ipswich	83
3	Man Utd	78
4	Tottenham	71
5	Arsenal	71
6	Swansea	69
7	Southampton	66
8	Everton	64
9	West Ham	58
10	Man City	58
11	Aston Villa	57
12	Nottm For	57
13	Brighton	52
14	Coventry	50
15	Notts Co	47
16	Birmingham	44
17	West Brom	44
18	Stoke	44
19	Sunderland	44
20	Leeds	42
21	Wolves	40
22	Middlesbro	39

DIVISION 2

1	Luton	88
2	Watford	80
3	Norwich	71
4	Sheff Wed	70
5	QPR	69
6	Barnsley	67
7	Rotherham	67
8	Leicester	66
9	Newcastle	62
10	Blackburn	59
11	Oldham	59
12	Chelsea	57
13	Charlton	51
14	Cambridge	48
15	C.Palace	48
16	Derby	48
17	Grimsby	46
18	Shrewsbury	46
19	Bolton	46
20	Cardiff	44
21	Wrexham	44
22	L.Orient	39

1980-81
DIVISION 1

1	Aston Villa	60
2	Ipswich	56
3	Arsenal	53
4	West Brom	52
5	Liverpool	51
6	Southampton	50
7	Nottm For	50
8	Man Utd	48
9	Leeds	44
10	Tottenham	43
11	Stoke	42
12	Man City	39
13	Birmingham	38
14	Middlesbro	38
15	Everton	36
16	Coventry	36
17	Sunderland	35
18	Wolves	35
19	Brighton	35
20	Norwich	33
21	Leicester	32
22	C.Palace	19

DIVISION 2

1	West Ham	66
2	Notts Co	53
3	Swansea	50
4	Blackburn	50
5	Luton	48
6	Derby	45
7	Grimsby	45
8	QPR	43
9	Watford	43
10	Sheff Wed	42
11	Newcastle	42
12	Chelsea	40
13	Cambridge	40
14	Shrewsbury	39
15	Oldham	39
16	Wrexham	38
17	L.Orient	38
18	Bolton	38
19	Cardiff	36
20	Preston	36
21	Bristol City	30
22	Bristol Rovers	23

WHAT A STAR ⭐ IAN RUSH

Ian Rush broke just about every Liverpool scoring record going, as well as those for the FA Cup, FA Cup Finals, and Wales, but he would have been a marvellous player even if he had never got a goal. Few strikers passed as well as he did, and none worked harder at being the first defender as well as the last attacker. He deserved every one of the honours he won in his career, for his pleasant temperament meant that he was no problem for referees (or managers) and, allied to his skill, made him a role model for any youngster.

CHAMPIONS
Aston Villa 1980-81

Villa went out of the League Cup at the second stage and the FA Cup at the first hurdle. This left them free to concentrate on the League - and they won it despite a poor record against their greatest rivals: they won two, drew two and lost four of the matches against the four clubs who finished immediately below them. Their greatest strength was in teamwork, and a record seven players appeared in all 42 League games as the club won the Championship for the first time in 71 years. The following season Villa tasted success in the European Cup, beating German Champions Bayern Munich 1-0 in the Final.

1981-82 cont
DIVISION 3

1	Burnley	80
2	Carlisle	80
3	Fulham	78
4	Lincoln	77
5	Oxford	71
6	Gillingham	71
7	Southend	69
8	Brentford	68
9	Millwall	67
10	Plymouth	65
11	Chesterfield	64
12	Reading	62
13	Portsmouth	61
14	Preston	61
15	Bristol Rovers	61
16	Newport	58
17	Huddersfield	57
18	Exeter	57
19	Doncaster	56
20	Walsall	53
21	Wimbledon	53
22	Swindon	52
23	Bristol City	46
24	Chester	32

DIVISION 4

1	Sheff Utd	96
2	Bradford	91
3	Wigan	91
4	Bournemouth	88
5	Peterborough	82
6	Colchester	72
7	Port Vale	70
8	Hull	69
9	Bury	68
10	Hereford	67
11	Tranmere	60
12	Blackpool	58
13	Darlington	58
14	Hartlepool	55
15	Torquay	55
16	Aldershot	54
17	York	50
18	Stockport	49
19	Halifax	49
20	Mansfield	47
21	Rochdale	46
22	Northampton	42
23	Scunthorpe	42
24	Crewe	27

1982-83
DIVISION 1

1	Liverpool	82
2	Watford	71
3	Man Utd	70
4	Tottenham	69
5	Nottm For	69
6	Aston Villa	68
7	Everton	64
8	West Ham	64
9	Ipswich	58
10	Arsenal	58
11	West Brom	57
12	Southampton	57
13	Stoke	57
14	Norwich	54
15	Notts Co	52
16	Sunderland	50
17	Birmingham	50
18	Luton	49
19	Coventry	48
20	Man City	47
21	Swansea	41
22	Brighton	40

DIVISION 2

1	QPR	85
2	Wolves	75
3	Leicester	70
4	Fulham	69
5	Newcastle	67
6	Sheff Wed	63
7	Oldham	61
8	Leeds	60
9	Shrewsbury	59
10	Barnsley	57
11	Blackburn	57
12	Cambridge	51
13	Derby	49
14	Carlisle	48
15	C.Palace	48
16	Middlesbro	48
17	Charlton	48
18	Chelsea	47
19	Grimsby	47
20	Rotherham	45
21	Burnley	44
22	Bolton	44

DIVISION 3

1	Portsmouth	91
2	Cardiff	86
3	Huddersfield	82
4	Newport	78
5	Oxford	78
6	Lincoln	76
7	Bristol Rovers	75
8	Plymouth	65
9	Brentford	64
10	Walsall	64
11	Sheff Utd	64
12	Bradford	61
13	Gillingham	61
14	Bournemouth	61
15	Southend	59
16	Preston	58
17	Millwall	55
18	Wigan	54
19	Exeter	54
20	L.Orient	54
21	Reading	53
22	Wrexham	51
23	Doncaster	38
24	Chesterfield	37

DIVISION 4

1	Wimbledon	98
2	Hull	90
3	Port Vale	88
4	Scunthorpe	83
5	Bury	81
6	Colchester	81
7	York	79
8	Swindon	68
9	Peterborough	64
10	Mansfield	61
11	Halifax	60
12	Torquay	58
13	Chester	56
14	Bristol City	56
15	Northampton	54
16	Stockport	54
17	Darlington	52
18	Aldershot	51
19	Tranmere	50
20	Rochdale	49
21	Blackpool	49
22	Hartlepool	48
23	Crewe	41
24	Hereford	41

Goal-den Garth

Spurs beat Liverpool 1-0 three times in 1984-85, twice in the League and once in the League Cup, and Garth Crooks scored all three goals.

Strange but true!

Leicester beat Burnley 4-2 in December 1982 in a match that contained four goalkeepers (two of them deputies because of injury), three penalties (two missed) and two sendings-off.

WHAT A STAR ⭐ KENNY DALGLISH

A star with Celtic, he succeeded a star when he replaced Kevin Keegan at Liverpool, and became an even bigger star. "The first few yards are in his head," Bob Paisley used to say, and Kenny usually seemed to be a move or two in front of the others. A good finisher, too, with a century of goals for a single club in both Scotland and England, and Scotland's most-capped player with 102 caps. He would have appeared in a fourth World Cup, at 35, but for injury. To think that Rangers passed up on the chance to sign him as a kid.

1983-84

DIVISION 1		DIVISION 2	
1 Liverpool	80	1 Chelsea	88
2 Southampton	77	2 Sheff Wed	88
3 Nottm For	74	3 Newcastle	80
4 Man Utd	74	4 Man City	70
5 QPR	73	5 Grimsby	70
6 Arsenal	63	6 Blackburn	67
7 Everton	62	7 Carlisle	64
8 Tottenham	61	8 Shrewsbury	61
9 West Ham	60	9 Brighton	60
10 Aston Villa	60	10 Leeds	60
11 Watford	57	11 Fulham	57
12 Ipswich	53	12 Huddersfield	57
13 Sunderland	52	13 Charlton	57
14 Norwich	51	14 Barnsley	52
15 Leicester	51	15 Cardiff	51
16 Luton	51	16 Portsmouth	49
17 West Brom	51	17 Middlesbro	49
18 Stoke	50	18 C.Palace	47
19 Coventry	50	19 Oldham	47
20 Birmingham	48	20 Derby	42
21 Notts Co	41	21 Swansea	29
22 Wolves	29	22 Cambridge	24

Strange but true!

Newcastle drew four successive away matches in 1984-85 by different scores - 5-5, 1-1, 3-3 and 2-2.

DIVISION 3		DIVISION 4	
1 Oxford	95	1 York	101
2 Wimbledon	87	2 Doncaster	85
3 Sheff Utd	83	3 Reading	82
4 Hull	83	4 Bristol City	82
5 Bristol Rovers	79	5 Aldershot	75
6 Walsall	75	6 Blackpool	72
7 Bradford	71	7 Peterborough	68
8 Gillingham	70	8 Colchester	67
9 Millwall	67	9 Torquay	67
10 Bolton	64	10 Tranmere	66
11 L.Orient	63	11 Hereford	63
12 Burnley	62	12 Stockport	63
13 Newport	62	13 Chesterfield	60
14 Lincoln	61	14 Darlington	59
15 Wigan	61	15 Bury	59
16 Preston	56	16 Crewe	59
17 Bournemouth	55	17 Swindon	58
18 Rotherham	54	18 Northampton	53
19 Plymouth	51	19 Mansfield	52
20 Brentford	49	20 Wrexham	48
21 Scunthorpe	46	21 Halifax	48
22 Southend	44	22 Rochdale	46
23 Port Vale	43	23 Hartlepool	40
24 Exeter	33	24 Chester	34

Birthday Joy

Stuart Rimmer's 21st birthday was on October 11, 1985, and it's one he will never forget because he celebrated by scoring four goals for Chester against Preston.

CHAMPIONS
Liverpool 1983-84

Even Liverpool had their doubts about completing only the third hat-trick of League titles, after Huddersfield in the 20s and Arsenal in the 30s. Yet they did it with something to spare, giving new manager Joe Fagan - at 63 - an historic 'double treble' in his first season after succeeding Paisley. In addition to the League success, Liverpool also won the League Cup and the European Cup. Only a surprise FA Cup defeat by Second Division Brighton marred the season. Very much a team effort, of course, but Ian Rush was the main man, with 32 League goals and 47 in all matches.

Pro-File: Alan Hansen

Alan Hansen was one of the cornerstones on which the great Liverpool team of the late 70s and early 80s was built.

His partnership in the centre of defence with Mark Lawrenson was one of the meanest around, and proved that you don't necessarily have to be big and strong to be a world class defender.

Hansen was competent enough in the air, but it was on the ground that he and Lawrenson excelled as their cultured style helped Liverpool to sweep all before them.

They were more like two midfield players filling in at the back and that meant that Liverpool could build from deep positions and, more importantly, meant that they hardly ever gave the ball away.

Hansen enjoyed phenomenal success at Anfield, the likes of which no individual is ever likely to repeat.

He won virtually every honour there is to win - most of them more than once - and has a medal collection which would make a museum curator proud.

The only surprise was that he was never recognised more by his country and his 26 caps for Scotland is a paltry reward for a player of his class.

Still, while he was being left out of international matches, he was concentrating on Liverpool's quest to become the biggest and the best.

And, without a doubt, Liverpool's gain was Scotland's loss.

Career details

● **Represented:** Scotland, Partick Thistle, Liverpool. ● **Position:** Defender ● **Born:** Alloa, 13.06.55 ● **Height:** 6ft 1in ● **Weight:** 13st ● **Club Honours:** League Championship: 1978-79, 1979-80, 1981-82, 1982-83, 1983-84, 1985-86, 1987-88, 1989-90; FA Cup: 1986, 1989; League Cup: 1981, 1983, 1984; European Cup: 1978, 1981, 1984 ● **International Honours:** Scotland 3 U23, 26 full caps.

Club League Record

Club	Games	Goals
Partick Thistle	86	6
Liverpool	436	7

League Highlights

May 1979: Hansen wins his first Championship trophy as Liverpool begin a period of total dominance.

May 1986: He captains the Liverpool side which becomes only the third this century to complete the League and Cup double.

May 1990: Hansen collects his eighth Championship medal, a record he shares with former Liverpool team-mate Phil Neal.

HANSEN ON:

● I never liked pundits before I became one.

Hansen on his change of career to TV analyst

● You'll never win anything with kids.

Hansen's verdict on the Manchester United side which kicked off the 1995-96 season with a 0-3 defeat at Aston Villa. Nine months later, they did the double.

DID YOU KNOW THAT...

● Hansen's nickname at Anfield was Jocky.

● His best mate in football is Newcastle boss Kenny Dalglish.

● His main hobby away from football is golf. His regular playing partner is Dalglish.

● Hansen's tally of eight League Championship titles is a record. He shares the honour with his former Liverpool team-mate Phil Neal.

● He has always stressed that he would never ever become a football manager.

● Hansen did once fool his Liverpool team-mates into believing that he had taken over as Anfield boss. After an hour, he owned up to the prank.

● As well as being a BBC TV pundit, Hansen has started to make his own shows. His first attempt, called the Sack Race, charted the pressures on football managers and was a big success.

Strange but true!

Cambridge lost 4-1 at home to QPR in November 1982, but did not concede a goal in their next 12 home games. Then they lost 4-1 to Oldham, conceding all four goals in just eight minutes.

1984-85
DIVISION 1

1 Everton	90
2 Liverpool	77
3 Tottenham	77
4 Man Utd	76
5 Southampton	68
6 Chelsea	66
7 Arsenal	66
8 Sheff Wed	65
9 Nottm For	64
10 Aston Villa	56
11 Watford	55
12 West Brom	55
13 Luton	54
14 Newcastle	52
15 Leicester	51
16 West Ham	51
17 Ipswich	50
18 Coventry	50
19 QPR	50
20 Norwich	49
21 Sunderland	40
22 Stoke	17

1984-85 cont
DIVISION 2

1 Oxford	84
2 Birmingham	82
3 Man City	74
4 Portsmouth	74
5 Blackburn	73
6 Brighton	72
7 Leeds	69
8 Shrewsbury	65
9 Fulham	65
10 Grimsby	62
11 Barnsley	58
12 Wimbledon	58
13 Huddersfield	55
14 Oldham	53
15 C.Palace	48
16 Carlisle	47
17 Charlton	45
18 Sheff Utd	44
19 Middlesbro	40
20 Notts Co	37
21 Cardiff	35
22 Wolves	33

DIVISION 3

1 Bradford	94
2 Millwall	90
3 Hull	87
4 Gillingham	83
5 Bristol City	81
6 Bristol Rovers	75
7 Derby	70
8 York	69
9 Reading	69
10 Bournemouth	68
11 Walsall	67
12 Rotherham	65
13 Brentford	62
14 Doncaster	59
15 Plymouth	59
16 Wigan	59
17 Bolton	54
18 Newport	52
19 Lincoln	51
20 Swansea	47
21 Burnley	46
22 L.Orient	46
23 Preston	46
24 Cambridge	21

DIVISION 4

1 Chesterfield	91
2 Blackpool	86
3 Darlington	85
4 Bury	84
5 Hereford	77
6 Tranmere	75
7 Colchester	74
8 Swindon	72
9 Scunthorpe	71
10 Crewe	66
11 Peterborough	62
12 Port Vale	60
13 Aldershot	59
14 Mansfield	57
15 Wrexham	54
16 Chester	54
17 Rochdale	53
18 Exeter	53
19 Hartlepool	52
20 Southend	50
21 Halifax	50
22 Stockport	47
23 Northampton	47
24 Torquay	41

1985-86
DIVISION 1

1 Liverpool	88
2 Everton	86
3 West Ham	84
4 Man Utd	76
5 Sheff Wed	73
6 Chelsea	71
7 Arsenal	69
8 Nottm For	68
9 Luton	66
10 Tottenham	65
11 Newcastle	63
12 Watford	59
13 QPR	52
14 Southampton	46
15 Man City	45
16 Aston Villa	44
17 Coventry	43
18 Oxford	42
19 Leicester	42
20 Ipswich	41
21 Birmingham	29
22 West Brom	24

Peter Reid and Paul Bracewell

WHAT A STAR ⭐ BRYAN ROBSON

His strength as a midfield player and his inspirational leadership made him one of the outstanding captains of post-war British football. His long list of successes at club level were supplemented by a splendid England record - 90 appearances, 65 of them as skipper, with 26 goals. All this despite continuing misfortune with various injuries that kept him out of many matches, notably in the final stages of two World Cups. Somehow he found the strength, mental as well as physical, to keep fighting back. Captain Marvel, indeed. Now, as manager of Middlesbrough, he has proved his desire to succeed by bringing in top foreign names and surely he will get that success.

CHAMPIONS
Everton 1984-85

After losing their first two matches of the season, Everton went on to double glory and nearly a treble. They won the First Division title with a then-record 90 points, then took the European Cup-Winners' Cup by beating Rapid Vienna 3-1. But three days later they were beaten by ten-man Man Utd in the FA Cup Final. Despite that disappointment, this was still a marvellous season for The Toffeemen. Sadly, the ban on English clubs which followed 1985's Heysel Stadium Disaster meant that they could not defend their European trophy.

1985-86 cont

DIVISION 2	
1 Norwich	84
2 Charlton	77
3 Wimbledon	76
4 Portsmouth	73
5 C.Palace	66
6 Hull	64
7 Sheff Utd	62
8 Oldham	60
9 Millwall	59
10 Stoke	57
11 Brighton	56
12 Barnsley	56
13 Bradford	54
14 Leeds	53
15 Grimsby	52
16 Huddersfield	52
17 Shrewsbury	51
18 Sunderland	50
19 Blackburn	49
20 Carlisle	46
21 Middlesbro	45
22 Fulham	36

DIVISION 3	
1 Reading	94
2 Plymouth	87
3 Derby	84
4 Wigan	83
5 Gillingham	79
6 Walsall	75
7 York	71
8 Notts Co	71
9 Bristol City	68
10 Brentford	66
11 Doncaster	64
12 Blackpool	63
13 Darlington	58
14 Rotherham	57
15 Bournemouth	54
16 Bristol Rovers	54
17 Chesterfield	53
18 Bolton	53
19 Newport	51
20 Bury	49
21 Lincoln	45
22 Cardiff	45
23 Wolves	43
24 Swansea	43

Geddis Can

Wimbledon drew 3-3 with Barnsley and lost 2-1 to Birmingham in successive home matches in 1984. David Geddis scored twice for the visiting team in both games.

DIVISION 4	
1 Swindon	102
2 Chester	84
3 Mansfield	81
4 Port Vale	79
5 L.Orient	72
6 Colchester	70
7 Hartlepool	70
8 Northampton	64
9 Southend	64
10 Hereford	64
11 Stockport	64
12 Crewe	63
13 Wrexham	60
14 Burnley	59
15 Scunthorpe	59
16 Aldershot	58
17 Peterborough	56
18 Rochdale	55
19 Tranmere	54
20 Halifax	54
21 Exeter	54
22 Cambridge	54
23 Preston	43
24 Torquay	37

1986-87

DIVISION 1	
1 Everton	86
2 Liverpool	77
3 Tottenham	71
4 Arsenal	70
5 Norwich	68
6 Wimbledon	66
7 Luton	66
8 Nottm For	65
9 Watford	63
10 Coventry	63
11 Man Utd	56
12 Southampton	52
13 Sheff Wed	52
14 Chelsea	52
15 West Ham	52
16 QPR	50
17 Newcastle	47
18 Oxford	46
19 Charlton	44
20 Leicester	42
21 Man City	39
22 Aston Villa	36

Premium Bond

Kevin Bond of Norwich scored for both sides in two successive games in March 1980 - a 2-1 defeat by Stoke and a 1-1 draw with West Brom.

WHAT A STAR ⭐ GLENN HODDLE

One of the most naturally talented players English football has ever produced, Hoddle became a cult hero at Tottenham where he guided the club to three FA Cup Finals in the 1980s, scoring the winner in the 1982 replay victory over QPR. His stylish skills lit up the midfield for club and country and although he won 53 international caps for England, many felt he should have been closer to 100. He moved to France with Monaco in 1987 before returning to run first Swindon, then Chelsea - and finally becoming national team manager in 1996.

Pro-File: GARY LINEKER

Gary Linekar will be remembered as the greatest English striker of his era.

Although he ultimately finished one goal short of Bobby Charlton's all-time England scoring record of 49, he still more than deserves his place in English football's history books.

He scored goals wherever he played throughout his career, for Leicester, Everton, Barcelona, Tottenham and Grampus Eight in Japan, and always played the game in the right spirit.

Incredibly, for a striker at the cutting edge of the game, he was never booked or sent-off in a distinguished career.

The one disappointment for him, perhaps, was that he never won as many honours as his talents deserved.

Despite playing for both Everton and Spurs, he had only the 1991 FA Cup to show for his efforts - and even then he missed a penalty in the Final against Nottingham Forest.

That was the only domestic honour he won, although he finished League and FA Cup runner-up with Everton in 1985-86, and did win the Spanish Cup and the European Cup-Winners' Cup with Barcelona.

Career details

●**Represented:** England, Leicester City, Everton, Barcelona (Spain), Tottenham, Nagoya Grampus Eight (Japan) ●**Position:** Striker
●**Born:** Leicester, 30.11.60 ●**Height:** 5ft 9in ●**Weight:** 11st 10lb
●**Club Honours:** FWA Footballer of the Year 1986, 1992, Golden Boot 1986 (30 goals for Everton); Spanish Cup 1988; European Cup-Winners' Cup 1989; FA Cup 1991; Awarded OBE 1992. ●**International Honours:** England 'B', 80 full caps (48 goals). Golden Boot for top scorer in 86 World Cup.

Club League Record

Era	Club	Games	Goals
78/79 - 84/85	Leicester	194	95
85/86	Everton	41	30
86/87 - 88/89	Barcelona	99	44
89/90 - 91/92	Tottenham	105	67
92/93 - 93/94	Grampus 8	N/A	N/A

League Highlights

May 1986: The closest Lineker comes to a League Championship medal as Everton finished runners-up to Liverpool.

May 1992: Lineker collects his second Golden Boot award, scoring 28 League goals for Spurs. He won his first award in 1986.

On Lineker:

● After I've been in Japan for two days I start to get depressed and want to go home. The people get on my nerves and I just want to say 'stop bowing will you?'. There is no cigarettes, drugs and drink. Everyone's too nice - no wonder Gary Lineker went there. **Noel Gallagher (Oasis)**

● Taking Gary off against Sweden was the right decision. I thought Alan Smith would offer us something different in attack. **Graham Taylor, on his decision to substitute Lineker in his last international**

DID YOU KNOW THAT...

● His middle name is Winston, after Winston Churchill.

● His dad, Barry, runs a fruit stall at Leicester Market, while brother Wayne is the owner of a bar called 'Linekers' on Tenerife.

● Gary never shot at goal during the warm-up, and if he went for a long spell without scoring he would have a haircut to change his luck.

● Troubled with poor circulation in his feet he would always stand in a hot bath about half-an-hour before a match to get the blood flowing.

● Gary is a member of the MCC (Marylebone Cricket Club) and regularly represents the Lord's Taverners Charity team.

● A real-life 'Roy of the Rovers' character himself, Gary wrote a regular soccer column in the children's comic of the same name.

● He played cricket for Leicestershire 2nd X1.

● The BBC quiz show 'They Think It's All Over' features Gary and his pal David Gower as opposing skippers.

● He spent many hours visiting sick patients in Great Ormond St Hospital, not knowing that one day his own son, George, would be having treatment there for leukaemia.

● Gary picks out his first goal against Poland in the 1986 World Cup as his most memorable saying: "It was special because it was so vital. We had to win to stay in the competition."

WHAT A STAR ⭐ LIAM BRADY

He was contemporary with Johnny Giles for a time, then took over from him as the Republic of Ireland's main playmaker. Ironically, he missed the 1988 European Championship, and the 1990 World Cup arrived too late for him. Before then he had been one of the world's outstanding midfield players, first with Arsenal, then with four Italian clubs. Even in his final flourish, with West Ham when he was in his mid-thirties, he was better than most, threading passes through the narrowest of gaps, a complete master of the ball.

Empty Pool

Liverpool competed for seven trophies in 1984-85 - League, FA Cup, League Cup, European Cup, European Super Cup, World Club Championship and Charity Shield - and did not win any.

1986-87 cont
DIVISION 2

1	Derby	84
2	Portsmouth	78
3	Oldham	75
4	Leeds	68
5	Ipswich	64
6	C.Palace	62
7	Plymouth	61
8	Stoke	58
9	Sheff Utd	58
10	Bradford	55
11	Barnsley	55
12	Blackburn	55
13	Reading	53
14	Hull	53
15	West Brom	51
16	Millwall	51
17	Huddersfield	51
18	Shrewsbury	51
19	Birmingham	50
20	Sunderland	48
21	Grimsby	44
22	Brighton	39

DIVISION 3

1	Bournemouth	97
2	Middlesbro	94
3	Swindon	87
4	Wigan	85
5	Gillingham	78
6	Bristol City	77
7	Notts Co	76
8	Walsall	75
9	Blackpool	64
10	Mansfield	61
11	Brentford	60
12	Port Vale	57
13	Doncaster	57
14	Rotherham	57
15	Chester	56
16	Bury	55
17	Chesterfield	54
18	Fulham	53
19	Bristol Rovers	51
20	York	49
21	Bolton	45
22	Carlisle	38
23	Darlington	37
24	Newport	37

1986-87 cont
DIVISION 4

1	Northampton	99
2	Preston	90
3	Southend	80
4	Wolves	79
5	Colchester	70
6	Aldershot	70
7	L.Orient	69
8	Scunthorpe	66
9	Wrexham	66
10	Peterborough	65
11	Cambridge	62
12	Swansea	62
13	Cardiff	61
14	Exeter	56
15	Halifax	55
16	Hereford	53
17	Crewe	53
18	Hartlepool	51
19	Stockport	51
20	Tranmere	50
21	Rochdale	50
22	Burnley	49
23	Torquay	48
24	Lincoln	48

1987-88
DIVISION 1

1	Liverpool	90
2	Man Utd	81
3	Nottm For	73
4	Everton	70
5	QPR	67
6	Arsenal	66
7	Wimbledon	57
8	Newcastle	56
9	Luton	53
10	Coventry	53
11	Sheff Wed	53
12	Southampton	50
13	Tottenham	47
14	Norwich	45
15	Derby	43
16	West Ham	42
17	Charlton	42
18	Chelsea	42
19	Portsmouth	35
20	Watford	32
21	Oxford	31

Strange but true!

Kevin Bremner scored against Reading three times in 1982-83 - once for Wrexham, once for Plymouth and once for Millwall.

CHAMPIONS
Swindon 1985-86

A total of 102 points gave Swindon a League record that still stands. Their 1-0 win over Crewe on the last day took them past the 101 set by York two years earlier, also in the old Division Four. It was Town's 32nd victory, to go with six draws and eight defeats, five of which came in the first eight games. Under Lou Macari, Swindon played football suited to a higher division, but their feats have been marred by fines, suspensions and a demotion for financial irregularities.

CHAMPIONS
Arsenal 1988-89

Roy of the Rovers couldn't have timed it any better than Michael of the Gunners. In the season's last fixture, Arsenal needed a victory at Anfield by two goals to snatch the title from Liverpool's grasp. However, The Reds had not lost by such a margin at home for three years, were unbeaten in 18 matches and had just won the FA Cup. Yet incredibly Arsenal managed it. Alan Smith gave them the lead and they scored their second through Michael Thomas - who was later to become a Liverpool player - in the very last minute to take the crown on goals scored, after the clubs had finished with identical points and goal differences.

1987-88 cont

DIVISION 2

1	Millwall	82
2	Aston Villa	78
3	Middlesbro	78
4	Bradford	77
5	Blackburn	77
6	C.Palace	75
7	Leeds	69
8	Ipswich	66
9	Man City	65
10	Oldham	65
11	Stoke	62
12	Swindon	59
13	Leicester	59
14	Barnsley	57
15	Hull	57
16	Plymouth	56
17	Bournemouth	49
18	Shrewsbury	49
19	Birmingham	48
20	West Brom	47
21	Sheff Utd	46
22	Reading	42
23	Huddersfield	28

DIVISION 3

1	Sunderland	93
2	Brighton	84
3	Walsall	82
4	Notts Co	81
5	Bristol City	75
6	Northampton	73
7	Wigan	72
8	Bristol Rovers	66
9	Fulham	66
10	Blackpool	65
11	Port Vale	65
12	Brentford	62
13	Gillingham	59
14	Bury	59
15	Chester	58
16	Preston	58
17	Southend	55
18	Chesterfield	55
19	Mansfield	54
20	Aldershot	53
21	Rotherham	52
22	Grimsby	50
23	York	33
24	Doncaster	33

DIVISION 4

1	Wolves	90
2	Cardiff	85
3	Bolton	78
4	Scunthorpe	77
5	Torquay	77
6	Swansea	70
7	Peterborough	70
8	L.Orient	69
9	Colchester	67
10	Burnley	67
11	Wrexham	66
12	Scarborough	65
13	Darlington	65
14	Tranmere	64
15	Cambridge	61
16	Hartlepool	59
17	Crewe	58
18	Halifax	55
19	Hereford	54
20	Stockport	51
21	Rochdale	48
22	Exeter	46
23	Carlisle	44
24	Newport	25

1988-89

DIVISION 1

1	Arsenal	76
2	Liverpool	76
3	Nottm For	64
4	Norwich	62
5	Derby	58
6	Tottenham	57
7	Coventry	55
8	Everton	54
9	QPR	53
10	Millwall	53
11	Man Utd	51
12	Wimbledon	51
13	Southampton	45
14	Charlton	42
15	Sheff Wed	42
16	Luton	41
17	Aston Villa	40
18	Middlesbro	39
19	West Ham	38
20	Newcastle	31

DIVISION 2

1	Chelsea	99
2	Man City	82
3	C.Palace	81
4	Watford	78
5	Blackburn	77
6	Swindon	76
7	Barnsley	74
8	Ipswich	73
9	West Brom	72
10	Leeds	67
11	Sunderland	63
12	Bournemouth	62
13	Stoke	59
14	Bradford	56
15	Leicester	55
16	Oldham	54
17	Oxford	54
18	Plymouth	54
19	Brighton	51
20	Portsmouth	51
21	Hull	47
22	Shrewsbury	42
23	Birmingham	35
24	Walsall	31

Michael Thomas steals the title for Arsenal

1988-89 cont

DIVISION 3
1	Wolves	92
2	Sheff Utd	84
3	Port Vale	84
4	Fulham	75
5	Bristol Rovers	74
6	Preston	72
7	Brentford	68
8	Chester	68
9	Notts Co	67
10	Bolton	64
11	Bristol City	63
12	Swansea	61
13	Bury	61
14	Huddersfield	60
15	Mansfield	59
16	Cardiff	57
17	Wigan	56
18	Reading	56
19	Blackpool	55
20	Northampton	54
21	Southend	54
22	Chesterfield	49
23	Gillingham	40
24	Aldershot	37

DIVISION 4
1	Rotherham	82
2	Tranmere	80
3	Crewe	78
4	Scunthorpe	77
5	Scarborough	77
6	L.Orient	75
7	Wrexham	71
8	Cambridge	68
9	Grimsby	66
10	Lincoln	64
11	York	64
12	Carlisle	60
13	Exeter	60
14	Torquay	59
15	Hereford	58
16	Burnley	55
17	Peterborough	54
18	Rochdale	53
19	Hartlepool	52
20	Stockport	51
21	Halifax	50
22	Colchester	50
23	Doncaster	49
24	Darlington	42

1989-90

DIVISION 1
1	Liverpool	79
2	Aston Villa	70
3	Tottenham	63
4	Arsenal	62
5	Chelsea	60
6	Everton	59
7	Southampton	55
8	Wimbledon	55
9	Nottm For	54
10	Norwich	53
11	QPR	50
12	Coventry	49
13	Man Utd	48
14	Man City	48
15	C.Palace	48
16	Derby	46
17	Luton	43
18	Sheff Wed	43
19	Charlton	30
20	Millwall	26

DIVISION 2
1	Leeds	85
2	Sheff Utd	85
3	Newcastle	80
4	Swindon	74
5	Blackburn	74
6	Sunderland	74
7	West Ham	72
8	Oldham	71
9	Ipswich	69
10	Wolves	67
11	Port Vale	61
12	Portsmouth	61
13	Leicester	59
14	Hull	58
15	Watford	57
16	Plymouth	55
17	Oxford	54
18	Brighton	54
19	Barnsley	54
20	West Brom	51
21	Middlesbro	50
22	Bournemouth	48
23	Bradford	41
24	Stoke	37

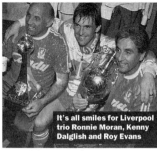

It's all smiles for Liverpool trio Ronnie Moran, Kenny Dalglish and Roy Evans

DIVISION 3
1	Bristol Rovers	93
2	Bristol City	91
3	Notts Co	87
4	Tranmere	80
5	Bury	74
6	Bolton	69
7	Birmingham	66
8	Huddersfield	65
9	Rotherham	64
10	Reading	64
11	Shrewsbury	63
12	Crewe	62
13	Brentford	61
14	L.Orient	58
15	Mansfield	55
16	Chester	54
17	Swansea	54
18	Wigan	53
19	Preston	52
20	Fulham	51
21	Cardiff	50
22	Northampton	47
23	Blackpool	46
24	Walsall	41

DIVISION 4
1	Exeter	89
2	Grimsby	79
3	Southend	75
4	Stockport	74
5	Maidstone	73
6	Cambridge	73
7	Chesterfield	71
8	Carlisle	71
9	Peterborough	68
10	Lincoln	68
11	Scunthorpe	66
12	Rochdale	66
13	York	64
14	Gillingham	62
15	Torquay	57
16	Burnley	56
17	Hereford	55
18	Scarborough	55
19	Hartlepool	55
20	Doncaster	51
21	Wrexham	51
22	Aldershot	50
23	Halifax	49
24	Colchester	43

Ups and Downs

Lincoln City became the first club to be relegated to the Vauxhall Conference in 1987. A year later, they bounced back.

WHAT A STAR ⭐ NEVILLE SOUTHALL

Southall has been trying to keep things empty all his working life - first as a binman in north Wales, then as a world-class goalkeeper with Everton, seemingly feeling a personal insult every time he had to empty a net. In 15 years at Goodison he won two Championships, two FA Cups and the European Cup-Winners' Cup, as well as making more appearances for the club than anyone else in history, and becoming his country's most-capped player. A big, burly 'keeper with remarkable agility for a man of his size, he has an unsurpassed knowledge of angles and timing and that has enabled him to remain at the top for so long - and he shows no sign of stopping.

1990-1997

UNITED AT THE DOUBLE DOUBLE

If the 1980s belonged to Liverpool, then the 1990s certainly belong to Manchester United. It may have taken the Old Trafford club 26 years to get their hands back on the League Championship, but they show no signs of letting it go again and became the first club to win the double twice when they clinched the League and FA Cup in 1996 to follow on from their 1994 dual success.

When they finally won the trophy - the first Premiership title - in 1993 it ended a long and painful 26-year wait to be called Champions again. Since then, they have had a stranglehold on the English game which has been broken only once, by Blackburn in 1995, and even then most people felt that the title had been lost by United rather than won by Blackburn. It has been an extraordinary period of dominance, particularly in an age when clubs are throwing money around like confetti in a bid to buy success.

Under the shrewd management of Alex Ferguson, United have developed into a team for all occasions, and one which never knows when it is beaten. They have quality throughout the side, and in Eric Cantona they had the kind of special talent that illuminates games.

The Gallic genius is a fiery, temperamental character but in Ferguson he had found an ally and someone who seems to understand him and his moods. Together they turned United into a magnificent unit and while Old Trafford might be the Theatre of Dreams for Reds' fans, it is the stuff of nightmares for their opponents. But with Cantona retiring at the end of the 1997 season, the stage is set for the young stars of Old Trafford to take first billing with David Beckham just one of the many kids ready to grow into world class performers.

Arsenal and Leeds won the first two titles of the 90s, and of course Blackburn grabbed it in '95, but other than that the crown has sat proudly on Ferguson's head. And the taciturn Scot has given no indication that he is willing to abdicate from his throne as he looks to build a new dynasty at Old Trafford, a dynasty to rival that of Liverpool in the 70s and 80s.

LEAGUE TABLES
1990-91 to 1996-97

1990-91

DIVISION 1			DIVISION 2	
1	Arsenal*	83	1 Oldham	88
2	Liverpool	76	2 West Ham	87
3	C.Palace	69	3 Sheff Wed	82
4	Leeds	64	4 Notts Co	80
5	Man City	62	5 Millwall	73
6	Man Utd*	59	6 Brighton	70
7	Wimbledon	56	7 Middlesbro	69
8	Nottm For	54	8 Barnsley	69
9	Everton	51	9 Bristol City	67
10	Tottenham	49	10 Oxford	61
11	Chelsea	49	11 Newcastle	59
12	QPR	46	12 Wolves	58
13	Sheff Utd	46	13 Bristol Rovers	58
14	Southampton	45	14 Ipswich	57
15	Norwich	45	15 Port Vale	57
16	Coventry	44	16 Charlton	56
17	Aston Villa	41	17 Portsmouth	53
18	Luton	37	18 Plymouth	53
19	Sunderland	34	19 Blackburn	52
20	Derby	24	20 Watford	51
			21 Swindon	50
			22 Leicester	50
			23 West Brom	48
			24 Hull	45

Arsenal were deducted 2 points and Man Utd 1 after a brawl between the players in an clash at Old Trafford.

CHAMPIONS
Leeds United 1991-92

Leeds signed off the history of the old First Division by becoming the competition's final Champions, with the all-new Premier League set to take over from the following season. They finished strongly while Man Utd, beaten only once in 15 matches, suddenly lost three in a row to finish four points adrift of top spot. Leeds were inspired by Gordon Strachan and newcomer Eric Cantona - one signed from United, the other destined to go to Old Trafford.

DIVISION 3			DIVISION 4	
1	Cambridge	86	1 Darlington	83
2	Southend	85	2 Stockport	82
3	Grimsby	83	3 Hartlepool	82
4	Bolton	83	4 Peterborough	80
5	Tranmere	78	5 Blackpool	79
6	Brentford	76	6 Burnley	79
7	Bury	73	7 Torquay	72
8	Bradford	70	8 Scunthorpe	71
9	Bournemouth	70	9 Scarborough	69
10	Wigan	69	10 Northampton	67
11	Huddersfield	67	11 Doncaster	65
12	Birmingham	65	12 Rochdale	62
13	L.Orient	64	13 Cardiff	60
14	Stoke	60	14 Lincoln	59
15	Reading	59	15 Gillingham	54
16	Exeter	57	16 Walsall	53
17	Preston	56	17 Hereford	53
18	Shrewsbury	52	18 Chesterfield	53
19	Chester	51	19 Maidstone	51
20	Swansea	48	20 Carlisle	48
21	Fulham	46	21 York	46
22	Crewe	44	22 Halifax	46
23	Rotherham	42	23 Aldershot	41
24	Mansfield	38	24 Wrexham	40

Strange but true!

Reading's 6-4 away win over Exeter in October 1993 is thought to be unique in League soccer history, because five players scored two goals each.

How's Rat?

Kevin Ratcliffe played more than 450 games for Everton and scored only two goals, then joined Cardiff in 1993 and scored on his debut for the club.

WHAT A STAR ⭐ PAUL GASCOIGNE

Gazza will long be remembered for what might have been as much as for what was. Although blessed with remarkable talents, his inability to cope with the pressures of stardom prevented him from making full use of them. Whether with England, Newcastle, Spurs, Lazio in Italy or Rangers in Glasgow, his career was dotted with scores of escapades and misdemeanours, all of which detracted from his marvellous ability. The self-confessed 'daft lad' achieved a great deal, but he could, and should have, achieved a great deal more.

WHAT A STAR ⭐ CHRIS WADDLE

Waddle's career seemed to be in decline when he returned to England after a successful spell with Marseille, but he surprised a great many people by doing so well with Sheffield Wednesday that he was voted Footballer of the Year in 1993, when he helped his club to the Finals of both domestic Cups. Waddle, who had been an unorthodox and entertaining winger with Newcastle, Spurs and England, gaining 62 caps, had few equals at the art of beating his man, or men, and he scored plenty of spectacular goals. It was just a pity he couldn't score from the penalty spot against Germany in the 1990 World Cup Semi-Final shoot-out.

Leeds on their way to glory in 1992

1991-92 cont
DIVISION 4

1	Burnley	83
2	Rotherham	77
3	Mansfield	77
4	Blackpool	76
5	Scunthorpe	72
6	Crewe	70
7	Barnet	69
8	Rochdale	67
9	Cardiff	66
10	Lincoln	62
11	Gillingham	57
12	Scarborough	57
13	Chesterfield	53
14	Wrexham	51
15	Walsall	49
16	Northampton	46
17	Hereford	44
18	Maidstone	42
19	York	40
20	Halifax	38
21	Doncaster	35
22	Carlisle	34

1991-92
DIVISION 1

1	Leeds	82
2	Man Utd	78
3	Sheff Wed	75
4	Arsenal	72
5	Man City	70
6	Liverpool	64
7	Aston Villa	60
8	Nottm For	59
9	Sheff Utd	57
10	C.Palace	57
11	QPR	54
12	Everton	53
13	Wimbledon	53
14	Chelsea	53
15	Tottenham	52
16	Southampton	52
17	Oldham	51
18	Norwich	45
19	Coventry	44
20	Luton	42
21	Notts Co	40
22	West Ham	38

DIVISION 2

1	Ipswich	84
2	Middlesbro	80
3	Derby	78
4	Leicester	77
5	Cambridge	74
6	Blackburn	74
7	Charlton	71
8	Swindon	69
9	Portsmouth	69
10	Watford	65
11	Wolves	64
12	Southend	62
13	Bristol Rovers	62
14	Tranmere	61
15	Millwall	61
16	Barnsley	59
17	Bristol City	54
18	Sunderland	53
19	Grimsby	53
20	Newcastle	52
21	Oxford	50
22	Plymouth	48
23	Brighton	47
24	Port Vale	45

DIVISION 3

1	Brentford	82
2	Birmingham	81
3	Huddersfield	78
4	Stoke	77
5	Stockport	76
6	Peterborough	74
7	West Brom	71
8	Bournemouth	71
9	Fulham	70
10	L.Orient	65
11	Hartlepool	65
12	Reading	61
13	Bolton	59
14	Hull	59
15	Wigan	59
16	Bradford	58
17	Preston	57
18	Chester	56
19	Swansea	56
20	Exeter	53
21	Bury	51
22	Shrewsbury	47
23	Torquay	47
24	Darlington	37

Wright On

Arsenal scored only 40 goals in their 42 League games during the 1992-93 season, Ian Wright getting 15 of them, but scored in all their 17 Cup matches (Wright getting 15 goals out of a total of 33) and won both the FA and League Cups.

Strange but true!

Steve Morrow scored only two goals during his seven years with Arsenal - both against Sheffield Wednesday, in the 1993 League Cup Final and in a 1994 Premiership match.

1992-93
FA PREMIER LEAGUE

1	Man Utd	84
2	Aston Villa	74
3	Norwich	72
4	Blackburn	71
5	QPR	63
6	Liverpool	59
7	Sheff Wed	59
8	Tottenham	59
9	Man City	57
10	Arsenal	56
11	Chelsea	56
12	Wimbledon	54
13	Everton	53
14	Sheff Utd	52
15	Coventry	52
16	Ipswich	52
17	Leeds	51
18	Southampton	50
19	Oldham	49
20	C.Palace	49
21	Middlesbro	44
22	Nottm For	40

1992-93
DIVISION 1

1	Newcastle	96
2	West Ham	88
3	Portsmouth	88
4	Tranmere	79
5	Swindon	76
6	Leicester	76
7	Millwall	70
8	Derby	66
9	Grimsby	64
10	Peterborough	62
11	Wolves	61
12	Charlton	61
13	Barnsley	60
14	Oxford	56
15	Bristol City	56
16	Watford	55
17	Notts Co	52
18	Southend	52
19	Birmingham	51
20	Luton	51
21	Sunderland	50
22	Brentford	49
23	Cambridge	49
24	Bristol Rovers	41

1992-93
DIVISION 2 cont

1	Stoke	93
2	Bolton	90
3	Port Vale	89
4	West Brom	85
5	Swansea	73
6	Stockport	72
7	L.Orient	72
8	Reading	69
9	Brighton	69
10	Bradford	68
11	Rotherham	65
12	Fulham	65
13	Burnley	61
14	Plymouth	60
15	Huddersfield	60
16	Hartlepool	54
17	Bournemouth	53
18	Blackpool	51
19	Exeter	50
20	Hull	50
21	Preston	47
22	Mansfield	44
23	Wigan	41
24	Chester	29

1992-93
DIVISION 3 cont

1	Cardiff	83
2	Wrexham	80
3	Barnet	79
4	York	75
5	Walsall	73
6	Crewe	70
7	Bury	63
8	Lincoln	63
9	Shrewsbury	62
10	Colchester	59
11	Rochdale	58
12	Chesterfield	56
13	Scarborough	54
14	Scunthorpe	54
15	Darlington	50
16	Doncaster	47
17	Hereford	45
18	Carlisle	44
19	Torquay	43
20	Northampton	41
21	Gillingham	40
22	Halifax	36

Cleaning Up

Gillingham's 46 Third Division games in 1995-96 contained only 69 goals - 49 for and 20 against. Goalkeeper Jim Stannard, who turned 34 during the season, kept a League record 29 clean sheets during the campaign.

Alex Ferguson and Brian Kidd celebrate another United success

WHAT A STAR ⭐ ROY KEANE

Manchester United's signing of Roy Keane from Nottingham Forest in 1993 was a record for a deal between English clubs, some £3.6 million. At the time it seemed a huge amount to pay for a midfielder who had just turned 22, but in the current cash-dominated world of top soccer, he has proved a wonderful bargain. Despite a low flashpoint threshold, Keane is a talented and influential player of great skill and stamina, a star with the Republic of Ireland as well as United. His manager Alex Ferguson labels him the 'heartbeat' of the United side.

CHAMPIONS
Manchester United 1993-94

In the new money-led Premier League, Manchester United - the richest club of all - achieved the double with contemptuous ease. They had not won the First Division for 26 years, but soon showed that the Premiership was theirs as if by divine right. They won it by a mile in 1992-93, and a year later completed the double, with 92 points - the highest in top-division history - and a 4-0 defeat of Chelsea at Wembley in the FA Cup Final. Costly signings such as Schmeichel, Ince, Irwin and Pallister all proved worth the money. So too did Cantona, signed from Leeds for a mere £1.2 million.

1993-94 PREMIERSHIP

1	Man Utd	92
2	Blackburn	84
3	Newcastle	77
4	Arsenal	71
5	Leeds	70
6	Wimbledon	65
7	Sheff Wed	64
8	Liverpool	60
9	QPR	60
10	Aston Villa	57
11	Coventry	56
12	Norwich	53
13	West Ham	52
14	Chelsea	51
15	Tottenham	45
16	Man City	45
17	Everton	44
18	Southampton	43
19	Ipswich	43
20	Sheff Utd	42
21	Oldham	40
22	Swindon	30

1993-94 DIVISION 1 cont

1	C.Palace	90
2	Nottm For	83
3	Millwall	74
4	Leicester	73
5	Tranmere	72
6	Derby	71
7	Notts Co	68
8	Wolves	68
9	Middlesbro	67
10	Stoke	67
11	Charlton	65
12	Sunderland	65
13	Bristol City	64
14	Bolton	59
15	Southend	59
16	Grimsby	59
17	Portsmouth	58
18	Barnsley	55
19	Watford	54
20	Luton	53
21	West Brom	51
22	Birmingham	51
23	Oxford	49
24	Peterborough	37

Keep out

Alan Shearer was on the books of Newcastle as a kid but was let go after playing in goal in a trial match!

DIVISION 2

1	Reading	89
2	Port Vale	88
3	Plymouth	85
4	Stockport	85
5	York	75
6	Burnley	73
7	Bradford	70
8	Bristol Rovers	70
9	Hull	68
10	Cambridge	66
11	Huddersfield	65
12	Wrexham	62
13	Swansea	60
14	Brighton	59
15	Rotherham	58
16	Brentford	58
17	Bournemouth	57
18	L.Orient	56
19	Cardiff	54
20	Blackpool	53
21	Fulham	52
22	Exeter	45
23	Hartlepool	36
24	Barnet	28

DIVISION 3

1	Shrewsbury	79
2	Chester	74
3	Crewe	73
4	Wycombe	70
5	Preston	67
6	Torquay	67
7	Carlisle	64
8	Chesterfield	62
9	Rochdale	60
10	Walsall	60
11	Scunthorpe	59
12	Mansfield	55
13	Bury	53
14	Scarborough	53
15	Doncaster	52
16	Gillingham	51
17	Colchester	49
18	Lincoln	47
19	Wigan	45
20	Hereford	42
21	Darlington	41
22	Northampton	38

Wad's start

Chris Waddle began his working life in a sausage factory before being picked up by Newcastle.

Blackburn, Premier Champions 94-95

Top Kev

Former Stockport, and now Birmingham striker Kevin Francis is the tallest player in English football at 6ft 7in.

Pro-File: ERIC CANTONA

Love him or loathe him, you certainly cannot ignore Eric Cantona. Nor can you ignore the impact the controversial striker has made on the English game.

Since he first swaggered into Elland Road in 1991, there has never been a dull moment where the Frenchman is concerned.

There have been some fantastic times, both with Leeds and Manchester United, and there have been some desperate times.

But his record in this country is nothing short of remarkable and entitles him to the title of the greatest ever import to these shores.

He helped Leeds land the League title in his first season, albeit playing only 15 games, but his stay at Elland Road was brief and after just 28 League appearances he was on his way out.

Surely no-one could have predicted what was to follow, as he became the catalyst of a Manchester United side which has totally dominated the English game in the 90s.

He soared to new heights at Old Trafford, and plunged to new depths as he showed on that fateful night when he attacked a spectator at Crystal Palace in January 1995.

Cantona came back from that lengthy ban better than ever and lifted the Cup and League double in 1996, was voted Footballer of the Year, then stayed around for another title success before shocking the soccer world by quitting United in May 1997 to take up an acting career.

Career details

● **Represented:** France, Auxerre (twice), Martigues, Marseille (twice), Bordeaux, Montpellier, Nimes, Leeds, Manchester United. ● **Position:** Striker ● **Born:** Paris,24.05.66 ● **Height:** 6ft 2in ● **Weight:** 14st 3lb ● **Club Honours:** League Championship: 1991-92, 1992-93, 1993-94, 1995-96, 1996-97; FA Cup: 1994, 1996; Football Writers' Footballer of the Year 1996. ● **International Honours:** France 45 full caps

Club League Record

Era	Club	Games	Goals
1983-85	Auxerre	13	2
1985-86	Martigues	0	0
1986-88	Auxerre	68	21
1988-89	Marseille	22	5
1988-89	Bordeaux	11	6
1989-90	Montpellier	33	10
1990-91	Marseille	18	8
1991-92	Nimes	17	2
1991-93	Leeds	28	9
1993-97	Manchester United	143	64

League Highlights

May 1992: Cantona claims his first Championship medal in England when he helps Leeds win the last First Division title in 1992.

May 1993: Now wearing the red of Manchester United, he helps them win the first ever Premiership trophy.

May 1994: Another Premiership crown, and this time the FA Cup to go with it.

May 1996: Surely Cantona's finest hour. His goals in the second half of the season steer United to their third Premiership title almost single-handed. Add an FA Cup winning goal to complete the 'double double', and the Football Writers' Footballer of the Year award and you have the perfect season.

May 1997: Just for good measure, Cantona makes it four titles out of five.

On Cantona:

● He is so mild-mannered when the volcano is not erupting inside him and so patient with the youngsters. **Alex Ferguson defends his wayward superstar**

●1966 was a great year for English football. Eric was born. **A Nike advertising slogan in 1994**

DID YOU KNOW THAT...

● Cantona is a great fan of painting and poetry.

● He was originally due to join Sheffield Wednesday before he signed for Leeds, but he walked out when Trevor Francis asked him to stay for a week's trial.

● Alex Ferguson paid just £1.2 million to sign him for United, surely the transfer bargain of all time.

● Cantona was banned from football for eight months after attacking Crystal Palace fan Matthew Simmons at Selhurst Park in January 1995. It was the longest suspension in modern times.

● The Frenchman was sentenced to two weeks in prison for the assault but an appeal led to 120 hours community service as punishment.

● He has part-ownership of a French theatre company and has dreams of Hollywood success in his new career in acting.

CHAMPIONS
Blackburn 1994-95

Blackburn's Jack Walker, one of Britain's wealthiest men, enabled manager Kenny Dalglish to piece together a team capable of winning the title. Rovers hit a winning streak and came through to deprive Man Utd of the crown, as United failed to win at West Ham on the final day. Although Blackburn lost at Liverpool, against Dalglish's old club, they still finished a point in front. Much of their success was due to 34-goal Alan Shearer, a record signing from Southampton.

1994-95 PREMIERSHIP			1994-95 DIVISION 1	
1 Blackburn	89		1 Middlesbro	82
2 Man Utd	88		2 Reading	79
3 Nottm For	77		3 Bolton	77
4 Liverpool	74		4 Wolves	76
5 Leeds	73		5 Tranmere	76
6 Newcastle	72		6 Barnsley	72
7 Tottenham	62		7 Watford	70
8 QPR	60		8 Sheff Utd	68
9 Wimbledon	56		9 Derby	66
10 Southampton	54		10 Grimsby	65
11 Chelsea	54		11 Stoke	63
12 Arsenal	51		12 Millwall	62
13 Sheff Wed	51		13 Southend	62
14 West Ham	50		14 Oldham	61
15 Everton	50		15 Charlton	59
16 Coventry	50		16 Luton	58
17 Man City	49		17 Port Vale	58
18 Aston Villa	48		18 Portsmouth	58
19 C.Palace	45		19 West Brom	58
20 Norwich	43		20 Sunderland	54
21 Leicester	29		21 Swindon	48
22 Ipswich	27		22 Burnley	46
			23 Bristol City	45
			24 Notts Co	40

Strange but true!

Peter Beardsley, Steve Bruce and Alan Shearer all went to the same soccer boys club in their native Newcastle.

Alan Shearer

Upton Spark

West Ham's 1-1 draw with Man United in 1995 was the second time The Hammers had denied The Reds the title in four years after beating them 1-0 at home in 1992.

WHAT A STAR ⭐ ALAN SHEARER

His transfers from Southampton to Blackburn and Blackburn to Newcastle smashed the British record, and he might do it again yet. Few players of the modern era have matched him for all-round ability in the striking role, for he is strong and compact, difficult to dispossess, a born goalscorer with a fighter's heart. He showed his class and consistency by topping the League scorers list three seasons in a row - 1994-95 , 1995-96 and 1996-97 - and is one of those players who tends to relish the really big occasion, notably the European Championship of 1996, when he finished top scorer with five goals.

WHAT A STAR ⭐ STEVE BRUCE

Why did Steve Bruce never gain an England cap? With Norwich and then with Manchester United he was one of the outstanding central defenders in the game, brave and strong, a commanding presence and a sleeves-up captain. But although he did so well at club level, collecting plenty of silverware, he was always passed over by a succession of his country's managers. His move to Birmingham in 1996, when 35, was not just for the money - it proved yet again the big Geordie was determined to show he could still do the business. A career in soccer management now beckons for Mr Nice Guy.

Strange but true!

In March 1996, Ipswich Town were losing 3-0 at Barnsley with five minutes to go before grabbing a 3-3

1995-96

PREMIERSHIP			DIVISION 1		
1	Man Utd	82	1	Sunderland	83
2	Newcastle	78	2	Derby	79
3	Liverpool	71	3	C.Palace	75
4	Aston Villa	63	4	Stoke	73
5	Arsenal	63	5	Leicester	71
6	Everton	61	6	Charlton	71
7	Blackburn	61	7	Ipswich	69
8	Tottenham	61	8	Huddersfield	63
9	Nottm For	58	9	Sheff Utd	62
10	West Ham	51	10	Barnsley	60
11	Chelsea	50	11	West Brom	60
12	Middlesbro	43	12	Port Vale	60
13	Leeds	43	13	Tranmere	59
14	Wimbledon	41	14	Southend	59
15	Sheff Wed	40	15	Birmingham	58
16	Coventry	38	16	Norwich	57
17	Southampton	38	17	Grimsby	56
18	Man City	38	18	Oldham	56
19	QPR	33	19	Reading	56
20	Bolton	29	20	Wolves	55
			21	Portsmouth	52
			22	Millwall	52
			23	Watford	48
			24	Luton	45

1994-95 cont

DIVISION 2			DIVISION 3		
1	Birmingham	89	1	Carlisle	91
2	Brentford	85	2	Walsall	83
3	Crewe	83	3	Chesterfield	81
4	Bristol Rovers	82	4	Bury	80
5	Huddersfield	81	5	Preston	67
6	Wycombe	78	6	Mansfield	65
7	Oxford	75	7	Scunthorpe	62
8	Hull	74	8	Fulham	62
9	York	72	9	Doncaster	61
10	Swansea	71	10	Colchester	58
11	Stockport	65	11	Barnet	56
12	Blackpool	64	12	Lincoln	56
13	Wrexham	63	13	Torquay	55
14	Bradford	60	14	Wigan	52
15	Peterborough	60	15	Rochdale	50
16	Brighton	59	16	Hereford	49
17	Rotherham	56	17	Northampton	44
18	Shrewsbury	53	18	Hartlepool	43
19	Bournemouth	50	19	Gillingham	41
20	Cambridge	48	20	Darlington	41
21	Plymouth	46	21	Scarborough	34
22	Cardiff	38	22	Exeter	34
23	Chester	29			
24	L.Orient	26			

The force B with you

In the 1996-97 season Blackpool fielded eight players in a number of games whose surname started with the letter B.

CHAMPIONS
Manchester United 1995-96

With Blackburn's success proving a flash in the pan and Liverpool a long way short of their old power, Newcastle provided the biggest opposition to Alex Ferguson and his team, but United still managed to record an historic second double. The team was even stronger than before, with youngsters such as Beckham, Butt, Scholes and the Neville brothers reinforcing seniors now including Andy Cole, a controversial £7 million capture from Newcastle.

Pro-File: TONY ADAMS

Tony Adams has been at the heart of the Arsenal defence for the past ten or so years and shows no signs of going anywhere for a good while yet.

The big defender has had his share of problems during his distinguished Highbury career, but no-one could ever accuse him of not giving 100 per cent every time he steps on to the pitch.

He was compared with the legendary Bobby Moore earlier in his career and, while that would have been a momumental task for anyone to live up to, Adams has gone a fair way to doing it.

Not only has he played for one of England's top clubs for the past decade, but he has also captained them for much of that time, and that in itself leads to added pressure in these days of high finance.

Maybe that pressure explains why Adams felt the need to turn to drink and a much publicised spell in prison for drink-driving was merely a prequel to his admission that he was suffering from alcoholism.

But, typically, he has met the problem head on and beaten it as you would expect from a man who had led from the front throughout his career, both with Arsenal and England.

Career details
● **Represented:** England, Arsenal ● **Position:** Defender ● **Born:** Romford, 10.10.1966 ● **Height:** 6ft 3in ● **Weight:** 13st 11lbs ● **Club Honours:** ● League Championship: 1988-89, 1990-91; FA Cup 1993; League Cup 1987, 1993; European Cup-Winners' Cup: 1994; PFA Young Player of the Year 1987 ● **International Honours:** England 18 Youth, 5 U21, 4 B, 47 full caps

Club League Record

Era	Club	Games	Goals
1983-97	Arsenal	385	27

League Highlights

May 1989: Arsenal travel to Anfield for the last game of the season needing to win, and score at least two goals, to snatch the title from Liverpool's grasp. Incredibly, they win 2-0 with the winner from Michael Thomas coming in the very last minute.

May 1991: Adams lifts the Championship trophy for the second time as The Gunners win the League crown for the second time in three years

On Adams:

● I'll never forget the day he was sent to prison for drink-driving. Just after he was sentenced he whispered to me: "I have done wrong and I'm going to take the punishment. I don't want to appeal." That's Tony. If you're in a battle on the pitch, he's the first bloke you'd want on your side. **Former Arsenal star David O'Leary on Adams facing up to his prison term.**

Adams on:

● Dennis (Bergkamp) is such a nice man, such a tremendous gentleman, with such a lovely family - it's going to be very hard for me to kick him. **Adams preparing to face his Arsenal team-mate Dennis Bergkamp in the England-Holland clash in Euro 96.**

DID YOU KNOW THAT...

● Adams made his League debut against Sunderland on November 5, 1983.

● He spent six weeks inside Wormwood Scrubs prison after being convicted of drink driving.

● He admitted to being an alcoholic after England were knocked out of the Euro 96 Semi-Finals on a penalty shoot-out against Germany.

● Early in his career he had to live with taunts of 'Donkey' as opposing fans questioned his ability. Curiously, no-one shouts it now.

● Manchester United have twice attempted to sign him.

● He made his England debut against Spain in February 1987. England won 4-2 in Madrid with a certain Gary Lineker netting all four goals.

● When David Seaman saved Gary McAllister's penalty in the England-Scotland match at Euro 96, Adams was the first to reach him and planted a huge kiss on his cheek.

● Adams scored the only goal of the 1993 FA Cup Semi-Final against Tottenham Hotspur, as The Gunners gained revenge for their 3-1 defeat by their great North London rivals at the same stage two years earlier.

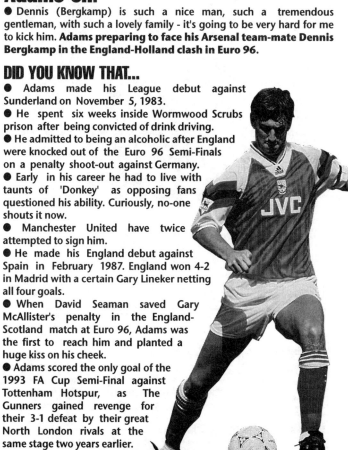

CHAMPIONS
Bolton 1996-97

The Premiership predictably went to Old Trafford for the fourth time in five seasons, while nearby Bolton also took their share of the limelight by winning the First Division Championship a year after being relegated from the Premiership. In truth the title was a stroll for the Wanderers, who scored 100 League goals - 22 more than any other team in the division. The international strike-force of John McGinlay (Scotland) and Nathan Blake (Wales) contributed 54 goals as Bolton finished the campaign a massive 18 points clear of second placed Barnsley and only two points short of the magic ton.

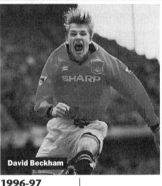

David Beckham

1995-96 cont
DIVISION 2

1	Swindon	92
2	Oxford	83
3	Blackpool	82
4	Notts Co	78
5	Crewe	73
6	Bradford	73
7	Chesterfield	72
8	Wrexham	70
9	Stockport	70
10	Bristol Rvrs	70
11	Walsall	69
12	Wycombe	60
13	Bristol City	60
14	Bournemouth	58
15	Brentford	58
16	Rotherham	56
17	Burnley	55
18	Shrewsbury	53
19	Peterborough	52
20	York	52
21	Carlisle	49
22	Swansea	47
23	Brighton	40
24	Hull	31

DIVISION 3

1	Preston	86
2	Gillingham	83
3	Bury	79
4	Plymouth	78
5	Darlington	78
6	Hereford	74
7	Colchester	72
8	Chester	70
9	Barnet	70
10	Wigan	70
11	Northampton	67
12	Scunthorpe	60
13	Doncaster	59
14	Exeter	57
15	Rochdale	55
16	Cambridge	54
17	Fulham	53
18	Lincoln	53
19	Mansfield	53
20	Hartlepool	49
21	L.Orient	47
22	Cardiff	45
23	Scarborough	40
24	Torquay	29

1996-97
PREMIER

1	Man Utd	75
2	Newcastle	68
3	Arsenal	68
4	Liverpool	68
5	Aston Villa	61
6	Chelsea	59
7	Sheff Wed	57
8	Wimbledon	56
9	Leicester	47
10	Tottenham	46
11	Leeds	46
12	Derby	46
13	Blackburn	42
14	West Ham	42
15	Everton	42
16	Southampton	41
17	Coventry	41
18	Sunderland	40
19	Middlesbro*	39
20	Nottm For	34

DIVISION 1

1	Bolton	98
2	Barnsley	80
3	Wolves	76
4	Ipswich	74
5	Sheff Utd	73
6	C.Palace	71
7	Portsmouth	68
8	Port Vale	67
9	QPR	66
10	Birmingham	66
11	Tranmere	65
12	Stoke	64
13	Norwich	63
14	Man City	61
15	Charlton	59
16	West Brom	57
17	Oxford	57
18	Reading	57
19	Swindon	54
20	Huddersfield	54
21	Bradford	48
22	Grimsby	46
23	Oldham	43
24	Southend	39

Middlesbrough were deducted 3 points for failing to turn up for a match against Blackburn

1996-97 cont
DIVISION 2

1	Bury	84
2	Stockport	82
3	Luton	78
4	Brentford	74
5	Bristol City	73
6	Crewe	73
7	Blackpool	69
8	Wrexham	69
9	Burnley	68
10	Chesterfield	68
11	Gillingham	67
12	Walsall	67
13	Watford	67
14	Millwall	61
15	Preston	61
16	Bournemouth	60
17	Bristol Rvrs	56
18	Wycombe	55
19	Plymouth	54
20	York	52
21	Peterborough	47
22	Shrewsbury	46
23	Rotherham	35
24	Notts Co	35

DIVISION 3

1	Wigan	87
2	Fulham	87
3	Carlisle	84
4	Northampton	72
5	Swansea	71
6	Chester	70
7	Cardiff	69
8	Colchester	68
9	Lincoln	66
10	Cambridge	65
11	Mansfield	64
12	Scarborough	63
13	Scunthorpe	63
14	Rochdale	58
15	Barnet	58
16	L.Orient	57
17	Hull	57
18	Darlington	52
19	Doncaster	52
20	Hartlepool	51
21	Torquay	50
22	Exeter	48
23	Brighton**	47
24	Hereford	47

**Brighton deducted two points for crowd trouble*

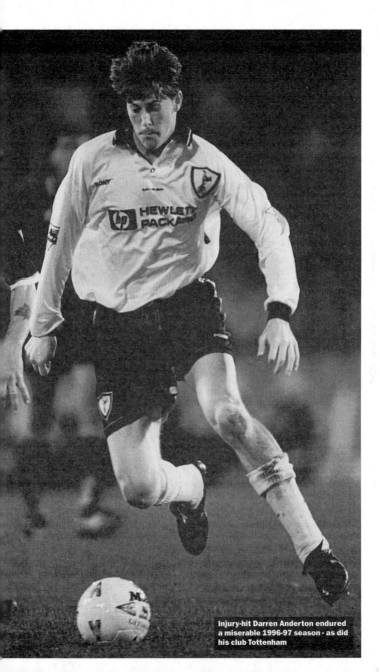

Injury-hit Darren Anderton endured
a miserable 1996-97 season - as did
his club Tottenham

Everything you wanted to know about...

YOUR CLUB

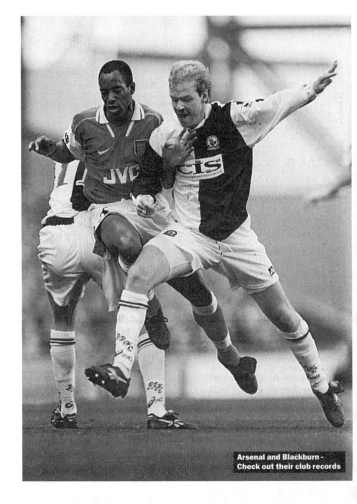

Arsenal and Blackburn -
Check out their club records

ARSENAL

FIRST TIME

First League Game:
Home v Newcastle Utd
(02-Sep-1893)
Result: D2-2
Final position: 9th

KICKIN' OFF

Successive wins at start of season: 8 (1903/04)
Successive defeats at start of season: 4 (1923/24)
Successive unbeaten games at start of season: 23 (1990/91)

HIGHS AND LOWS

Biggest home win: 12-0 v Loughborough Town (12-Mar-1900)
Biggest away win: 7-1 v Wolverhampton W. (05-Nov-1932), 6-0 v Tottenham Hotspur (06-Mar-1935), 7-1 v Aston Villa (14-Dec-1935)
Biggest home defeat: 0-5 v Liverpool (28-Oct-1893) 0-5 v Huddersfield Town (14-Feb-1925)
Biggest away defeat: 0-8 v Loughborough Town (12-Dec-1896)
Most points (3 for a win): 83, Division 1 (1990/91)
Most points (2 for a win): 66, Division 1 (1930/31)
Least points (3 for a win): 51, Premier (1994/95)
Least points (2 for a win): 18, Division 1 (1912/13)
Highest finish: 1, Division 1 (1930/31), (1932/33), (1933/34), (1934/35), (1937/38), (1947/48), (1952/53), (1970/71), (1988/89), (1990/91)
Lowest finish: 10, Division 2 (1896/97)

GOALS, GOALS, GOALS

Most goals scored (in a season): 127 (1930/31)
Fewest goals scored: 26 (1912/13)
Most goals conceded: 86 (1926/27), (1927/28)
Fewest goals conceded: 18 (1990/91)
Most clean sheets: 25 (1970/71)
Fewest clean sheets: 3 (1927/28)

Their roots

The club was founded at the government's Royal Arsenal arms factory in Woolworth Arsenal, South London in 1886. In those early days they would wheel off their injured players in a milk cart for treatment on the side of the pitch.

Friendly Forest

Arsenal used to wear all red until 1933. Their first kit was donated to the club, then known as Dial Square, by Nottingham Forest because former Forest player Fred Beardsley was involved with The Gunners.

ON THE RUN

Successive games unbeaten: 26 (28-Apr-1980)*
Successive games without a win: 23 (28-Sep-1912)
Successive wins: 10 (12-Sep-1987)
Successive defeats: 7 (12-Feb-1977)
Successive draws: 6 (04-Mar-1961)
Successive games without scoring: 6 (25-Feb-1987)
Successive games without conceding: 8 (10-Apr-1903)

*date in brackets indicates the start of the run

WIN, LOSE OR DRAW

Most wins (in a season): 29 (1970/71)
Fewest wins: 3 (1912/13)
Most draws: 18 (1969/70)
Fewest draws: 4 (1893/94), (1895/96), (1896/97), (1899/1900), (1906/07)
Most defeats: 23 (1912/13), (1924/25)
Fewest defeats: 1 (1990/91)

THEIR LEAGUE RECORD

P	W	D	L	F	A
3726	1619	933	1174	6101	4906

ASTON VILLA

HIGHS AND LOWS

Biggest home win: 12-2 v Accrington (12-Mar-1892), 10-0 v The Wednesday (05-Oct-1912), 10-0 v Wolves (29-Aug-1925), 11-1 v Charlton Athletic (14-Nov-1959)
Biggest away win: 6-0 v Manchester Utd (14-Mar-1914), 6-0 v Oldham Athletic (27-Nov-1971)
Biggest home defeat: 0-7 v West Brom (19-Oct-1935)
Biggest away defeat: 0-7 v Blackburn Rovers (19-Oct-1889), 0-7 v Everton (04-Jan-1890), 0-7 v Manchester Utd (08-Mar-1950), 0-7 v Manchester Utd (24-Oct-1964)
Most points (3 for a win): 78, Division 2 (1987/88)
Most points (2 for a win): 70, Division 3 (1971/72)
Least points (3 for a win): 36, Division 1 (1986/87)
Least points (2 for a win): 29, Division 1 (1888/89), (1966/67), (1969/70)
Highest finish: 1, Division 1 (1893/94), (1895/96), (1896/97), (1898/99), (1899/1900), (1909/10), (1980/81)
Lowest finish: 4, Division 3 (1970/71)

FIRST TIME

First League Game:
Away v Wolves
(08-Sep-1888)
Result: Drew 1-1
Final position: 2nd

Savo Milosevic

GOALS, GOALS, GOALS

Most goals scored (in a season): 128 (1930/31)
Fewest goals scored: 36 (1969/70)
Most goals conceded: 110 (1935/36)
Fewest goals conceded: 32 (1971/72), (1974/75)
Most clean sheets: 26 (1971/72)
Fewest clean sheets: 1 (1888/89)

Strange but true!

Savo Milosevic joined Aston Villa in a record deal at £3.5 million in June 1995 without manager Brian Little seeing him play live. The Villa boss made his decision after watching Savo on video.

ON THE RUN

Successive games unbeaten: 15 (16-Jan-1897), (18-Mar-1909), (12-Mar-1949)
Successive games without a win: 12 (10-Nov-1973), (27-Dec-1986)
Successive wins: 9 (22-Mar-1897), (15-Oct-1910)
Successive defeats: 11 (23-Mar-1963)
Successive draws: 6 (12-Sep-1981)
Successive games without scoring: 5 (23-Dec-1961), (01-Mar-1989), (11-Jan-1992), (29-Jan-1992)
Successive games without conceding: 7 (27-Oct-1923)

WIN, LOSE OR DRAW

Most wins (in a season): 32 (1971/72)
Fewest wins: 8 (1969/70) (1986/87)
Most draws: 17 (1975/76)
Fewest draws: 3 (1892/93) (1902/03) (1921/22)
Most defeats: 24 (1966/67)
Fewest defeats: 7 (1912/13)

THEIR LEAGUE RECORD

P	W	D	L	F	A
3862	1639	882	1341	6500	5671

BARNET

FIRST TIME
First League Game:
Home v Crewe Alexandra
(17-Aug-1991)
Result: Lost 4-7
Final position: 7th

HIGHS AND LOWS
Biggest home win: 5-0 v Aldershot (03-Mar-1992), 5-0 v Wigan (17-Feb-1996)
Biggest away win: 6-0 v Lincoln City (04-Sep-1991)
Biggest home defeat: 1-5 v York City (13-Mar-1993), 0-4 v Rochdale (8-Apr-1996)
Biggest away defeat: 0-6 v Port Vale (21-Aug-1993)
Most points (3 for a win): 79, Division 3 (1992/93)
Least points (3 for a win): 28, Division 2 (1993/94)
Highest finish: 24, Division 2 (1993/94)
Lowest finish: 15, Division 3 (1996/97)

KICKIN' OFF
Successive wins at start of season: 2 (1992/93)
Successive defeats at start of season: 10 (1993/94)
Successive unbeaten games at start of season: 3 (1992/93)

Naked truth
Two Barnet players had to escort a streaker off their Underhill pitch during the club's 4-0 win over Torquay in the 1995-96 season.

GOALS, GOALS, GOALS
Most goals scored (in a season): 81 (1991/92)
Fewest goals scored: 41 (1993/94)
Most goals conceded: 86 (1993/94)
Fewest goals conceded: 48 (1992/93)
Most clean sheets: 16 (1991/92)
Fewest clean sheets: 6 (1993/94)

Fry Up!
Police once caught someone mowing the Underhill pitch at 4.00am - it was manager Barry Fry, unable to sleep through tension and wanting to do something useful!

Bee stings
After winning promotion to the Football League in 1991, Barnet's first match ended in a 7-4 defeat at home to Crewe! Their first season included 6-0, 4-0, 4-2, 5-1, 4-1 and three 3-0 wins. The Bees also lost 5-2, 4-2, and 3-0 three times in that campaign.

ON THE RUN
Successive games unbeaten: 12 (05-Dec-1992)
Successive games without a win: 14 (24-Apr-1993), (11-Dec-1993)
Successive wins: 5 (29-Jan-1993)
Successive defeats: 11 (08-May-1993)
Successive draws: 4 (22-Jan-1994)
Successive games without scoring: 3 (15-Jan-1994), (12-Feb-1994), (04-Apr-1994), (14-Feb-1995)
Successive games without conceding: 4 (05-Sep-1992)

Run over
Barnet's 16 match unbeaten run at home in the League was ended by Scarborough's first ever win at Underhill in October, 1996

WIN, LOSE OR DRAW
Most wins (in a season): 23 (1992/93)
Fewest wins: 5 (1993/94)
Most draws: 13 (1993/94)
Fewest draws: 6 (1991/92)
Most defeats: 28 (1993/94)
Fewest defeats: 9 (1992/93)

THEIR LEAGUE RECORD

P	W	D	L	F	A
264	96	72	96	355	354

BARNSLEY

HIGHS AND LOWS

Biggest home win: 9-0 v Loughborough Town (28-Jan-1899)

Biggest away win: 9-0 v Accrington Stanley (03-Feb-1934)

Biggest home defeat: 1-6 v Bolton (26-Dec-1899), 2-7 v Middlesbrough (22-Feb-1902), 0-5 v Birmingham (14-Feb-1920), 0-5 v Liverpool (10-Mar-1956), 1-6 v Sheffield Utd (01-Sep-1956), 0-5 v Huddersfield Town (10-Nov-1956), 0-5 v Newcastle Utd (04-May-1983)

Biggest away defeat: 0-9 v Notts County (19-Nov-1927)

Most points (3 for a win): 80, Division 1 (1996/97)

Most points (2 for a win): 67, Division 3(N) (1938/39)

Least points (3 for a win): 52, Division 2 (1983/84)

Least points (2 for a win): 18, Division 2 (1952/53)

Highest finish: 2, Division 1 (1996/97)

Lowest finish: 16, Division 4 (1965/66), (1966/67)

FIRST TIME

First League Game:
Away v Lincoln City
(01-Sep-1898)
Result: Lost 0-1
Final position: 11th

KICKIN' OFF

Successive wins at start of season: 5 (1921/22), (1978/79), (1996/97)
Successive defeats at start of season: 6 (1986/87)
Successive unbeaten games at start of season: 10 (1946/47)

Long stayers

The Tykes spent more time in Division Two (now called Division One) than any other club - 65 years.

GOALS, GOALS, GOALS

Most goals scored (in a season): 118 (1933/34)

Fewest goals scored: 32 (1971/72)

Most goals conceded: 108 (1952/53)

Fewest goals conceded: 34 (1938/39)

Most clean sheets: 20 (1984/85)

Fewest clean sheets: 1 (1952/53)

No Oldham back!

On the 13th January, 1996, Barnsley won 1-0 at Oldham, their first victory there in 61 years

Saints alive!

Barnsley may have called Danny Wilson St Danny when he took them into the Premiership for the first time ever in 1997, but 110 years earlier they had actually been called Barnsley St Peter's.

WIN, LOSE OR DRAW

Most wins (in a season): 30 (1938/39), (1954/55)

Fewest wins: 5 (1952/53)

Most draws: 18 (1971/72), (1995-96)

Fewest draws: 3 (1914/15)

Most defeats: 29 (1952/53)

Fewest defeats: 5 (1938/39)

ON THE RUN

Successive games unbeaten: 21 (01-Jan-1934)

Successive games without a win: 26 (13-Dec-1952)

Successive wins: 10 (05-Mar-1955)

Successive defeats: 9 (14-Mar-1953)

Successive draws: 7 (28-Mar-1911)

Successive games without scoring: 6 (07-Oct-1899), (27-Nov-1971)

Successive games without conceding: 8 (05-Mar-1955)

THEIR LEAGUE RECORD

P	W	D	L	F	A
3734	1361	946	1427	5305	5576

BIRMINGHAM

FIRST TIME

First League Game:
Home v Burslem Port Vale
(03-Sep-1892)
Result: Won 5-1
Final position: 1st

KICKIN' OFF

Successive wins at start of
season: 5 (1984/85)
Successive defeats at start
of season: 6 (1895/96)
Successive unbeaten
games at start of season:
15 (1900/01)

HIGHS AND LOWS

Biggest home win: 12-0 v Walsall Town S. (17-Dec-1892), 12-0 v Doncaster Rovers (11-Apr-1903)
Biggest away win: 7-0 v Northwich Victoria (06-Jan-1894)
Biggest home defeat: 1-7 v Burnley (10-Apr-1926), 0-6 v West Bromwich Alb. (03-Sep-1958), 1-7 v West Bromwich Alb. (18-Apr-1960), 0-6 v Crystal Palace (05-Sep-1987)
Biggest away defeat: 1-9 v Blackburn (05-Jan-1895), 0-8 v Derby County (30-Nov-1895), 0-8 v Newcastle Utd (23-Nov-1907), 1-9 v Sheffield Wed. (13-Dec-1930), 0-8 v Preston North End (01-Feb-1958)
Most points (3 for a win): 89, Division 2 (1994/95)
Most points (2 for a win): 59, Division 2 (1947/48)
Least points (3 for a win): 29, Division 1 (1985/86)
Least points (2 for a win): 22, Division 1 (1978/79)
Highest finish: 6, Division 1 (1955/56)
Lowest finish: 12, Division 3 (1990/91)

GOALS, GOALS, GOALS

Most goals scored (in a season): 103 (1893/94)
Fewest goals scored: 30 (1985/86)
Most goals conceded: 96 (1964/65)
Fewest goals conceded: 24 (1900/01), (1947/48)
Most clean sheets: 24 (1947/48)
Fewest clean sheets: 3 (1896/97)

Still counting

Manager Barry Fry created history in the 1995-96 season by using the most number of players any club has ever fielded in a League season since the War, 46.

On the move

Everything changed for Birmingham in 1905-06 when they moved from Muntz Street to St Andrews and changed their name from Small Heath to Birmingham City.

ON THE RUN

Successive games unbeaten: 20 (03-Sep-1994)
Successive games without a win: 17 (28-Sep-1985)
Successive wins: 13 (17-Dec-1892)
Successive defeats: 8 (26-Dec-1922), (02-Dec-1978), (28-Sep-1985)
Successive draws: 8 (18-Sep-1990)
Successive games without scoring: 6 (01-Oct-1949), (26-Oct-1985), (11-Feb-1989)
Successive games without conceding: 7 (29-Oct-1994)

WIN, LOSE OR DRAW

Most wins (in a season):
25 (1946/47), (1984/85), (1994/95)
Fewest wins: 6 (1978/79)
Most draws: 18 (1937/38), (1971/72)
Fewest draws: 4 (1895/96), (1897/98), (1926/27)
Most defeats: 29 (1985/86)
Fewest defeats: 5 (1900/01), (1947/48), (1971/72)

THEIR LEAGUE RECORD

P	W	D	L	F	A
3808	1423	932	1453	5595	5564

BLACKBURN

FIRST TIME

First League Game:
Home v Accrington
(15-Sep-1888)
Result: Drew 5-5
Final position: 4th

KICKIN' OFF

Successive wins at start of season: 5 (1913/14)
Successive defeats at start of season: 3 (1897/98), (1925/26), (1947/48), (1951/52)
Successive unbeaten games at start of season: 10 (1913/14), (1989/90)

HIGHS AND LOWS

Biggest home win: 9-0 v Middlesbrough (06-Nov-1954)
Biggest away win: 7-1 v Burnley (03-Nov-1888), 7-1 v Newcastle Utd (09-Sep-1925), 8-2 v West Ham Utd (26-Dec-1963)
Biggest home defeat: 1-7 v Notts County (14-Mar-1891), 1-7 v Middlesbrough (29-Nov-1947)
Biggest away defeat: 0-8 v Arsenal (25-Feb-1933), 0-8 v Lincoln City (29-Aug-1953)
Most points (3 for a win): 89, Premier (1994/95)
Most points (2 for a win): 60, Division 3 (1974/75)
Least points (3 for a win): 42, Premier (1996/97)
Least points (2 for a win): 20, Division 1 (1965/66)
Highest finish: 1, Division 1 (1911/12), (1913/14) 1, Premier (1994/95)
Lowest finish: 13, Division 3 (1973/74)

GOALS, GOALS, GOALS

Most goals scored (in a season): 114 (1954/55)
Fewest goals scored: 37 (1970/71)
Most goals conceded: 102 (1932/33)
Fewest goals conceded: 29 (1980/81)
Most clean sheets: 23 (1980/81)
Fewest clean sheets: 3 (1897/98)

Chris Sutton

Costly Chris

Chris Sutton became the most expensive player in British football when he joined Blackburn from Norwich City in July 1994 for £5 million. His strike partnership with Alan Shearer took Rovers to the League title that season.

ON THE RUN

Successive games unbeaten: 23 (30-Sep-1987)
Successive games without a win: 16 (11-Nov-1978)
Successive wins: 8 (01-Mar-1980)
Successive defeats: 7 (12-Mar-1966)
Successive draws: 5 (06-Apr-1974), (11-Oct-1975)
Successive games without scoring: 4 (12 times)
Successive games without conceding: 6 (11-Apr-1981)

WIN, LOSE OR DRAW

Most wins (in a season): 27 (1994/95)
Fewest wins: 6 (1970/71)
Most draws: 18 (1980/81)
Fewest draws: 4 (1899/00)
Most defeats: 30 (1965/66)
Fewest defeats: 7 (1889/90), (1913/14), (1994/95)

THEIR LEAGUE RECORD

P	W	D	L	F	A
3902	1541	940	1421	6126	5882

BLACKPOOL

FIRST TIME
First League Game:
Away v Lincoln City
(05-Sep-1896)
Result: Lost 1-3
Final position: 8th

KICKIN' OFF
Successive wins at start of
season: 4 (1946/47)
Successive defeats at start
of season: 4 (1898/99)
Successive unbeaten
games at start of season:
11 (1900/01)

HIGHS AND LOWS
Biggest home win: 7-0 v Reading (10-Nov-1928),
7-0 v Sunderland (05-Oct-1957)
Biggest away win: 7-0 v Preston North End
(01-May-1948)
Biggest home defeat: 0-6 v Manchester Utd
(27-Feb-1960)
Biggest away defeat: 1-10 v Small Heath (02-Mar-1901)
1-10 v Huddersfield Town (13-Dec-1930)
Most points (3 for a win): 86, Division 4 (1984/85)
Most points (2 for a win): 58, Division 2 (1929/30)
58, Division 2 (1967/68)
Least points (3 for a win): 46, Division 3 (1989/90)
Least points (2 for a win): 21, Division 1 (1966/67)
Highest finish: 2, Division 1 (1955/56)
Lowest finish: 21, Division 4 (1982/83)

GOALS, GOALS, GOALS
Most goals scored (in a season): 98 (1929/30)
Fewest goals scored: 32 (1911/12)
Most goals conceded: 125 (1930/31)
Fewest goals conceded: 33 (1974/75)
Most clean sheets: 21 (1974/75)
Fewest clean sheets: 3 (1927/28)

Seaside Ton
Even if Blackpool leave Bloomfield Road for their
dream super-stadium, they will have completed
100 years at the ground, having first played
there in 1899.

Strange but true!
In 1992-93, Preston's Tony
Ellis scored six times in
three derby matches
against The Tangerines.
A year later, Blackpool
bought him. After three
derby games on the
other side, he had failed to
score and is now back
playing with the
seaside club.

ON THE RUN
Successive games unbeaten: 17 (06-Apr-1968)
Successive games without a win: 19 (19-Dec-1970)
Successive wins: 9 (21-Nov-1936)
Successive defeats: 8 (26-Nov-1898)
Successive draws: 5 (06-Sep-1902), (26-Jan-1907),
(26-Dec-1973), (04-Dec-1976)
Successive games without scoring: 5 (12-Apr-1975),
(11-Jan-1986), (25-Nov-1989)
Successive games without conceding: 5 (28-Aug-1922)

WIN, LOSE OR DRAW
Most wins (in a season): 27
(1929/30)
Fewest wins: 4 (1970/71)
Most draws: 17 (1974/75),
(1976/77)
Fewest draws: 4 (1898/99),
(1929/30)
Most defeats: 27 (1966/67)
Fewest defeats: 8
(1967/68), (1976/77),
(1984/85)

THEIR LEAGUE RECORD
P	W	D	L	F	A
3698	1376	913	1409	5407	5439

BOLTON

HIGHS AND LOWS

Biggest home win: 8-0 v Barnsley (06-Oct-1934)
Biggest away win: 7-1 v Aston Villa (26-Dec-1914)
Biggest home defeat: 0-6 v Manchester United (25-Feb-1996)
Biggest away defeat: 0-7 v Burnley (01-Mar-1890), 0-7 v The Wednesday (01-Mar-1915), 0-7 v Manchester City (21-Mar-1936)
Most points (3 for a win): 98, Division 1 (1996/97)
Most points (2 for a win): 61, Division 3 (1972/73)
Least points (3 for a win): 29, Premier (1995/96)
Least points (2 for a win): 24, Division 1 (1893/94) 24, Division 1 (1909/10), 24, Division 2 (1970/71)
Highest finish: 3, Division 1 (1891/92), (1920/21), (1924/25)
Lowest finish: 3, Division 4 (1987/88)

FIRST TIME

First League Game:
Home v Derby County (08-Sep-1888)
Result: Lost 3-6
Final position: 5th

KICKIN' OFF

Successive wins at start of season: 7 (1934/35)
Successive defeats at start of season: 7 (1902/03)
Successive unbeaten games at start of season: 7 (1896/97), (1906/07), (1934/35)

Going down, coming up!

When Bolton Wanderers went up to the Premiership in the 1995-96 season, they won only two matches before the New Year but they were relegated only a week from the end of the season after a stirring fightback. They bounced straight back to the top flight by winning the First Division title in 1997.

GOALS, GOALS, GOALS

Most goals scored (in a season): 100 (1996/97)
Fewest goals scored: 35 (1970/71)
Most goals conceded: 92 (1932/33)
Fewest goals conceded: 28 (1908/09)
Most clean sheets: 21 (1987/88)
Fewest clean sheets: 1 (1888/89)

Spotted!

Bolton were called the Reds early in their history because they wore red and white quartered shirts. Around 1883 they tried white shirts with red spots which supposedly made their players look bigger than they actually were!

ON THE RUN

Successive games unbeaten: 23 (13-Oct-1990)
Successive games without a win: 26 (07-Apr-1902)
Successive wins: 11 (05-Nov-1904)
Successive defeats: 11 (07-Apr-1902)
Successive draws: 6 (25-Jan-1913)
Successive games without scoring: 5 (03-Jan-1898) (16-Mar-1990)
Successive games without conceding: 7 (24-Feb-1900)

WIN, LOSE OR DRAW

Most wins (in a season): 28 (1996/97)
Fewest wins: 5 (1979/80)
Most draws: 17 (1991/92)
Fewest draws: 3 (1902/03), (1911/12)
Most defeats: 25 (1970/71)
Fewest defeats: 4 (1996/97)

THEIR LEAGUE RECORD

P	W	D	L	F	A
3928	1541	919	1468	5954	5690

BOURNEMOUTH

FIRST TIME

First League Game:
Away v Swindon Town
(25-Aug-1923)
Result: Lost 1-3
Final position: 21st

KICKIN' OFF

Successive wins at start of season: 4 (1947/48)
Successive defeats at start of season: 7 (1994/95)
Successive unbeaten games at start of season: 14 (1961/62)

HIGHS AND LOWS

Biggest home win: 7-0 v Swindon Town (22-Sep-1956)
Biggest away win: 6-1 v Norwich (26-Dec-1946), 6-1 v Brighton (19-Feb-1949), 5-0 v Mansfield (29-Oct-1971), 7-2 v Rotherham (10-Oct-1972), 5-0 v Tranmere (28-Sep-1979)
Biggest home defeat: 0-4 v Southend (24-Sep-1938), 0-4 v Exeter (23-Apr-1952), 0-4 v Carlisle (06-Feb-1965), 3-7 v Plymouth (11-Jan-1975), 0-4 v Crewe (16-Sep-1995)
Biggest away defeat: 0-9 v Lincoln City (18-Dec-1982)
Most points (3 for a win): 97, Division 3 (1986/87)
Most points (2 for a win): 62, Division 3 (1971/72)
Least points (3 for a win): 48, Division 2 (1989/90)
Least points (2 for a win): 27, Division 3(S) (1933/34)
Highest finish: 12, Division 2 (1988/89)
Lowest finish: 18, Division 4 (1978/79)

GOALS, GOALS, GOALS

Most goals scored (in a season): 88 (1956/57)
Fewest goals scored: 38 (1965/66)
Most goals conceded: 102 (1933/34)
Fewest goals conceded: 30 (1981/82)
Most clean sheets: 22 (1981/82)
Fewest clean sheets: 4 (1932/33)

Centre Court

England star Jamie Redknapp played only 13 times for Bournemouth before Kenny Dalglish took him to Liverpool for £350,000. The canny Scot had Jamie on trial at Anfield as a 15-year-old and watched the lad's progress. Jamie's dad, Harry, learned his management skills at Dean Court before taking over at West Ham.

Mac-nificent!

The Cherries are famous for producing personalities who went on to star elsewhere. Ted MacDougall scored a record nine times in one FA Cup tie v Margate in 1971 and moved on to great success with Norwich and Man City. But he never forgot Bournemouth and flew home from Canada to pledge his support to the club as they faced financial ruin in 1997.

ON THE RUN

Successive games unbeaten: 18 (06-Mar-1982)
Successive games without a win: 14 (06-Mar-1974)
Successive wins: 7 (22-Aug-1970)
Successive defeats: 7 (01-Nov-1952)
Successive draws: 5 (10-Nov-1979)
Successive games without scoring: 6 (01-Feb-1975)
Successive games without conceding: 7 (20-Oct-1984)

WIN, LOSE OR DRAW

Most wins (in a season): 29 (1986/87)
Fewest wins: 9 (1933/34)
Most draws: 19 (1981/82)
Fewest draws: 7 (1934/35), (1950/51), (1983/84)
Most defeats: 24 (1933/34)
Fewest defeats: 4 (1981/82)

THEIR LEAGUE RECORD

P	W	D	L	F	A
3000	1116	792	1092	4084	4026

BRADFORD

HIGHS AND LOWS

Biggest home win: 11-1 v Rotherham United (25-Aug-1928)
Biggest away win: 8-2 v Ashington (13-Oct-1928), 6-0 v New Brighton (03-Feb-1951)
Biggest home defeat: 1-7 v Stockport County (18-Sep-1965)
Biggest away defeat: 0-8 v Manchester City (07-May-1927), 1-9 v Colchester Utd (30-Dec-1961)
Most points (3 for a win): 94, Division 3 (1984/85)
Most points (2 for a win): 63, Division 3(N) (1928/29)
Least points (3 for a win): 41, Division 2 (1989/90)
Least points (2 for a win): 23, Division 2 (1926/27)
Highest finish: 5, Division 1 (1910/11)
Lowest finish: 23, Division 4 (1962/63), (1965/66)

FIRST TIME

First League Game:
Away v Grimsby Town (01-Sep-1903)
Result: Lost 0-2
Final position: 10th

KICKIN' OFF

Successive wins at start of season: 5 (1932/33)
Successive defeats at start of season: 5 (1949/50)
Successive unbeaten games at start of season: 8 (1954/55), (1979/80)

Schoolboy star

Bradford midfielder Shaun Murray holds the all-time record for winning the most England schoolboy caps. A teenage prodigy from Newcastle, Murray signed for Tottenham in 1987 but failed to make it into the first team and was sold to Portsmouth. His career continued to decline until an inspired spell with Scarborough earned him a move back up to Bradford and First Division football.

GOALS, GOALS, GOALS

Most goals scored (in a season): 128 (1928/29)
Fewest goals scored: 35 (1923/24)
Most goals conceded: 94 (1936/37), (1965/66)
Fewest goals conceded: 40 (1913/14)
Most clean sheets: 20 (1953/54)
Fewest clean sheets: 3 (1960/61)

On parade

The Queen visited Bradford in 1997 to officially open the club's new Midland Road stand and thus complete the rebuilding of Valley Parade after the fire of 1985. It was believed to be the first time she had visited a League ground.

ON THE RUN

Successive games unbeaten: 21 (11-Jan-1969)
Successive games without a win: 16 (28-Aug-1948)
Successive wins: 10 (26-Nov-1983)
Successive defeats: 8 (21-Jan-1933)
Successive draws: 6 (30-Jan-1976)
Successive games without scoring: 7 (18-Apr-1925), (15-Apr-1995)
Successive games without conceding: 5 (22-Apr-1905), (30-Oct-1909), (28-Feb-1911), (06-Mar-1929) (29-Aug-1953), (16-Jan-1954)

WIN, LOSE OR DRAW

Most wins (in a season): 28 (1984/85)
Fewest wins: 7 (1926/27)
Most draws: 20 (1968/69)
Fewest draws: 5 (1906/07), (1910/11)
Most defeats: 26 (1926/27), (1964/65)
Fewest defeats: 6 (1928/29)

THEIR LEAGUE RECORD

P	W	D	L	F	A
3606	1339	992	1345	5212	5171

BRENTFORD

FIRST TIME

First League Game:
Away v Exeter City
(28-Aug-1920)
Result: Lost 0-3
Final position: 21st

KICKIN' OFF

Successive wins at start of season: 7 (1932/33)
Successive defeats at start of season: 6 (1961/62)
Successive unbeaten games at start of season: 14 (1932/33)

HIGHS AND LOWS

Biggest home win: 9-0 v Wrexham (15-Oct-1963),
Biggest away win: 6-0 v Southampton (09-Mar-1959),
7-1 v Exeter City (23-Apr-1983)
Biggest home defeat: 1-6 v Brighton & Hove A.
(12-Sep-1925), 0-5 v Bristol Rovers (05-Feb-1966)
Biggest away defeat: 0-7 v Swansea Town
(08-Nov-1924), 0-7 v Walsall (19-Jan-1957)
Most points (3 for a win): 85, Division 2 (1994/95)
Most points (2 for a win): 62, Division 3(S) (1932/33)
62, Division 4 (1962/63)
Least points (3 for a win): 49, Division 3 (1983/84)
49, Division 1 (1992/93)
Least points (2 for a win): 25, Division 3(S) (1924/25)
25, Division 1 (1946/47)
Highest finish: 5, Division 1 (1935/36)
Lowest finish: 19, Division 4 (1973/74)

GOALS, GOALS, GOALS

Most goals scored (in a season): 98 (1962/63)
Fewest goals scored: 38 (1924/25)
Most goals conceded: 94 (1925/26)
Fewest goals conceded: 39 (1969/70), (1994/95)
Most clean sheets: 22 (1971/72), (1994/95)
Fewest clean sheets: 5 (1936/37)

Home sweet home

In the 1929-30 season, while in the Third Division, Brentford became the only club to win all their 21 home League games, and yet still finished runners-up.

Strange but true!

In 1937-38, the Bees fielded a forward line of internationals; Idris Hopkins (Wales), Bill Scott and George Eastham (both England) and Dave McCulloch and Bobby Reid (both Scotland).

ON THE RUN

Successive games unbeaten: 16 (30-Apr-1932),
(14-Jan-1967)
Successive games without a win: 16 (19-Feb-1994)
Successive wins: 9 (30-Apr-1932)
Successive defeats: 9 (13-Apr-1925), (20-Oct-1928)
Successive draws: 5 (16-Mar-1957)
Successive games without scoring: 5 (17-Feb-1923),
(26-Mar-1949), (21-Nov-1953), (22-Apr-1967)
Successive games without conceding: 7 (01-Oct-1957)

WIN, LOSE OR DRAW

Most wins (in a season): 28
(1929/30), (09-Dec-1961)
Fewest wins: 9 (1920/21),
(1924/25), (1946/47)
Most draws: 19 (1980/81),
(1993/94)
Fewest draws: 5 (1929/30)
Most defeats: 26
(1924/25), (1946/47)
Fewest defeats: 6
(1932/33)

THEIR LEAGUE RECORD

P	W	D	L	F	A
3112	1196	785	1131	4525	4349

BRIGHTON

HIGHS AND LOWS

Biggest home win: 9-1 v Newport County (18-Apr-1951), 9-1 v Southend Utd (27-Nov-1965)
Biggest away win: 8-2 v Merthyr Town (01-Feb-1930)
Biggest home defeat: 0-6 v Plymouth Argyle (18-Nov-1950), 2-8 v Bristol Rovers (01-Dec-1973)
Biggest away defeat: 0-9 v Middlesbrough (23-Aug-1958)
Most points (3 for a win): 84, Division 3 (1987/88)
Most points (2 for a win): 65, Division 3(S) (1955/56) 65, Division 3 (1971/72)
Least points (3 for a win): 39, Division 2 (1986/87)
Least points (2 for a win): 29, Division 2 (1972/73)
Highest finish: 13, Division 1 (1981/82)
Lowest finish: 23rd, Division 3 (1997/98)

FIRST TIME

First League Game:
Away v Southend Utd (28-Aug-1920)
Result: Lost 0-2
Final position: 18th

KICKIN' OFF

Successive wins at start of season: 5 (1953/54)
Successive defeats at start of season: 6 (1988/89)
Successive unbeaten games at start of season: 8 (1953/54), (1977/78)

Better late than never

Brighton survived relegation to the Vauxhall Conference in 1997 when they drew 1-1 at Hereford in the final game, which sent their opponents down instead. They still ended the year groundless after selling the Goldstone Ground to developers, though.

GOALS, GOALS, GOALS

Most goals scored (in a season): 112 (1955/56)
Fewest goals scored: 37 (1986/87)
Most goals conceded: 90 (1958/59)
Fewest goals conceded: 34 (1922/23), (1984/85)
Most clean sheets: 21 (1923/24)
Fewest clean sheets: 4 (1972/73)

Strange but true!

The club's first hat-trick in the League was scored by Irish international Jack Doran in 1921-22 in a 3-0 win at Exeter. He repeated the feat at home to Exeter only seven days later!

ON THE RUN

Successive games unbeaten: 16 (08-Oct-1930)
Successive games without a win: 15 (20-Sep-1947), (21-Oct-1972)
Successive wins: 9 (02-Oct-1926)
Successive defeats: 12 (11-Nov-1972)
Successive draws: 6 (16-Feb-1980)
Successive games without scoring: 6 (22-Apr-1922), (08-Nov-1924), (23-Sep-1970)
Successive games without conceding: 5 (22-Dec-1923), (08-Mar-1924), (13-Dec-1969), (29-Jan-1977), (25-Feb-1995)

WIN, LOSE OR DRAW

Most wins (in a season): 29 (1955/56)
Fewest wins: 8 (1972/73)
Most draws: 18 (1948/49)
Fewest draws: 5 (1936/37)
Most defeats: 26 (1995/96)
Fewest defeats: 8 (1971/72), (1977/78), (1987/88)

THEIR LEAGUE RECORD

P	W	D	L	F	A
3068	1209	769	1090	4525	4238

BRISTOL CITY

FIRST TIME

First League Game:
Away v Blackpool
(07-Sep-1901)
Result: Won 2-0
Final position: 6th

KICKIN' OFF

Successive wins at start of
season: 5 (1902/03),
(1927/28)
Successive defeats at start
of season: 4 (1933/34),
(1966/67), (1967/68),
(1985/86)
Successive unbeaten
games at start of season:
13 (1954/55)

HIGHS AND LOWS

Biggest home win: 9-0 v Aldershot (28-Dec-1946)
Biggest away win: 8-2 v Walsall (26-Feb-1938)
Biggest home defeat: 0-8 v Derby County
(29-Sep-1923)
Biggest away defeat: 0-9 v Coventry City (28-Apr-1934)
Most points (3 for a win): 91, Division 3 (1989/90)
Most points (2 for a win): 70, Division 3(S) (1954/55)
Least points (3 for a win): 45, Division 1 (1994/95)
Least points (2 for a win): 23, Division 2 (1931/32)
Highest finish: 2, Division 1 (1906/07)
Lowest finish: 14, Division 4 (1982/83)

Hats off

Bristol City beat Luton 5-0 in 1996-97 to record their
best win since 1983. Hatters boss Lennie Lawrence
called his side 'gutless' after the defeat.

GOALS, GOALS, GOALS

Most goals scored (in a season): 104 (1926/27)
Fewest goals scored: 29 (1980/81)
Most goals conceded: 97 (1959/60)
Fewest goals conceded: 28 (1905/06)
Most clean sheets: 24 (1920/21)
Fewest clean sheets: 3 (1932/33)

Four star

In 1996-97, City fielded
internationals Paul
Agostino (Australia),
Clayton Blackmore (Wales),
Greg Goodridge
(Barbados), and Shaun
Goater (Bermuda) - but still
lost in the Second Division
play-offs to Brentford at
the Semi-Final stage.

Three's Company

In 1905-06, City got promoted to Division One thanks
to three players scoring over 20 League goals: William
Maxwell (25), Walter Bennett (20) and Sammy
Gilligan (20).

ON THE RUN

Successive games unbeaten: 24 (09-Sep-1905)
Successive games without a win: 15 (29-Apr-1933)
Successive wins: 14 (09-Sep-1905)
Successive defeats: 7 (05-Sep-1931)
Successive draws: 4 (20-Mar-1920), (21-Mar-1953),
(07-Sep-1968), (03-May-1980), (30-Oct-1982),
(17-Apr-1993)
Successive games without scoring: 6 (10-Sep-1910),
(20-Dec-1980)
Successive games without conceding: 5 (1996-97)

WIN, LOSE OR DRAW

Most wins (in a season): 30
(1905/06), (1954/55)
Fewest wins: 6 (1931/32)
Most draws: 17 (1919/20),
(1965/66), (1982/83)
Fewest draws: 5 (1910/11),
(1959/60)
Most defeats: 26 (1959/60)
Fewest defeats: 2
(1905/06)

THEIR LEAGUE RECORD

P	W	D	L	F	A
3602	1391	914	1297	5201	5004

BRISTOL ROVERS

HIGHS AND LOWS

Biggest home win: 7-0 v Brighton & Hove A. (29-Nov-1952), 7-0 v Swansea Town (02-Oct-1954), 7-0 v Shrewsbury Town (21-Mar-1964)
Biggest away win: 8-2 v Brighton & Hove A. (01-Dec-1973)
Biggest home defeat: 0-7 v Grimsby Town (14-Dec-1957)
Biggest away defeat: 0-12 v Luton Town (13-Apr-1936)
Most points (3 for a win): 93, Division 3 (1989/90)
Most points (2 for a win): 64, Division 3(S) (1952/53)
Least points (3 for a win): 41, Division 1 (1992/93)
Least points (2 for a win): 23, Division 2 (1980/81)
Highest finish: 6, Division 2 (1955/56), (1958/59)
Lowest finish: 22, Division 3(S) (1938/39)

FIRST TIME

First League Game:
Away v Millwall Athletic
(28-Aug-1920)
Result: Lost 0-2
Final position: 10th

KICKIN' OFF

Successive wins at start of season: 4 (1936/37)
Successive defeats at start of season: 7 (1961/62)
Successive unbeaten games at start of season: 27 (1973/74)

Rover the moon!

Joe Riley scored a hat-trick on his debut when Rovers beat Bournemouth 4-1 on January 2nd 1932, the first Rover to do so.

GOALS, GOALS, GOALS

Most goals scored (in a season): 92 (1952/53)
Fewest goals scored: 34 (1980/81)
Most goals conceded: 95 (1935/36)
Fewest goals conceded: 33 (1973/74)
Most clean sheets: 22 (1973/74)
Fewest clean sheets: 3 (1960/61)

Top fee

Rovers picked up a record fee for a goalkeeper of £1 million when Nigel Martyn left the club to join Crystal Palace in November 1989.

Strange but true!

Rovers were first called the Purdown Poachers but changed their name later in 1893 to the Black Arabs because they wore black shirts. They became Bristol Rovers via Eastville Rovers in 1898.

ON THE RUN

Successive games unbeaten: 32 (07-Apr-1973)
Successive games without a win: 20 (05-Apr-1980)
Successive wins: 12 (18-Oct-1952)
Successive defeats: 8 (29-Apr-1961)
Successive draws: 5 (18-Mar-1967), (01-Nov-1975)
Successive games without scoring: 6 (14-Oct-1922)
Successive games without conceding: 6 (15-Sep-1973) (12-May-1984), (05-Mar-1988), (12-Apr-1988), (16-Sep-1989)

WIN, LOSE OR DRAW

Most wins (in a season): 26 (1952/53), (1989/90)
Fewest wins: 5 (1980/81)
Most draws: 17 (1973/74), (1988/89)
Fewest draws: 4 (1927/28), (1936/37)
Most defeats: 25 (1992/93)
Fewest defeats: 5 (1989/90)

THEIR LEAGUE RECORD

P	W	D	L	F	A
3064	1153	772	1139	4530	4519

BURNLEY

FIRST TIME
First League Game:
Away v Preston
(08-Sep-1888)
Result: Lost 2-5
Final position: 9th

KICKIN' OFF
Successive wins at start of season: 4 (1911/12)
Successive defeats at start of season: 5 (1927/28)
Successive unbeaten games at start of season: 16 (1972/73)

HIGHS AND LOWS
Biggest home win: 9-0 v Darwen (09-Jan-1892)
Biggest away win: 7-1 v Birmingham (10-Apr-1926)
Biggest home defeat: 1-7 v Blackburn Rovers
(03-Nov-1888), 0-6 v Hereford Utd (24-Jan-1987)
Biggest away defeat: 0-10 v Aston Villa (29-Aug-1925)
0-10 v Sheffield Utd (19-Jan-1929)
Most points (3 for a win): 83, Division 4 (1991/92)
Most points (2 for a win): 62, Division 2 (1972/73)
Least points (3 for a win): 44, Division 2 (1982/83)
Least points (2 for a win): 27, Division 1 (1895/96)
27, Division 1 (1899/00), 27, Division 1 (1970/71)
27, Division 2 (1979/80)
Highest finish: 1, Division 1 (1920/21), (1959/60)
Lowest finish: 22, Division 4 (1986/87)

GOALS, GOALS, GOALS
Most goals scored (in a season): 102 (1960/61)
Fewest goals scored: 29 (1970/71)
Most goals conceded: 108 (1925/26)
Fewest goals conceded: 29 (1900/01), (1946/47)
Most clean sheets: 21 (1980/81)
Fewest clean sheets: 1 (1890/91)

Six appeal
Only 17 players - a club record - were used when Burnley won promotion to Division One in 1973 and six were ever-presents - Alan Stevenson, Keith Newton, Colin Waldron, Jimmy Thompson, Frank Casper and Leighton James.

The only way is up!
In 1987, Burnley hit rock bottom, needing to win their last game of the season at home to Leyton Orient to stay in the Football League. They did, and seven years later were in Division One.

ON THE RUN
Successive games unbeaten: 30 (06-Sep-1920)
Successive games without a win: 24 (16-Apr-1979)
Successive wins: 10 (16-Nov-1912)
Successive defeats: 8 (09-Nov-1889), (16-Mar-1895),
(02-Jan-1995)
Successive draws: 6 (21-Feb-1931)
Successive games without scoring: 5 (22-Aug-1970)
Successive games without conceding: 7 (06-Sep-1980)

WIN, LOSE OR DRAW
Most wins (in a season): 25 (1991/92)
Fewest wins: 6 (1896/97), (1902/03), (1979/80)
Most draws: 17 (1981/82)
Fewest draws: 4 (1891/92), (1892/93), (1893/94), (1894/95), (1900/01), (1953/54)
Most defeats: 23 (1975/76)
Fewest defeats: 4 (1972/73)

THEIR LEAGUE RECORD

P	W	D	L	F	A
3932	1531	937	1464	5940	5865

BURY

HIGHS AND LOWS

Biggest home win: 8-0 v Tranmere Rovers (10-Jan-1970)
Biggest away win: 7-1 v Millwall (21-Feb-1948), 7-1 v Tranmere Rovers (01-Oct-1960)
Biggest home defeat: 0-6 v Stoke City (13-Mar-1954), 0-6 v Huddersfield Town (01-Apr-1989)
Biggest away defeat: 0-8 v Sheffield Utd (06-Apr-1896), 0-8 v Swindon Town (08-Dec-1979)
Most points (3 for a win): 84, Division 4 (1984/85), 84, (1996/97)
Most points (2 for a win): 68, Division 3 (1960/61)
Least points (3 for a win): 49, Division 3 (1985/86)
Least points (2 for a win): 21, Division 1 (1911/12)
Highest finish: 4, Division 1 (1925/26)
Lowest finish: 15, Division 4 (1983/84)

FIRST TIME

First League Game: Home v Manchester City (01-Sep-1894)
Result: Won 4-2
Final position: 1st

KICKIN' OFF

Successive wins at start of season: 5 (1957/58)
Successive defeats at start of season: 4 (1895/96), (1904/05), (1928/29), (1949/50)
Successive unbeaten games at start of season: 10 (1975/76)

Shake Up

The Shakers equalled their highest ever points total when they gained 84 to top Division Two in 1996-97. They got the same total in Division Four in 1984-85 but still ended behind Chesterfield.

GOALS, GOALS, GOALS

Most goals scored (in a season): 108 (1960/61)
Fewest goals scored: 32 (1911/12)
Most goals conceded: 99 (1928/29)
Fewest goals conceded: 35 (1923/24)
Most clean sheets: 22 (1923/24), (1996-97)
Fewest clean sheets: 1 (1954/55)

Neville ending story!

When Bury went from Divisions Three to One in successive seasons between 1995-97, their backroom staff included Gary and Phil Neville's dad - Neville Neville - mum, sister, uncle, auntie and cousin!

Bury 'em

Bury's 2-0 win over Millwall in 1997 set a new club record run of 25 unbeaten home games.

ON THE RUN

Successive games unbeaten: 18 (04-Feb-1961)
Successive games without a win: 19 (01-Apr-1911)
Successive wins: 9 (26-Sep-1960)
Successive defeats: 6 (10-Jan-1903), (04-May-1949), (03-Oct-1953), (14-Jan-1967)
Successive draws: 4 (11 times)
Successive games without scoring: 6 (11-Jan-1969)
Successive games without conceding: 8 (09-Feb-1924)

WIN, LOSE OR DRAW

Most wins (in a season): 30 (1960/61)
Fewest wins: 6 (1911/12)
Most draws: 20 (1978/79)
Fewest draws: 3 (1895/96), (1902/03), (1930/31)
Most defeats: 25 (1956/57), (1966/67)
Fewest defeats: 8 (1960/61), (1994/95)

THEIR LEAGUE RECORD

P	W	D	L	F	A
3840	1459	903	1478	5696	5654

CAMBRIDGE

FIRST TIME

First League Game: Home v Lincoln City (15-Aug-1970)
Result: Drew 1-1
Final position: 20th

KICKIN' OFF

Successive wins at start of season: 3 (1991/92)
Successive defeats at start of season: 4 (1992/93)
Successive unbeaten games at start of season: 9 (1986/87)

HIGHS AND LOWS

Biggest home win: 6-0 v Darlington (18-Sep-1971), 6-0 v Hartlepool Utd (11-Feb-1989)
Biggest away win: 5-0 v Exeter City (04-Apr-1994), 7-2 v Cardiff City (30-Apr-1994)
Biggest home defeat: 0-4 v York City (09-Feb-1985), 0-4 v Bradford City (23-Apr-1985), 0-4 v Burnley (09-Nov-1985)
Biggest away defeat: 0-6 v Aldershot (13-Apr-1974), 0-6 v Darlington (28-Sep-1974), 0-6 v Chelsea (15-Jan-1983), 0-6 v Brentford (28-Jan-1995)
Most points (3 for a win): 86, Division 3 (1990/91)
Most points (2 for a win): 65, Division 4 (1976/77)
Least points (3 for a win): 21, Division 3 (1984/85)
Least points (2 for a win): 35, Division 3 (1973/74)
Highest finish: 5, Division 2 (1991/92)
Lowest finish: 22, Division 4 (1985/86)

GOALS, GOALS, GOALS

Most goals scored (in a season): 87 (1976/77)
Fewest goals scored: 28 (1983/84)
Most goals conceded: 95 (1984/85)
Fewest goals conceded: 40 (1976/77)
Most clean sheets: 22 (1976/77), (1977/78), (1990/91)
Fewest clean sheets: 5 (1984/85)

Beck and call

Former manager John Beck left United for Preston in 1992 and then took no less than nine former United players to Deepdale.

Strange but true!

United were on the verge of the top flight in 1992 but lost in a play-off to Leicester - just 22 years after coming into the Football League. Five years later they were struggling to stay in the League.

Out now

In the 1996-97 season, Paul Clark resigned as caretaker manager after one game in charge - a 2-1 win over Swansea.

ON THE RUN

Successive games unbeaten: 13 (14-Mar-1975)
Successive games without a win: 31 (08-Oct-1983)
Successive wins: 7 (19-Feb-1977)
Successive defeats: 7 (08-Oct-1983), (11-Feb-1984), (29-Dec-1984), (08-Apr-1985)
Successive draws: 6 (06-Sep-1986)
Successive games without scoring: 5 (29-Sep-1973)
Successive games without conceding: 5 (23-Jan-1982), (22-Feb-1987)

WIN, LOSE OR DRAW

Most wins (in a season): 26 (1976/77)
Fewest wins: 4 (1983/84), (1984/85)
Most draws: 17 (1972/73), (1991/92)
Fewest draws: 6 (1980/81)
Most defeats: 33 (1984/85)
Fewest defeats: 7 (1976/77)

THEIR LEAGUE RECORD

P	W	D	L	F	A
1218	430	334	454	1576	1670

CARDIFF

HIGHS AND LOWS

Biggest home win: 7-0 v Burnley (01-Sep-1928), 9-2 v Thames (06-Feb-1932), 7-0 v Barnsley (07-Dec-1957)
Biggest away win: 5-1 v Burnley (30-Mar-1923), 4-0 v Brighton & Hove A. (28-Sep-1946), 4-0 v Port Vale (12-Oct-1946), 4-0 v Liverpool (19-Dec-1959), 6-2 v Preston North End (29-Sep-1962), 4-0 v Newcastle Utd (09-Nov-1963), 5-1 v Derby County (01-Sep-1965), 5-1 v Fulham (07-Dec-1968), 4-0 v Sunderland (13-Feb-1971), 4-0 v Millwall (05-Sep-1982), 4-0 v Lincoln City (14-Dec-1985)
Biggest home defeat: 1-9 v Wolverhampton W. (03-Sep-1955)
Biggest away defeat: 2-11 v Sheffield Utd (01-Jan-1926) 0-9 v Preston North End (07-May-1966)
Most points (3 for a win): 86, Division 3 (1982/83)
Most points (2 for a win): 66, Division 3(S) (1946/47)
Least points (3 for a win): 35, Division 2 (1984/85)
Least points (2 for a win): 24, Division 3(S) (1933/34)
Highest finish: 2, Division 1 (1923/24)
Lowest finish: 22, Division 3 (1995/96)

FIRST TIME

First League Game:
Away v Stockport County (28-Aug-1920)
Result: Won 5-2
Final position: 2nd

KICKIN' OFF

Successive wins at start of season: 2 (1923/24), (1933/34), (1934/35), (1959/60), (1965/66), (1993/94)
Successive defeats at start of season: 6 (1921/22)
Successive unbeaten games at start of season: 11 (1923/24)

Up and down Dale

In 1995-96, Carl Dale became the first Bluebird to score more than half the club's total goals, with 21 out of their 41 strikes. Despite his amazing efforts, Dale and Cardiff finished 90th in the League.

GOALS, GOALS, GOALS

Most goals scored (in a season): 93 (1946/47)
Fewest goals scored: 36 (1974/75)
Most goals conceded: 105 (1933/34)
Fewest goals conceded: 30 (1946/47)
Most clean sheets: 23 (1946/47)
Fewest clean sheets: 2 (1933/34)

Homes and Gardens

About 100 years ago, Cardiff played their home games at Sophia Gardens, which is now home to Glamorgan county cricket club. They changed their name from Riverside Albion to Cardiff City in 1908 and moved to Ninian Park two years later.

WIN, LOSE OR DRAW

Most wins (in a season): 30 (1946/47)
Fewest wins: 8 (1928/29), (1930/31)
Most draws: 16 (1950/51), (1973/74), (1986/87)
Fewest draws: 6 (1933/34), (1946/47), (1983/84)
Most defeats: 27 (1933/34)
Fewest defeats: 6 (1946/47)

ON THE RUN

Successive games unbeaten: 21 (21-Sep-1946)
Successive games without a win: 15 (21-Nov-1936)
Successive wins: 9 (26-Oct-1946)
Successive defeats: 7 (04-Nov-1933)
Successive draws: 6 (29-Nov-1980)
Successive games without scoring: 8 (20-Dec-1952)
Successive games without conceding: 7 (07-Apr-1976)

THEIR LEAGUE RECORD

P	W	D	L	F	A
2988	1078	745	1165	4114	4479

CARLISLE

FIRST TIME
First League Game:
Away v Accrington Stanley
(25-Aug-1928)
Result: Won 3-2
Final position: 8th

KICKIN' OFF
Successive wins at start of
season: 3 (1974/75)
Successive defeats at start
of season: 5 (1957/58)
Successive unbeaten
games at start of season:
10 (1989/90)

HIGHS AND LOWS
Biggest home win: 8-0 v Hartlepools Utd
(01-Sep-1928), 8-0 v Scunthorpe Utd (25-Dec-1952)
Biggest away win: 6-0 v Hartlepools Utd (16-Sep-1963)
Biggest home defeat: 1-8 v Rotherham United
(04-Dec-1948)
Biggest away defeat: 1-11 v Hull City (14-Jan-1939)
Most points (3 for a win): 91, Division 3 (1994/95)
Most points (2 for a win): 62, Division 3(N) (1950/51)
Least points (3 for a win): 34, Division 4 (1991/92)
Least points (2 for a win): 23, Division 3(N) (1934/35)
Highest finish: 22, Division 1 (1974/75)
Lowest finish: 23, Division 4 (1987/88)

Light up
United were the first team
outside of London to install
floodlights. Brunton Park lit
up in 1952.

GOALS, GOALS, GOALS
Most goals scored (in a season): 113 (1963/64)
Fewest goals scored: 39 (1986/87)
Most goals conceded: 111 (1938/39)
Fewest goals conceded: 31 (1994/95)
Most clean sheets: 19 (1978/79), (1983/84)
Fewest clean sheets: 4 (1938/39)

Out of town
Carlisle were formed through a merger between local
clubs Shaddongate United and Carlisle Red Rose.
They were admitted to the Lancashire Combination
in 1905, despite being about 80 miles north of the
county.

Peter the Great
Former England and
Liverpool star Peter
Beardsley made his name
with the Cumbrian club and
became their record sale
at £275,000 to Canadian
side Vancouver Whitecaps
in April 1981.

ON THE RUN
Successive games unbeaten: 19 (01-Oct-1994)
Successive games without a win: 14 (19-Jan-1935)
Successive wins: 6 (27-Feb-1937), (14-Nov-1981),
(27-Aug-1994)
Successive defeats: 8 (19-Jan-1935), (08-Nov-1986)
Successive draws: 6 (11-Feb-1978)
Successive games without scoring: 5 (24-Aug-1968)
Successive games without conceding: 7 (09-Oct-1968)

WIN, LOSE OR DRAW
Most wins (in a season): 27
(1994/95)
Fewest wins: 7 (1991/92)
Most draws: 22 (1978/79)
Fewest draws: 5 (1930/31),
(1965/66), (1974/75)
Most defeats: 28 (1986/87)
Fewest defeats: 5
(1994/95)

THEIR LEAGUE RECORD

P	W	D	L	F	A
2708	992	647	1069	3911	4147

CHARLTON

HIGHS AND LOWS
Biggest home win: 8-1 v Middlesbrough (12-Sep-1953)
Biggest away win: 6-1 v Luton Town (10-Feb-1962)
Biggest home defeat: 0-7 v Everton (07-Feb-1931)
Biggest away defeat: 1-11 v Aston Villa (14-Nov-1959)
Most points (3 for a win): 77, Division 2 (1985/86)
Most points (2 for a win): 61, Division 3(S) (1934/35)
Least points (3 for a win): 30, Division 1 (1989/90)
Least points (2 for a win): 22, Division 1 (1956/57)
22, Division 2 (1979/80)
Highest finish: 2, Division 1 (1936/37)
Lowest finish: 21, Division 3(S) (1925/26)

FIRST TIME
First League Game:
Home v Exeter City
(27-Aug-1921)
Result: Won 1-0
Final position: 16th

KICKIN' OFF
Successive wins at start of season: 4 (1992/93)
Successive defeats at start of season: 5 (1956/57)
Successive unbeaten games at start of season: 12 (1927/28)

Strange but true
The Addicks' 4-3 win at Birmingham on January 14th, 1996 was their first win at St Andrews since 1939, when they also won 4-3

GOALS, GOALS, GOALS
Most goals scored (in a season): 107 (1957/58)
Fewest goals scored: 31 (1989/90)
Most goals conceded: 120 (1956/57)
Fewest goals conceded: 44 (1980/81)
Most clean sheets: 20 (1980/81)
Fewest clean sheets: 2 (1956/57)

Live Action
Charlton home League ground, The Valley, became the first stadium to host a live televised FA Cup match (outside the Final) when Charlton met Blackburn in the Fifth Round in 1947 with the cameras primed for action.

London calling
Charlton played host to rugby league in 1996 when London Broncos staged their First Division matches there. After an opening crowd of around 10,000, attendances dropped and the Broncos moved to the Stoop in Richmond for the Super League.

ON THE RUN
Successive games unbeaten: 15 (04-Oct-1980)
Successive games without a win: 16 (26-Feb-1955)
Successive wins: 7 (07-Oct-1980)
Successive defeats: 10 (11-Apr-1990)
Successive draws: 6 (13-Dec-1992)
Successive games without scoring: 5 (06-Sep-1922)
Successive games without conceding: 7 (22-Dec-1923)

WIN, LOSE OR DRAW
Most wins (in a season): 27 (1934/35)
Fewest wins: 6 (1979/80)
Most draws: 20 (1995/96)
Fewest draws: 4 (1956/57)
Most defeats: 29 (1956/57)
Fewest defeats: 8 (1934/35)

THEIR LEAGUE RECORD
P	W	D	L	F	A
2932	1060	734	1138	4293	4555

CHELSEA

FIRST TIME

First League Game:
Away v Stockport County
(02-Sep-1905)
Result: Lost 0-1
Final position: 3rd

KICKIN' OFF

Successive wins at start of season: 6 (1928/29)
Successive defeats at start of season: 3 (1907/08), (1912/13), (1973/74)
Successive unbeaten games at start of season: 14 (1925/26)

HIGHS AND LOWS

Biggest home win: 7-0 v Burslem Port Vale (03-Mar-1906), 9-2 v Glossop (01-Sep-1906), 7-0 v Lincoln City (29-Oct-1910), 7-0 v Portsmouth (21-May-1963)
Biggest away win: 7-0 v Walsall (04-Feb-1989)
Biggest home defeat: 0-6 v Notts County (09-Feb-1924)
Biggest away defeat: 1-8 v Wolverhampton W. (26-Sep-1953), 0-7 v Leeds Utd (07-Oct-1967), 0-7 v Nottingham Forest (20-Apr-1991)
Most points (3 for a win): 99, Division 2 (1988/89)
Most points (2 for a win): 57, Division 2 (1906/07)
Least points (3 for a win): 42, Division 1 (1987/88)
Least points (2 for a win): 20, Division 1 (1978/79)
Highest finish: 1, Division 1 (1954/55)
Lowest finish: 18, Division 2 (1982/83)

GOALS, GOALS, GOALS

Most goals scored (in a season): 98 (1960/61)
Fewest goals scored: 31 (1923/24)
Most goals conceded: 100 (1960/61)
Fewest goals conceded: 34 (1906/07), (1911/12)
Most clean sheets: 19 (1925/26)
Fewest clean sheets: 1 (1960/61)

Roberto Di Matteo

Slick start

Roberto Di Matteo became Chelsea's record buy when he joined the club from Lazio for a £4.5 million fee in the summer of 1996 but he repaid that fee a few times over with Chelsea's opening goal after 43 seconds in their 2-0 FA Cup Final win over Middlesbrough.

ON THE RUN

Successive games unbeaten: 27 (29-Oct-1988)
Successive games without a win: 21 (03-Nov-1987)
Successive wins: 8 (06-Oct-1927) (15-Mar-1989)
Successive defeats: 7 (01-Nov-1952)
Successive draws: 6 (20-Aug-1969)
Successive games without scoring: 9 (14-Mar-1981)
Successive games without conceding: 9 (04-Nov-1905)

WIN, LOSE OR DRAW

Most wins (in a season): 29 (1988/89)
Fewest wins: 5 (1978/79)
Most draws: 18 (1922/23)
Fewest draws: 4 (1958/59), (1962/63)
Most defeats: 27 (1978/79)
Fewest defeats: 4 (1983/84)

THEIR LEAGUE RECORD

P	W	D	L	F	A
3348	1279	887	1182	5016	4902

CHESTER

HIGHS AND LOWS

Biggest home win: 12-0 v York City (01-Feb-1936)
Biggest away win: 5-0 v Rotherham United (07-Jan-1933), 5-0 v Rochdale (15-Mar-1952), 5-0 v Swansea Town (26-Dec-1968), 5-0 v Fulham (24-Jan-1987), 5-0 v Hereford Utd (06-Nov-1993)
Biggest home defeat: 0-5 v Northampton Town (15-Aug-1987)
Biggest away defeat: 0-9 v Barrow (10-Feb-1934), 2-11 v Oldham Athletic (19-Jan-1952)
Most points (3 for a win): 84, Division 4 (1985/86)
Most points (2 for a win): 57, Division 4 (1974/75)
Least points (3 for a win): 29, Division 2 (1992/93) 29, Division 2 (1994/95)
Least points (2 for a win): 26, Division 4 (1961/62)
Highest finish: 2, Division 3(N) (1935/36)
Lowest finish: 24, Division 4 (1960/61), (1983/84)

FIRST TIME

First League Game:
Home v Wrexham
(02-Sept-1931)
Result: Drew 1-1
Final position: 3rd

KICKIN' OFF

Successive wins at start of season: 4 (1934/35)
Successive defeats at start of season: 7 (1994/95)
Successive unbeaten games at start of season: 9 (1936/37)

Rush start

Chester's old Sealand Road home was the breeding ground for Ian Rush. He scored 14 times in 34 games as a teenager before moving to Liverpool in 1980.

Same again

Their League record for the seasons 1995-96 and 1996-97 both read: won 18, drew 16, lost 12, points 70

WIN, LOSE OR DRAW

Most wins (in a season): 25 (1946/47), (1964/65)
Fewest wins: 6 (1994/95)
Most draws: 22 (1977/78)
Fewest draws: 5 (1992/93)
Most defeats: 33 (1992/93)
Fewest defeats: 8 (1934/35), (1977/78), (1985/86)

GOALS, GOALS, GOALS

Most goals scored (in a season): 119 (1964/65)
Fewest goals scored: 36 (1981/82)
Most goals conceded: 104 (1960/61)
Fewest goals conceded: 38 (1974/75)
Most clean sheets: 20 (1974/75)
Fewest clean sheets: 5 (1983/84)

Out of bounds

City's new ground, the Deva Stadium, is half in England, half in Wales. But due to a ruling by the Welsh FA, they are no longer permitted to enter the Welsh Cup, which they won in 1908, 1933 and 1947

ON THE RUN

Successive games unbeaten: 18 (27-Oct-1934)
Successive games without a win: 26 (19-Sep-1961)
Successive wins: 8 (21-Apr-1934), (01-Feb-1936), (18-Sep-1978), (12-Apr-1978)
Successive defeats: 9 (07-Apr-1993), (30-Apr-1994)
Successive draws: 6 (11-Oct-1986)
Successive games without scoring: 5 (17-Nov-1951), (11-Apr-1955), (15-Apr-1972), (21-Oct-1980), (03-Apr-1982), (03-Nov-1990)
Successive games without conceding: 5 (12-Oct-1946), (21-Sep-1974)

THEIR LEAGUE RECORD

P	W	D	L	F	A
2658	924	674	1060	3736	3940

CHESTERFIELD

FIRST TIME
First League Game:
Away v Wednesday
(02-Sep-1899)
Result: Lost 1-5
Final position: 7th

KICKIN' OFF
Successive wins at start of season: 4 (1954/55), (1984/85)
Successive defeats at start of season: 3 (1929/30), (1938/39), (1961/62) (1982/83), (1994/95)
Successive unbeaten games at start of season: 9 (1935/36)

HIGHS AND LOWS
Biggest home win: 10-0 v Glossop North End (17-Jan-1903)
Biggest away win: 5-0 v Nelson (04-Apr-1931)
5-0 v Bradford Park Ave. (03-Sep-1955)
Biggest home defeat: 1-7 v Manchester Utd (13-Nov-1937), 0-6 v Wrexham (11-Sep-1976)
Biggest away defeat: 0-10 v Gillingham (05-Sep-1987)
Most points (3 for a win): 91, Division 4 (1984/85)
Most points (2 for a win): 64, Division 4 (1969/70)
Least points (3 for a win): 37, Division 3 (1982/83)
Least points (2 for a win): 23, Division 2 (1907/08)
Highest finish: 4, Division 2 (1946/47)
Lowest finish: 20, Division 4 (1965/66), (1968/69)

Inspired Effort
The Spireites leapt from the middle of Division Two to the Semi-Final of the FA Cup in 1996-97. They came closer to reaching the Final than any other 'Third' Division team before them, taking Middlesbrough to a replay after a stunning 3-3 draw at Old Trafford which they led 2-0 at one stage, with Boro down to ten men. Unfortunately they lost the replay 3-0.

GOALS, GOALS, GOALS
Most goals scored (in a season): 102 (1930/31)
Fewest goals scored: 37 (1903/04), (1908/09)
Most goals conceded: 92 (1907/08)
Fewest goals conceded: 32 (1969/70)
Most clean sheets: 22 (1994/95)
Fewest clean sheets: 5 (1965/66)

Kid Kev
Striker Kevin Davies was only 16 when he made his first team debut in 1993 and held onto his place throughout the next four years before a £1 million move to Southampton in May 1997.

ON THE RUN
Successive games unbeaten: 21 (26-Dec-1994)
Successive games without a win: 16 (22-Oct-1960) (26-Feb-1983)
Successive wins: 10 (06-Sep-1933)
Successive defeats: 9 (22-Oct-1960)
Successive draws: 5 (19-Sep-1990)
Successive games without scoring: 7 (23-Sep-1977)
Successive games without conceding: 6 (14-Mar-1936)

WIN, LOSE OR DRAW
Most wins (in a season): 27 (1933/34), (1969/70)
Fewest wins: 6 (1907/08)
Most draws: 17 (1948/49), (1970/71)
Fewest draws: 3 (1921/22)
Most defeats: 25 (1982/83), (1988/89)
Fewest defeats: 6 (1935/36)

THEIR LEAGUE RECORD

P	W	D	L	F	A
3412	1327	815	1270	4937	4767

COLCHESTER

HIGHS AND LOWS

Biggest home win: 9-1 v Bradford City (30-Dec-1961)
Biggest away win: 4-0 v Accrington Stanley (13-Jan-1962), 4-0 v Darlington (03-Dec-1966), 4-0 v Torquay Utd (19-Sep-1973), 4-0 v Chester (14-Nov-1973), 5-1 v Tranmere Rovers (09-May-1979), 5-1 v Exeter City (23-Mar-1985)
Biggest home defeat: 0-4 v Norwich City (02-May-1953), 0-4 v Brentford (21-Mar-1959), 0-4 v Walsall (31-Mar-1961), 0-4 v Shrewsbury Town (17-Apr-1965), 1-5 v Peterborough Utd (11-May-1968), 0-4 v Scunthorpe Utd (26-Aug-1968)
Biggest away defeat: 0-8 v Leyton Orient (15-Oct-1988)
Most points (3 for a win): 81, Division 4 (1982/83)
Most points (2 for a win): 60, Division 4 (1973/74)
Least points (3 for a win): 43, Division 4 (1989/90)
Least points (2 for a win): 30, Division 3(S) (1953/54) 30, Division 3 (1964/65)
Highest finish: 3, Division 3(S) (1956/57)
Lowest finish: 24, Division 4 (1989/90)

FIRST TIME

First League Game:
Away v Gillingham
(19-Aug-1950)
Result: Drew 0-0
Final position: 16th

KICKIN' OFF

Successive wins at start of season: 3 (1977/78)
Successive defeats at start of season: 4 (1975/76), (1994/95)
Successive unbeaten games at start of season: 9 (1961/62)

Wembley wonders

United won nothing until they reached a low in their history with relegation to the Conference. Ironically, in 1992, they then won the non-League double - Conference and FA Trophy - and returned to Wembley in 1997 only to lose the Auto Windscreens Shield to Carlisle on penalties.

GOALS, GOALS, GOALS

Most goals scored (in a season): 104 (1961/62)
Fewest goals scored: 41 (1975/76)
Most goals conceded: 101 (1960/61)
Fewest goals conceded: 36 (1973/74)
Most clean sheets: 21 (1973/74)
Fewest clean sheets: 4 (1964/65)

Start and finish

When winning at Torquay on New Year's Day 1996, Colchester scored 15 seconds from the start and 15 seconds from the end to clinch a dramatic 3-2 win.

WIN, LOSE OR DRAW

Most wins (in a season): 25 (1976/77)
Fewest wins: 9 (1954/55) (1967/68)
Most draws: 19 (1963/64)
Fewest draws: 5 (1992/93)
Most defeats: 26 (1953/54), (1964/65)
Fewest defeats: 10 (1956/57), (1973/74, (1995/96)

ON THE RUN

Successive games unbeaten: 20 (22-Dec-1956)
Successive games without a win: 20 (02-Mar-1968)
Successive wins: 7 (29-Nov-1968)
Successive defeats: 8 (09-Oct-1954)
Successive draws: 6 (21-Mar-1977)
Successive games without scoring: 5 (07-Apr-1981)
Successive games without conceding: 4 (04-Apr-1969), (14-Sep-1974), (01-Nov-1976), (09-Oct-1987)

THEIR LEAGUE RECORD

P	W	D	L	F	A
2056	757	545	754	2949	2992

COVENTRY

FIRST TIME

First League Game:
Home v Tottenham Hotspur
(30-Aug-1919)
Result: Lost 0-5
Final position: 20th

KICKIN' OFF

Successive wins at start of season: 5 (1964/65)
Successive defeats at start of season: 9 (1919/20)
Successive unbeaten games at start of season: 15 (1937/38)

HIGHS AND LOWS

Biggest home win: 9-0 v Bristol City (28-Apr-1934)
Biggest away win: 7-0 v Aberdare Athletic (18-Apr-1927)
Biggest home defeat: 0-5 v Tottenham Hotspur (30-Aug-1919), 0-5 v Everton (27-Sep-1980), 1-6 v Liverpool (05-May-1990)
Biggest away defeat: 1-9 v Millwall (19-Nov-1927), 2-10 v Norwich City (15-Mar-1930)
Most points (3 for a win): 63, Division 1 (1986/87)
Most points (2 for a win): 60, Division 4 (1958/59), 60, Division 3 (1963/64)
Least points (3 for a win): 38, Division 1 (1995/96)
Least points (2 for a win): 29, Division 2 (1919/20)
Highest finish: 6, Division 1 (1969/70)
Lowest finish: 2, Division 4 (1958/59)

GOALS, GOALS, GOALS

Most goals scored (in a season): 108 (1931/32)
Fewest goals scored: 35 (1919/20), (1991/92)
Most goals conceded: 97 (1931/32)
Fewest goals conceded: 38 (1970/71)
Most clean sheets: 18 (1938/39), (1958/59)
Fewest clean sheets: 5 (1971/72)

Gordon Bennett!

Coventry's only major trophy is the FA Cup which they won in 1987, beating Spurs 3-2 at Wembley. Only 12 months earlier, they had escaped the drop on the last day, thanks to a goal from Gary Bennett, who played a vital role in the Cup triumph and scored their first goal!

Great Escape - again!

City's last day escape from relegation in 1997 with a 2-1 win at Tottenham was the tenth time they've survived on the final day in their 30 years of top flight football.

ON THE RUN

Successive games unbeaten: 25 (26-Nov-1966)
Successive games without a win: 19 (30-Aug-1919)
Successive wins: 6 (20-Apr-1954), (25-Apr-1964)
Successive defeats: 9 (30-Aug-1919)
Successive draws: 5 (05-Apr-1930), (14-Nov-1987), (08-Feb-1992)
Successive games without scoring: 11 (11-Oct-1919)
Successive games without conceding: 6 (28-Apr-1934)

WIN, LOSE OR DRAW

Most wins (in a season): 24 (1935/36), (1958/59)
Fewest wins: 8 (1995/96)
Most draws: 17 (1962/63)
Fewest draws: 5 (1984/85)
Most defeats: 22 (1919/20), (1924/25), (1927/28), (1951/52), (1984/85)
Fewest defeats: 6 (1966/67)

THEIR LEAGUE RECORD

P	W	D	L	F	A
3008	1081	781	1146	4324	4419

CREWE

HIGHS AND LOWS

Biggest home win: 8-0 v Rotherham United (01-Oct-1932)

Biggest away win: 5-0 v Ashington (12-Jan-1929), 5-0 v Gateshead (24-Dec-1938), 6-1 v Hartlepools Utd (29-Apr-1950), 6-1 v Tranmere Rovers (09-Dec-1961), 5-0 v Hartlepool Utd (01-Oct-1986)

Biggest home defeat: 0-7 v Liverpool (28-Mar-1896) 1-8 v Rotherham United (08-Sep-1973)

Biggest away defeat: 1-11 v Lincoln City (29-Sep-1951)

Most points (3 for a win): 83, Division 2 (1994/95)

Most points (2 for a win): 59, Division 4 (1962/63)

Least points (3 for a win): 27, Division 4 (1981/82)

Least points (2 for a win): 21, Division 3(N) (1956/57)

Highest finish: 10, Division 2 (1892/93)

Lowest finish: 24, Division 4 (1971/72), (1978/79), (1981/82)

FIRST TIME

First League Game:
Away v Burton Swifts (03-Sep-1892)
Result: Lost 1-7
Final position: 10th

KICKIN' OFF

Successive wins at start of season: 5 (1994/95)
Successive defeats at start of season: 8 (1981/82)
Successive unbeaten games at start of season: 10 (1953/54)

Pieces of eight

On October 17th 1995, Crewe beat Hartlepool 8-0 in the Auto Windscreens Shield. Amazingly, there were eight different goalscorers in the match. Crewe also had matching League records in the 1995-96 and 1996-97 season.

GOALS, GOALS, GOALS

Most goals scored (in a season): 95 (1931/32)
Fewest goals scored: 29 (1981/82)
Most goals conceded: 110 (1956/57)
Fewest goals conceded: 38 (1922/23)
Most clean sheets: 18 (1996/97)
Fewest clean sheets: 1 (1894/95)

Alex in wonderland!

When Alex won the Second Division Play-Off in 1997, it was the first time they been in the 'Second' Division since they were among its original members in 1892.

ON THE RUN

Successive games unbeaten: 14 (27-Jan-1990)
Successive games without a win: 30 (22-Sep-1956)
Successive wins: 7 (08-Dec-1928), (04-Mar-1986), (30-Apr-1994)
Successive defeats: 10 (29-Sep-1923), (26-Dec-1957), (16-Apr-1979)
Successive draws: 5 (11-Feb-1924), (16-Mar-1968), (31-Aug-1987)
Successive games without scoring: 9 (06-Nov-1974)
Successive games without conceding: 5 (04-Apr-1959), (04-Nov-1972)

WIN, LOSE OR DRAW

Most wins (in a season): 25 (1994/95)
Fewest wins: 6 (1892/93), (1893/94), (1956/57), (1978/79), (1981/82)
Most draws: 19 (1987/88)
Fewest draws: 3 (1892/93), (1895/96), (1932/33)
Most defeats: 31 (1956/57), (1957/58), (1981/82)
Fewest defeats: 8 (1967/68)

THEIR LEAGUE RECORD

P	W	D	L	F	A
3172	1098	735	1339	4424	5134

CRYSTAL PALACE

FIRST TIME

First League Game:
Away v Merthyr Town
(28-Aug-1920)
Result: Lost 1-2
Final position: 1st

KICKIN' OFF

Successive wins at start of
season: 5 (1975/76)
Successive defeats at start
of season: 5 (1925/26)
Successive unbeaten
games at start of season:
11 (1978/79)

HIGHS AND LOWS

Biggest home win: 9-0 v Barrow (10-Oct-1959)
Biggest away win: 6-0 v Exeter City (26-Jan-1935)
6-0 v Birmingham City (05-Sep-1987)
Biggest home defeat: 1-6 v Millwall (07-May-1927),
1-6 v Nottingham Forest (27-Jan-1951), 0-5 v Norwich
City (18-Apr-1951), 0-5 v Wimbledon (24-Feb-1985),
1-6 v Liverpool (20-Aug-1994)
Biggest away defeat: 0-9 v Liverpool (12-Sep-1989)
Most points (3 for a win): 90, Division 1 (1993/94)
Most points (2 for a win): 64, Division 4 (1960/61)
Least points (3 for a win): 45, Premier (1994/95)
Least points (2 for a win): 19, Division 1 (1980/81)
Highest finish: 3, Division 1 (1990/91)
Lowest finish: 8, Division 4 (1959/60)

GOALS, GOALS, GOALS

Most goals scored (in a season): 110 (1960/61)
Fewest goals scored: 33 (1950/51)
Most goals conceded: 86 (1953/54)
Fewest goals conceded: 24 (1978/79)
Most clean sheets: 21 (1978/79)
Fewest clean sheets: 2 (1980/81)

Eagles have landed

When Palace won
promotion to the
Premiership via the play-
offs in 1997, it led to their
fourth spell in the top flight
in 17 years. They had David
Hopkin's last minute goal in
the Play-off Final against
Sheffield United to thank
for promotion. A year
earlier Palace had been
beaten in the Play-off Final
by a last gasp goal from
Leicester's Steve Claridge.

Poor Perry

Palace lost 9-0 to reigning Champions Liverpool in
September 1989. Perry Digweed was the unlucky
'keeper on a night when eight different players scored
for The Reds. Eight months later, Palace beat Liverpool
4-3 in an epic FA Cup Semi-Final to gain revenge for
that hammering.

ON THE RUN

Successive games unbeaten: 18 (22-Feb-1969)
Successive games without a win: 20 (03-Mar-1962)
Successive wins: 8 (09-Feb-1921)
Successive defeats: 8 (18-Apr-1925)
Successive draws: 5 (28-Mar-1921), (30-Dec-1978)
Successive games without scoring: 9 (19-Nov-1994)
Successive games without conceding: 6 (01-Sep-1920)

WIN, LOSE OR DRAW

Most wins (in a season): 29
(1960/61)
Fewest wins: 6 (1969/70),
(1980/81)
Most draws: 19 (1978/79)
Fewest draws: 3 (1925/26)
Most defeats: 29 (1980/81)
Fewest defeats: 4
(1978/79)

THEIR LEAGUE RECORD

P	W	D	L	F	A
3018	1118	812	1088	4274	4239

DARLINGTON

HIGHS AND LOWS

Biggest home win: 7-0 v Chesterfield (10-Sep-1921), 9-2 v Lincoln City (07-Jan-1928), 8-1 v Rotherham United (15-Feb-1930), 7-0 v Gateshead (19-Jan-1957)
Biggest away win: 5-0 v Crewe Alexandra (24-Jan-1925), 6-1 v Aldershot (01-Mar-1983)
Biggest home defeat: 0-7 v Southport (06-Jan-1973)
Biggest away defeat: 0-10 v Doncaster Rovers (25-Jan-1964)
Most points (3 for a win): 85, Division 4 (1984/85)
Most points (2 for a win): 59, Division 4 (1965/66)
Least points (3 for a win): 37, Division 3 (1986/87)
Least points (2 for a win): 28, Division 3(N) (1932/33)
Highest finish: 15, Division 2 (1925/26)
Lowest finish: 24, Division 4 (1972/73), (1988/89)

FIRST TIME

First League Game:
Home v Halifax Town
(27-Aug-1921)
Result: Won 2-0
Final position: 2nd

KICKIN' OFF

Successive wins at start of season: 4 (1929/30), (1948/49)
Successive defeats at start of season: 4 (1932/33), (1950/51)
Successive unbeaten games at start of season: 14 (1968/69)

Ten teams in a year!

Darlo striker Gary Innes amazingly played for ten teams within one year. He represented various school rep sides, England schoolboys, and Middlesbrough on trial before joining Darlo. Then he went on loan to Waterford in Ireland and Gateshead. Must have liked travelling!

GOALS, GOALS, GOALS

Most goals scored (in a season): 108 (1929/30)
Fewest goals scored: 40 (1973/74)
Most goals conceded: 109 (1932/33)
Fewest goals conceded: 33 (1924/25)
Most clean sheets: 21 (1921/22)
Fewest clean sheets: 3 (1932/33)

Little hero

Darlo's relegation to the Vauxhall Conference in 1989 unearthed the managerial talents of Brian Little, who took them straight back into the League before moving on to Leicester and then Aston Villa.

ON THE RUN

Successive games unbeaten: 17 (27-Apr-1968)
Successive games without a win: 19 (27-Apr-1988)
Successive wins: 5 (21-Jan-1922), (20-Sep-1924), (07-Jan-1928), (21-Apr-1975), (02-Mar-1985)
Successive defeats: 8 (31-Aug-1985)
Successive draws: 5 (03-Mar-1973), (24-Feb-1987), (31-Dec-1988)
Successive games without scoring: 7 (05-Sep-1975), (25-Feb-1995)
Successive games without conceding: 7 (16-Sep-1968), (02-Feb-1991)

WIN, LOSE OR DRAW

Most wins (in a season): 25 (1965/66)
Fewest wins: 7 (1972/73)
Most draws: 18 (1968/69), (1988/89), (1995-96)
Fewest draws: 4 (1931/32)
Most defeats: 29 (1991/92)
Fewest defeats: 7 (1990/91)

THEIR LEAGUE RECORD

P	W	D	L	F	A
3016	1024	728	1264	4283	4834

DERBY COUNTY

FIRST TIME

First League Game:
Away v Bolton Wanderers
(08-Sep-1888)
Result: Won 6-3
Final position: 10th

KICKIN' OFF

Successive wins at start of season: 5 (1905/06)
Successive defeats at start of season: 4 (1899/1900), (1965/66)
Successive unbeaten games at start of season: 16 (1948/49)

HIGHS AND LOWS

Biggest home win: 9-0 v Wolverhampton W. (10-Jan-1891), 9-0 v The Wednesday (21-Jan-1899)
Biggest away win: 8-0 v Bristol City (29-Sep-1923)
Biggest home defeat: 1-7 v Manchester City (29-Jan-1938), 1-7 v Middlesbrough (29-Aug-1959), 1-7 v Liverpool (23-Mar-1991)
Biggest away defeat: 0-8 v Blackburn Rovers (03-Jan-1891), 0-8 v Sunderland (01-Sep-1894)
Most points (3 for a win): 84, Division 3 (1985/86) 84, Division 2 (1986/87)
Most points (2 for a win): 63, Division 3(N) (1955/56), 1956/57
63, Division 2 (1968/69)
Least points (3 for a win): 24, Division 1 (1990/91)
Least points (2 for a win): 23, Division 1 (1894/95) 23, Division 2 (1954/55)
Highest finish: 1, Division 1 (1971/72), (1974/75)
Lowest finish: 7, Division 3 (1984/85)

GOALS, GOALS, GOALS

Most goals scored (in a season): 111 (1956/57)
Fewest goals scored: 32 (1920/21)
Most goals conceded: 90 (1936/37)
Fewest goals conceded: 28 (1911/12)
Most clean sheets: 23 (1971/72)
Fewest clean sheets: 1 (1890/91)

Gypsy Curse!

When Derby left the Baseball Ground to move to Pride Park in 1997, they wondered whether their ghosts would follow them. The ground was apparently haunted by romany gypsies, who cursed it after being moved off the ground in 1895 to make way for football!

Colour code

County were formed in 1884 by Derbyshire cricket club who wanted to raise some money through winter sport. They originally shared the cricket club colours of amber, chocolate and pale blue but changed to white and navy blue. They changed again in the eighties to wear white and black.

ON THE RUN

Successive games unbeaten: 22 (08-Mar-1969)
Successive games without a win: 20 (15-Dec-1990)
Successive wins: 9 (15-Mar-1969)
Successive defeats: 8 (29-Sep-1888), (17-Apr-1965), (12-Dec-1987)
Successive draws: 6 (26-Mar-1927)
Successive games without scoring: 8 (30-Oct-1920)
Successive games without conceding: 6 (08-Apr-1912)

WIN, LOSE OR DRAW

Most wins (in a season): 28 (1955/56)
Fewest wins: 5 (1920/21), (1990/91)
Most draws: 19 (1976/77), (1982/83)
Fewest draws: 4 (1891/92), (1893/94), (1896/97), (1907/08)
Most defeats: 26 (1954/55)
Fewest defeats: 5 (1968/69)

THEIR LEAGUE RECORD

P	W	D	L	F	A
3890	1543	931	1416	6197	5813

DONCASTER

HIGHS AND LOWS

Biggest home win: 10-0 v Darlington (25-Jan-1964)
Biggest away win: 6-0 v Hartlepool Utd (30-Sep-1989)
Biggest home defeat: 0-5 v Birmingham City (19-Jan-1952), 1-6 v Fulham (15-Mar-1958)
Biggest away defeat: 0-12 v Small Heath (11-Apr-1903)
Most points (3 for a win): 85, Division 4 (1983/84)
Most points (2 for a win): 72, Division 3(N) (1946/47)
Least points (3 for a win): 33, Division 3 (1987/88)
Least points (2 for a win): 24, Division 2 (1936/37)
Highest finish: 7, Division 2 (1901/02)
Lowest finish: 23, Division 4 (1988/89)

FIRST TIME

First League Game:
Home v Burslem Port Vale (07-Sep-1901)
Result: Drew 3-3
Final position: 7th

KICKIN' OFF

Successive wins at start of season: 5 (1946/47), (1990/91)
Successive defeats at start of season: 4 (1972/73), (1991/92)
Successive unbeaten games at start of season: 7 (1949/50), (1953/54) (1985/86)

Strange but true!

In 1991, bored fans sang 'Would you like a piece of cake?' to bemused away fans. Police intervened but gave up when they realised it was a harmless chant. But the next week, Rovers fans at Burnley offered cake to the police and sang: 'And so this is Burnley, and what have we done, We've lost here already, would you like a cream bun?' Bonkers!

GOALS, GOALS, GOALS

Most goals scored (in a season): 123 (1946/47)
Fewest goals scored: 30 (1936/37)
Most goals conceded: 117 (1966/67)
Fewest goals conceded: 38 (1949/50), (1968/69)
Most clean sheets: 22 (1968/69)
Fewest clean sheets: 3 (1904/05)

Famous faces

Rovers have had a series of famous faces in the manager's chair, including Lawrie McMenemy, Dave Mackay, Billy Bremner and Kerry Dixon, but have still been entrenched in the bottom two divisions since 1958.

ON THE RUN

Successive games unbeaten: 20 (26-Dec-1968)
Successive games without a win: 17 (14-Sep-1991)
Successive wins: 10 (22-Jan-1947)
Successive defeats: 9 (14-Jan-1905)
Successive draws: 4 (29-Oct-1932) (24-Dec-1938), (17-Jan-1953), (28-Feb-1970), (04-Mar-1978), (20-Apr-1987)
Successive games without scoring: 7 (27-Sep-1947)
Successive games without conceding: 7 (07-May-1994)

WIN, LOSE OR DRAW

Most wins (in a season): 33 (1946/47)
Fewest wins: 7 (1936/37)
Most draws: 17 (1949/50), (1968/69), (1977/78), (1981/82)
Fewest draws: 4 (1931/32)
Most defeats: 29 (1904/05), (1987/88)
Fewest defeats: 3 (1946/47)

THEIR LEAGUE RECORD

P	W	D	L	F	A
3052	1090	754	1208	4270	4645

EVERTON

FIRST TIME

First League Game:
Home v Accrington
(08-Sep-1888)
Result: Won 2-1
Final position: 8th

KICKIN' OFF

Successive wins at start of
season: 8 (1894/95)
Successive defeats at start
of season: 6 (1958/59)
Successive unbeaten
games at start of season:
19 (1978/79)

HIGHS AND LOWS

Biggest home win: 8-0 v Stoke (02-Nov-1889), 9-1 v
Manchester City (03-Sep-1906), 9-1 v Plymouth Argyle
(27-Dec-1930), 8-0 v Southampton (20-Nov-1971)
Biggest away win: 7-0 v Charlton Athletic (07-Feb-1931)
Biggest home defeat: 0-6 v Newcastle Utd
(26-Oct-1912)
Biggest away defeat: 0-7 v Sunderland (26-Dec-1934),
0-7 v Wolverhampton W. (22-Feb-1939), 0-7 v
Portsmouth (10-Sep-1949)
Most points (3 for a win): 90, Division 1 (1984/85)
Most points (2 for a win): 66, Division 1 (1969/70)
Least points (3 for a win): 42, Premier (1996/97)
Least points (2 for a win): 32, Division 1 (1902/03)
32, Division 1 (1950/51)
Highest finish: 1, Division 1 (1890/91), (1914/15),
(1927/28), (1931/32), (1938/39), (1962/63),
(1969/70), (1984/85), (1986/87)
Lowest finish: 16, Division 2 (1952/53)

GOALS, GOALS, GOALS

Most goals scored (in a season): 121 (1930/31)
Fewest goals scored: 37 (1971/72)
Most goals conceded: 92 (1929/30)
Fewest goals conceded: 27 (1987/88)
Most clean sheets: 21 (1969/70)
Fewest clean sheets: 2 (1888/89)

Strange but true

Everton director Bill Kenwright has appeared in
top TV soap Coronation Street as Betty Williams'
son, Gordon.

ON THE RUN

Successive games unbeaten: 20 (29-Apr-1978)
Successive games without a win: 14 (06-Mar-1937)
Successive wins: 12 (24-Mar-1894)
Successive defeats: 6 (06-Feb-1897), (10-Apr-1929),
(05-Mar-1930), (29-Mar-1958), (23-Aug-1958),
(04-Nov-1972)
Successive draws: 5 (15-Oct-1921), (05-Oct-1974), (04-May-1977)
Successive games without scoring: 6 (03-Mar-1951)
Successive games without conceding: 7
(01-Nov-1994), (06-May-1995)

What a cracker!

There wasn't a football in
sight at the opening of
Goodison Park in 1892.
The ceremony was
followed by an athletics
meeting and a firework
display to keep the
crowd happy.

WIN, LOSE OR DRAW

Most wins (in a season): 29
(1969/70)
Fewest wins: 9 (1888/89),
(1971/72), (1979/80)
Most draws: 18 (1925/26),
(1971/72), (1974/75)
Fewest draws: 4 (1891/92),
(1892/93), (1928/29),
(1931/32), (1958/59)
Most defeats: 22 (1950/51), (1993/94)
Fewest defeats: 5
(1889/90), (1969/70)

THEIR LEAGUE RECORD

P	W	D	L	F	A
3850	1602	939	1309	6265	5471

EXETER

HIGHS AND LOWS

Biggest home win: 8-1 v Coventry City (04-Dec-1926), 8-1 v Aldershot (04-May-1935), 7-0 v Crystal Palace (09-Jan-1954)

Biggest away win: 6-1 v Brighton & Hove A. (25-Dec-1946)

Biggest home defeat: 0-6 v Crystal Palace (26-Jan-1935), 0-6 v Walsall (21-Apr-1948), 1-7 v Leyton Orient (06-Nov-1954), 1-7 v Brentford (23-Apr-1983)

Biggest away defeat: 0-9 v Notts County (16-Oct-1948) 0-9 v Northampton Town (12-Apr-1958)

Most points (3 for a win): 89, Division 4 (1989/90)

Most points (2 for a win): 62, Division 4 (1976/77)

Least points (3 for a win): 33, Division 3 (1983/84)

Least points (2 for a win): 27, Division 3(S) (1935/36)

Highest finish: 2, Division 3(S) (1932/33)

Lowest finish: 22, Division 4 (1987/88) 22, Division 3 (1994/95)

FIRST TIME

First League Game: Home v Brentford (28-Aug-1920)

Result: Won 3-0

Final position: 19th

KICKIN' OFF

Successive wins at start of season: 3 (1924/25), (1987/88)

Successive defeats at start of season: 4 (1969/70)

Successive unbeaten games at start of season: 13 (1986/87)

Bell tolls

Jim 'Daisy' Bell was Exeter's top scorer in three Southern League seasons from 1908-09 to 1910-11 with 23,15 and 14 goals respectively.

GOALS, GOALS, GOALS

Most goals scored (in a season): 88 (1932/33)

Fewest goals scored: 36 (1994/95)

Most goals conceded: 104 (1982/83)

Fewest goals conceded: 37 (1963/64)

Most clean sheets: 24 (1975/76)

Fewest clean sheets: 2 (1983/84)

Saved!

The biggest cheer of the day at Exeter's 1-1 draw with Bury in April 1996 was after news came through that the local council had bought the ground to preserve the club's existence.

James the Second

Exeter share the name of their ground, St James Park, with Premiership club Newcastle. However its capacity is 26,000 less.

ON THE RUN

Successive games unbeaten: 13 (23-Aug-1986)

Successive games without a win: 18 (14-Jan-1984)

Successive wins: 7 (23-Apr-1977)

Successive defeats: 7 (19-Feb-1921), (07-Apr-1923), (24-Oct-1925), (22-Feb-1936), (14-Jan-1984)

Successive draws: 6 (13-Sep-1986)

Successive games without scoring: 6 (24-Nov-1923), (17-Jan-1986)

Successive games without conceding: 5 (16-Sep-1972), (20-Sep-1986)

WIN, LOSE OR DRAW

Most wins (in a season): 28 (1989/90)

Fewest wins: 6 (1983/84)

Most draws: 23 (1986/87)

Fewest draws: 5 (1925/26), (1989/90)

Most defeats: 26 (1957/58)

Fewest defeats: 8 (1932/33), (1963/64)

THEIR LEAGUE RECORD

P	W	D	L	F	A
3121	1042	807	1272	4226	4802

FULHAM

FIRST TIME

First League Game:
Home v Hull City
(03-Sep-1907)
Result: Lost 0-1
Final position: 4th

KICKIN' OFF

Successive wins at start of season: 6 (1958/59)
Successive defeats at start of season: 4 (1923/24), (1925/26), (1951/52), (1956/57)
Successive unbeaten games at start of season: 12 (1958/59)

GOALS, GOALS, GOALS

Most goals scored (in a season): 111 (1931/32)
Fewest goals scored: 39 (1973/74)
Most goals conceded: 98 (1967/68)
Fewest goals conceded: 32 (1922/23)
Most clean sheets: 20 (1996/97)
Fewest clean sheets: 3 (1953/54)

HIGHS AND LOWS

Biggest home win: 10-1 v Ipswich Town (26-Dec-1963)
Biggest away win: 8-0 v Halifax Town (16-Sep-1969)
Biggest home defeat: 0-6 v Port Vale (28-Mar-1987)
Biggest away defeat: 0-9 v Wolverhampton W. (16-Sep-1959)
Most points (3 for a win): 87, Division 3 (1996/97)
Most points (2 for a win): 60, Division 2 (1958/59) 60, Division 3 (1970/71)
Least points (3 for a win): 36, Division 2 (1985/86)
Least points (2 for a win): 25, Division 2 (1968/69)
Highest finish: 10, Division 1 (1959/60)
Lowest finish: 17, Division 3 (1995/96)

One and only

Fulham's only FA Cup Final appearance was in 1975. They were beaten 2-0 by West Ham and had former Hammer and England skipper Bobby Moore starring in their defence.

Spot on goalie

In December 1995, Fulham goalkeeper Tony Lange scored a penalty in a 4-1 FA Cup shoot-out win against Brighton, having remained unbeaten during the match.

Frank's alot!

Frank Newton is Fulham's leading League scorer in a season with 43 goals in the Third Division South in the 1931-32 campaign.

ON THE RUN

Successive games unbeaten: 15 (23-Mar-1957), (17-Jan-1970)
Successive games without a win: 15 (25-Feb-1950),
Successive wins: 8 (23-Feb-1963)
Successive defeats: 11 (02-Dec-1961)
Successive draws: 4 (07-Sep-1957), (15-Nov-1980)
Successive games without scoring: 6 (21-Aug-1971)
Successive games without conceding: 6 (21-Jan-1922), (03-Mar-1923), (28-Feb-1992)

WIN, LOSE OR DRAW

Most wins (in a season): 27 (1958/59)
Fewest wins: 7 (1968/69)
Most draws: 17 (1986/87), (1992/93)
Fewest draws: 4 (1956/57)
Most defeats: 26 (1985/86)
Fewest defeats: 9 (1931/32), (1948/49), (1958/59), (1996-97)

THEIR LEAGUE RECORD

P	W	D	L	F	A
3342	1238	835	1269	4946	4881

GILLINGHAM

HIGHS AND LOWS

Biggest home win: 10-0 v Chesterfield (05-Sep-1987)
Biggest away win: 4-0 v Port Vale (20-Feb-1965), 4-0 v Oxford Utd (20-Nov-1965), 4-0 v Orient (07-May-1968), 4-0 v Carlisle Utd (12-Mar-1991)
Biggest home defeat: 0-5 v Notts Co (28-Feb-1931), 0-5 v C.Palace (02-Apr-1934), 0-5 v Watford (11-Jan-1969)
Biggest away defeat: 0-8 v Luton Town (13-Apr-1929)
Most points (3 for a win): 83, Division 3 (1984/85), (1995/96)
Most points (2 for a win): 62, Division 4 (1973/74)
Least points (3 for a win): 40, Division 3 (1988/89) 40, Division 3 (1992/93)
Least points (2 for a win): 26, Division 3(S) (1937/38)
Highest finish: 4, Division 3(S) (1954/55) 4, Division 3 (1978/79), (1984/85)
Lowest finish: 21, Division 3 (1992/93)

FIRST TIME

First League Game:
Home v Southampton
(28-Aug-1920)
Result: Drew 1-1
Final position: 22nd

KICKIN' OFF

Successive wins at start of season: 4 (1995/96)
Successive defeats at start of season: 6 (1969/70)
Successive unbeaten games at start of season: 13 (1963/64)

Shut out

Gills' goalkeeper Jim Stannard set a new club record in 1995-96 when he kept 29 clean sheets during the season.

GOALS, GOALS, GOALS

Most goals scored (in a season): 90 (1973/74)
Fewest goals scored: 34 (1920/21)
Most goals conceded: 101 (1950/51)
Fewest goals conceded: 20 (1995/96)
Most clean sheets: 29 (1995/96)
Fewest clean sheets: 4 (1933/34)

571 and out!

John Simpson holds the record number of League appearances for Gillingham at 571. He was at Priestfield for 15 years between 1957 and 1972.

Strip please!

Gillingham allegedly signed Republic of Ireland striker Tony Cascarino from local Kent club Crockenhill for a set of shirts. It wasn't a bad buy as he went on to play for Millwall, Celtic and Marseille as well as winning over 65 caps for the Irish, three while with Gills.

ON THE RUN

Successive games unbeaten: 20 (13-Oct-1973)
Successive games without a win: 15 (01-Apr-1972)
Successive wins: 7 (18-Dec-1954)
Successive defeats: 10 (20-Sep-1988)
Successive draws: 5 (29-Dec-1990), (28-Aug-1993)
Successive games without scoring: 6 (06-Nov-1937), (11-Feb-1961)
Successive games without conceding: 5 (24-Feb-1954), (26-Dec-1963), (07-Apr-1969), (03-Apr-1981)

WIN, LOSE OR DRAW

Most wins (in a season): 25 (1973/74), (1984/85)
Fewest wins: 8 (1920/21)
Most draws: 20 (1977/78)
Fewest draws: 4 (1988/89)
Most defeats: 30 (1988/89)
Fewest defeats: 8 (1978/79)

THEIR LEAGUE RECORD

P	W	D	L	F	A
2900	1012	765	1123	3838	4189

GRIMSBY

FIRST TIME
First League Game:
Home v Northwich Victoria
(03-Sep-1892)
Result: Won 2-1
Final position: 4th

KICKIN' OFF
Successive wins at start of
season: 4 (1952/53)
Successive defeats at start
of season: 3 (1907/08)
Successive unbeaten
games at start of season:
10 (1960/61)

HIGHS AND LOWS
Biggest home win: 8-0 v Tranmere Rovers
(14-Sep-1925)
Biggest away win: 7-0 v Bristol Rovers (14-Dec-1957)
Biggest home defeat: 0-7 v Newton Heath
(26-Dec-1899)
Biggest away defeat: 1-9 v Arsenal (28-Jan-1931)
0-8 v Arsenal (01-May-1948)
Most points (3 for a win): 83, Division 3 (1990/91)
Most points (2 for a win): 68, Division 3(N) (1955/56)
Least points (3 for a win): 44, Division 2 (1986/87)
Least points (2 for a win): 22, Division 1 (1947/48)
Highest finish: 5, Division 1 (1934/35)
Lowest finish: 23, Division 4 (1968/69)

Strange but true
In Grimsby's early days when they played at Clee Park, the players had to change in bathing huts brought up from the beach.

GOALS, GOALS, GOALS
Most goals scored (in a season): 103 (1933/34)
Fewest goals scored: 34 (1919/20)
Most goals conceded: 111 (1947/48)
Fewest goals conceded: 29 (1955/56)
Most clean sheets: 25 (1955/56)
Fewest clean sheets: 3 (1950/51), (1958/59)

Out of town
When is a home game not a home game? Well Grimsby are the only English League club to have played League football for the last 90 odd years outside their home town. Blundell Park is based in nearby Cleethorpes and indeed the club's first home, Clee Park, was in the town.

Back with a bang
In April 1996 Clive Mendonca scored a hat-trick against Ipswich in only his second game after 15 months out with injury.

ON THE RUN
Successive games unbeaten: 19 (16-Feb-1980)
Successive games without a win: 18 (10-Oct-1981)
Successive wins: 11 (19-Jan-1952)
Successive defeats: 9 (30-Nov-1907)
Successive draws: 5 (25-Dec-1920), (06-Feb-1965)
Successive games without scoring: 5 (08-Apr-1983),
(21-Mar-1987)
Successive games without conceding: 8 (02-Apr-1956)

WIN, LOSE OR DRAW
Most wins (in a season): 31 (1955/56)
Fewest wins: 8 (1902/03), (1947/48), (1950/51)
Most draws: 20 (1993/94)
Fewest draws: 3 (1906/07)
Most defeats: 28 (1947/48)
Fewest defeats: 7 (1925/26)

THEIR LEAGUE RECORD

P	W	D	L	F	A
3860	1485	866	1509	5735	5820

HARTLEPOOL

HIGHS AND LOWS

Biggest home win: 10-1 v Barrow (04-Apr-1959)
Biggest away win: 6-1 v Southport (04-Sep-1956)
Biggest home defeat: 1-8 v Plymouth Argyle (07-May-1994)
Biggest away defeat: 1-10 v Wrexham (03-Mar-1962)
Most points (3 for a win): 82, Division 4 (1990/91)
Most points (2 for a win): 60, Division 4 (1967/68)
Least points (3 for a win): 36, Division 2 (1993/94)
Least points (2 for a win): 25, Division 3(N) (1923/24)
25, Division 4 (1962/63)
Highest finish: 2, Division 3(N) (1956/57)
Lowest finish: 24, Division 4 (1959/60), (1962/63)

FIRST TIME

First League Game:
Away v Wrexham
(27-Aug-1921)
Result: Won 2-0
Final position: 4th

KICKIN' OFF

Successive wins at start of season: 4 (1957/58)
Successive defeats at start of season: 5 (1938/39), (1989/90)
Successive unbeaten games at start of season: 6 (1992/93)

You're off - and you!

Hartlepool had two players sent-off at Torquay in 1996 in the first 32 minutes but still managed to draw 0-0.

GOALS, GOALS, GOALS

Most goals scored (in a season): 90 (1956/57)
Fewest goals scored: 33 (1923/24)
Most goals conceded: 116 (1932/33)
Fewest goals conceded: 39 (1921/22)
Most clean sheets: 20 (1967/68)
Fewest clean sheets: 3 (1928/29)

Strange but true!

Ambrose Fogarty is Hartlepool's most capped player, with one Republic of Ireland cap.

Hero Houchen

Former Hartlepool manager Keith Houchen, who quit the club in the 1996-97 season, has his name etched in the history of the FA Cup. His brilliant header for Coventry against Tottenham in 1987 helped the Sky Blues to their only major honour with a 3-2 win.

ON THE RUN

Successive games unbeaten: 17 (24-Feb-1968)
Successive games without a win: 18 (01-Dec-1962), (09-Jan-1993)
Successive wins: 7 (04-Sep-1956), (01-Apr-1968)
Successive defeats: 8 (08-Apr-1950)
Successive draws: 4 (18-Mar-1922), (15-Apr-1938), (29-Apr-1953)
(27-Jan-1973), (23-Aug-1986)
Successive games without scoring: 11 (09-Jan-1993)
Successive games without conceding: 6 (27-Jan-1973)

WIN, LOSE OR DRAW

Most wins (in a season): 26 (1955/56)
Fewest wins: 7 (1923/24), (1962/63)
Most draws: 19 (1968/69)
Fewest draws: 5 (1931/32), (1949/50), (1954/55), (1955/56)
Most defeats: 29 (1959/60)
Fewest defeats: 11 (1967/68)

THEIR LEAGUE RECORD

P	W	D	L	F	A
3070	1015	683	1372	4059	5080

HEREFORD

FIRST TIME
First League Game:
Away v Colchester Utd
(12-Aug-1972)
Result: Lost 0-1
Final position: 2nd

KICKIN' OFF
Successive wins at start of season: 4 (1984/85)
Successive defeats at start of season: 4 (1993/94)
Successive unbeaten games at start of season: 7 (1984/85)

HIGHS AND LOWS
Biggest home win: 5-0 v Chesterfield (28-Sep-1974), 5-0 v Chester (10-Mar-1976), 6-1 v Crewe Alexandra (16-Sep-1978), 5-0 v Hartlepool Utd (07-Mar-1984), 5-0 v Colchester Utd (16-Oct-1993)
Biggest away win: 6-0 v Burnley (24-Jan-1987)
Biggest home defeat: 1-6 v Wolverhampton W. (02-Oct-1976), 0-5 v Chester City (06-Nov-1993)
Biggest away defeat: 0-6 v Rotherham United (29-Apr-1989), 0-6 v Crewe Alexandra (09-Oct-1993), 1-7 v Mansfield Town (26-Dec-1994)
Most points (3 for a win): 77, Division 4 (1984/85)
Most points (2 for a win): 63, Division 3 (1975/76)
Least points (3 for a win): 41, Division 4 (1982/83)
Least points (2 for a win): 31, Division 2 (1976/77)
Highest finish: 22, Division 2 (1976/77)
Lowest finish: 24, Div 4 (1982/83), 24, Div 3 (1996/97)

GOALS, GOALS, GOALS
Most goals scored (in a season): 86 (1975/76)
Fewest goals scored: 34 (1977/78)
Most goals conceded: 79 (1982/83), (1993/94)
Fewest goals conceded: 38 (1972/73)
Most clean sheets: 22 (1972/73)
Fewest clean sheets: 5 (1985/86)

It's all over now
1997 saw Hereford draw with Brighton 0-0 at Edgar Street in a winner-takes-all survival battle. A draw meant Hereford were relegated to the Vauxhall Conference after 25 years in the Football League.

ON THE RUN
Successive games unbeaten: 14 (15-Feb-1984)
Successive games without a win: 13 (19-Nov-1977), (28-Mar-1978)
Successive wins: 5 (07-Mar-1984), (12-May-1984)
Successive defeats: 8 (07-Feb-1987)
Successive draws: 6 (12-Apr-1975)
Successive games without scoring: 5 (08-Apr-1978), (25-Mar-1980), (18-Sep-1982)
Successive games without conceding: 7 (25-Aug-1984)

What a shocker!
Hereford caused one of the biggest FA Cup upsets in history in 1972, when as a non-League side they beat Newcastle 2-1, in John Motson's first TV commentary in the FA Cup.

Proud Peacock
Darren Peacock is the club's record sale at £440,000 to QPR in December, 1990.

WIN, LOSE OR DRAW
Most wins (in a season): 26 (1975/76)
Fewest wins: 8 (1976/77)
Most draws: 19 (1981/82)
Fewest draws: 6 (1993/94)
Most defeats: 27 (1982/83)
Fewest defeats: 9 (1975/76)

THEIR LEAGUE RECORD

P	W	D	L	F	A
1130	363	317	450	1365	1513

HUDDERSFIELD

HIGHS AND LOWS

Biggest home win: 10-1 v Blackpool (13-Dec-1930)
Biggest away win: 7-1 v Sheffield Utd (12-Nov-1927),
6-0 v Manchester Utd (10-Sep-1930), 6-0 v Bury
(01-Apr-1989)
Biggest home defeat: 1-7 v Wolverhampton W.
(29-Sep-1951)
Biggest away defeat: 1-10 v Manchester City
(07-Nov-1987)
Most points (3 for a win): 82, Division 3 (1982/83)
Most points (2 for a win): 66, Division 4 (1979/80)
Least points (3 for a win): 28, Division 2 (1987/88)
Least points (2 for a win): 25, Division 1 (1971/72)
Highest finish: 1, Division 1 (1923/24), (1924/25),
(1925/26)
Lowest finish: 11, Division 4 (1977/78)

FIRST TIME

First League Game:
Away v Bradford Park Ave.
(03-Sep-1910)
Result: Won 1-0
Final position: 13th

KICKIN' OFF

**Successive wins at start of
season:** 4 (1924/25)
**Successive defeats at start
of season:** 6 (1992/93)
**Successive unbeaten
games at start of season:**
13 (1962/63)

Strange but true

In May 1951, Huddersfield
beat future European
Champions PSV Eindhoven
4-1 and French club Rennes
5-1 during the Festival of
Britain tournament.

GOALS, GOALS, GOALS

Most goals scored (in a season): 101 (1979/80)
Fewest goals scored: 27 (1971/72)
Most goals conceded: 100 (1987/88)
Fewest goals conceded: 28 (1924/25)
Most clean sheets: 23 (1922/23)
Fewest clean sheets: 6 (1960/61)

Top Bill

Billy Smith holds the
record number of League
appearances for the club
at 520 between 1914
and 1934.

Huddersfield hat-trick

Huddersfield won the Football League Championship
three times in a row, their only successes, in 1924,
1925 and 1926 under the guidance of former
Arsenal boss Herbert Chapman, rated as the best
boss in his era.

ON THE RUN

Successive games unbeaten: 27 (24-Jan-1925)
Successive games without a win: 22 (04-Dec-1971)
Successive wins: 11 (05-Apr-1920)
Successive defeats: 7 (06-Dec-1913), (08-Oct-1955)
Successive draws: 6 (03-Mar-1987)
Successive games without scoring: 7 (22-Jan-1972)
Successive games without conceding: 8 (13-Mar-1965)

WIN, LOSE OR DRAW

Most wins (in a season): 28
(1919/20)
Fewest wins: 6 (1971/72),
(1987/88)
Most draws: 17 (1926/27),
(1972/73)
Fewest draws: 5 (1937/38)
Most defeats: 28 (1987/88)
Fewest defeats: 5
(1924/25)

THEIR LEAGUE RECORD

P	W	D	L	F	A
3250	1260	839	1151	4680	4386

HULL CITY

FIRST TIME

First League Game:
Home v Barnsley
(02-Sep-1905)
Result: Won 4-1
Final position: 5th

KICKIN' OFF

Successive wins at start of season: 9 (1948/49)
Successive defeats at start of season: 3 (1934/35), (1955/56), (1990/91)
Successive unbeaten games at start of season: 11 (1948/49), (1983/84)

HIGHS AND LOWS

Biggest home win: 10-0 v Halifax Town (26-Dec-1930), 11-1 v Carlisle Utd (14-Jan-1939)
Biggest away win: 5-0 v Glossop (16-Mar-1915)
Biggest home defeat: 0-5 v Lincoln City (10-Oct-1959)
Biggest away defeat: 0-8 v Wolverhampton W. (04-Nov-1911)
Most points (3 for a win): 90, Division 4 (1982/83)
Most points (2 for a win): 69, Division 3 (1965/66)
Least points (3 for a win): 31, Division 2 (1995/96)
Least points (2 for a win): 20, Division 2 (1935/36)
Highest finish: 3, Division 2 (1909/10)
Lowest finish: 17, Division 3 (1996/97)

Strange but true

Hull University are the first Education establishment to sponsor a club when they backed Hull for the 1997-98 season.

GOALS, GOALS, GOALS

Most goals scored (in a season): 109 (1965/66)
Fewest goals scored: 34 (1977/78)
Most goals conceded: 111 (1935/36)
Fewest goals conceded: 28 (1948/49)
Most clean sheets: 22 (1948/49)
Fewest clean sheets: 4 (1935/36), (1955/56)

Tiger Feat

Hull's most capped player is Terry Neill, with 15 appearances for Northern Ireland. He later went on to manage Hull and then both North London giants, Tottenham and Arsenal.

Hull hell

Cash strapped Hull were close to going out of business during the 1996-97 season and their displays on the pitch didn't help matters. In their 2-0 home defeat by Scarborough, they had their lowest attendance in their history at 3,774 and they finished the term in their lowest ever League position - 17th in the Third Division.

ON THE RUN

Successive games unbeaten: 15 (12-Dec-1964), (23-Apr-1983)
Successive games without a win: 27 (27-Mar-1989)
Successive wins: 10 (01-May-1948), (23-Feb-1966)
Successive defeats: 8 (07-Apr-1934)
Successive draws: 5 (03-Feb-1921), (30-Mar-1929)
Successive games without scoring: 6 (13-Nov-1920)
Successive games without conceding: 6 (26-Sep-1908)

WIN, LOSE OR DRAW

Most wins (in a season): 31 (1965/66)
Fewest wins: 5 (1935/36), 5 (1995/95)
Most draws: 20 (1920/21)
Fewest draws: 4 (1907/08)
Most defeats: 27 (1935/36)
Fewest defeats: 4 (1948/49)

THEIR LEAGUE RECORD

P	W	D	L	F	A
3462	1314	911	1237	5033	4805

IPSWICH

HIGHS AND LOWS

Biggest home win: 7-0 v Portsmouth (07-Nov-1964), 7-0 v Southampton (02-Feb-1974), 7-0 v West Bromwich Alb. (06-Nov-1976)
Biggest away win: 6-0 v Notts County (25-Sep-1982)
Biggest home defeat: 1-6 v Millwall (21-Mar-1953), 2-7 v Manchester Utd (03-Sep-1963)
Biggest away defeat: 1-10 v Fulham (26-Dec-1963), 0-9 v Manchester Utd (04-Mar-1995)
Most points (3 for a win): 84, Division 2 (1991/92)
Most points (2 for a win): 64, Division 3(S) (1953/54) 64, Division 3(S) (1955/56)
Least points (3 for a win): 27, Premier (1994/95)
Least points (2 for a win): 25, Division 1 (1963/64)
Highest finish: 1, Division 1 (1961/62)
Lowest finish: 17, Division 3(S) (1949/50), (1951/52)

FIRST TIME

First League Game: Home v Southend Utd (27-Aug-1938)
Result: Won 4-2
Final position: 7th

KICKIN' OFF

Successive wins at start of season: 4 (1953/54), (1974/75)
Successive defeats at start of season: 3 (1949/50), (1956/57)
Successive unbeaten games at start of season: 14 (1980/81)

Strange but true!

Ipswich made eight appearances in the UEFA Cup in the ten seasons between 1973 and 1983, winning it in 1981. They were also the first English club to have an all-seater stadium.

GOALS, GOALS, GOALS

Most goals scored (in a season): 106 (1955/56)
Fewest goals scored: 32 (1985/86)
Most goals conceded: 121 (1963/64)
Fewest goals conceded: 39 (1976/77), (1979/80)
Most clean sheets: 20 (1979/80)
Fewest clean sheets: 3 (1994/95)

Town planner

Town have been managed by two past England managers, Sir Alf Ramsey and Bobby Robson.

Stevie Wonder

Steve Sedgley became Ipswich's first £1 million player when he joined the club from Tottenham in June 1994. A year earlier Town received their record transfer fee of £1.9 million for midfielder Jason Dozzell who headed for Tottenham.

ON THE RUN

Successive games unbeaten: 23 (08-Dec-1979)
Successive games without a win: 21 (28-Aug-1963)
Successive wins: 8 (23-Sep-1953)
Successive defeats: 10 (04-Sep-1954)
Successive draws: 7 (10-Nov-1990)
Successive games without scoring: 7 (28-Feb-1995)
Successive games without conceding: 5 (5-Apr-1997)

WIN, LOSE OR DRAW

Most wins (in a season): 27 (1953/54)
Fewest wins: 7 (1994/95)
Most draws: 18 (1990/91)
Fewest draws: 3 (1947/48)
Most defeats: 29 (1994/95)
Fewest defeats: 5 (1967/68)

THEIR LEAGUE RECORD

P	W	D	L	F	A
2234	898	553	783	3331	3139

LEEDS UNITED

FIRST TIME
First League Game:
Away v Port Vale
(28-Aug-1920)
Result: Lost 0-2
Final position: 14th

KICKIN' OFF
Successive wins at start of season: 7 (1973/74)
Successive defeats at start of season: 3 (1936/37)
Successive unbeaten games at start of season: 29 (1973/74)

HIGHS AND LOWS
Biggest home win: 8-0 v Leicester City (07-Apr-1934)
Biggest away win: 5-0 v Burnley (21-Nov-1931), 5-0 v Fulham (06-Jan-1968), 6-1 v Sheffield Wed. (12-Jan-1992), 5-0 v Swindon Town (07-May-1994)
Biggest home defeat: 0-5 v Arsenal (08-Nov-1980)
Biggest away defeat: 1-8 v Stoke City (27-Aug-1934)
Most points (3 for a win): 85, Division 2 (1989/90)
Most points (2 for a win): 67, Division 1 (1968/69)
Least points (3 for a win): 42, Division 1 (1981/82)
Least points (2 for a win): 18, Division 1 (1946/47)
Highest finish: 1, Division 1 (1968/69), (1973/74), (1991/92)
Lowest finish: 19, Division 2 (1961/62)

In no Rush
Ian Rush went four months without a goal before scoring his first strike for the club in a 2-0 win over Chelsea in 1996.

GOALS, GOALS, GOALS
Most goals scored (in a season): 98 (1927/28)
Fewest goals scored: 28 (1996/97)
Most goals conceded: 92 (1934/35), (1959/60)
Fewest goals conceded: 26 (1968/69)
Most clean sheets: 24 (1968/69), (1970/71)
Fewest clean sheets: 3 (1926/27), (1946/47)

Strange but true!
The Spion Kop at Elland Road is named after the huge hill in South Africa on which 322 British soldiers lost their lives in the Boer War.

Lucky Leeds
Leeds created a top flight record by scoring the fewest number of goals (28) without getting relegated in 1996/97.

Keeper capers
South African international Lucas Radebe made two stand-in appearances in goal as substitute 'keeper in 1996, keeping a clean sheet against Middlesbrough and conceding just one at Manchester United.

ON THE RUN
Successive games unbeaten: 34 (26-Oct-1968)
Successive games without a win: 17 (01-Feb-1947)
Successive wins: 9 (26-Sep-1931)
Successive defeats: 6 (26-Apr-1947), 6 (6-Apr-1996)
Successive draws: 5 (09-Apr-1962)
Successive games without scoring: 6 (30-Jan-1982)
Successive games without conceding: 9 (03-Mar-1928)

WIN, LOSE OR DRAW
Most wins (in a season): 27 (1968/69), (1970/71)
Fewest wins: 6 (1946/47)
Most draws: 21 (1982/83)
Fewest draws: 4 (1936/37)
Most defeats: 30 (1946/47)
Fewest defeats: 2 (1968/69)

THEIR LEAGUE RECORD

P	W	D	L	F	A
2938	1213	771	954	4418	3896

LEICESTER

HIGHS AND LOWS

Biggest home win: 10-0 v Portsmouth (20-Oct-1928)
Biggest away win: 5-0 v Burton Swifts (02-Mar-1895), 6-1 v Luton Town (14-Jan-1899), 5-0 v Charlton Athletic (28-Mar-1970)
Biggest home defeat: 0-6 v Derby County (28-Dec-1914), 0-6 v West Ham Utd (15-Feb-1923)
Biggest away defeat: 0-12 v Nottingham Forest (21-Apr-1909)
Most points (3 for a win): 77, Division 2 (1991/92)
Most points (2 for a win): 61, Division 2 (1956/57)
Least points (3 for a win): 29, Premier (1994/95)
Least points (2 for a win): 22, Division 2 (1903/04) 22, Division 1 (1977/78)
Highest finish: 2, Division 1 (1928/29)
Lowest finish: 22, Division 2 (1990/91)

FIRST TIME

First League Game:
Away v Grimsby Town (01-Sep-1894)
Result: Lost 3-4
Final position: 4th

KICKIN' OFF

Successive wins at start of season: 3 (1899/1900), (1906/07), (1922/23)
Successive defeats at start of season: 6 (1983/84)
Successive unbeaten games at start of season: 11 (1899/1900)

Lucky 13

Between 3rd September and 29th December 1906, Leicester won 13 consecutive home games in Division Two.

GOALS, GOALS, GOALS

Most goals scored (in a season): 109 (1956/57)
Fewest goals scored: 26 (1977/78)
Most goals conceded: 112 (1957/58)
Fewest goals conceded: 30 (1970/71)
Most clean sheets: 23 (1970/71)
Fewest clean sheets: 2 (1908/09)

In and out

Mark Draper was Leicester's record buy from Notts County for £1.25 million in 1994 and then became their record sale at £3.25 million to Aston Villa a year later.

Lovely bubbly!

When Leicester launched their plastic sheet pitch protector in the early 1980s as protection against the weather, it was possible to raise the bubble high enough for the players to train underneath it.

ON THE RUN

Successive games unbeaten: 19 (06-Feb-1971)
Successive games without a win: 18 (12-Apr-1975)
Successive wins: 7 (15-Feb-1908), (24-Jan-1925), (26-Dec-1962), (28-Feb-1993)
Successive defeats: 7 (28-Nov-1931), (28-Aug-1990)
Successive draws: 6 (21-Apr-1973), (21-Aug-1976)
Successive games without scoring: 7 (21-Nov-1987)
Successive games without conceding: 7 (14-Feb-1920)

WIN, LOSE OR DRAW

Most wins (in a season): 25 (1956/57)
Fewest wins: 5 (1977/78)
Most draws: 19 (1975/76)
Fewest draws: 4 (1895/96)
Most defeats: 25 (1977/78), (1994/95), (1913/14)
Fewest defeats: 6 (1956/57), (1970/71)

THEIR LEAGUE RECORD

P	W	D	L	F	A
3746	1391	946	1409	5746	5857

LEYTON ORIENT

FIRST TIME

First League Game:
Away v Leicester Fosse
(02-Sep-1905)
Result: Lost 1-2
Final position: 20th

KICKIN' OFF

Successive wins at start of season: 4 (1910/11)
Successive defeats at start of season: 4 (1965/66)
Successive unbeaten games at start of season: 8 (1968/69)

HIGHS AND LOWS

Biggest home win: 8-0 v Crystal Palace (12-Nov-1955), 8-0 v Rochdale (20-Oct-1987), 8-0 v Colchester Utd (15-Oct-1988)
Biggest away win: 7-1 v Exeter City (06-Nov-1954)
Biggest home defeat: 2-7 v Aldershot (25-Feb-1950)
Biggest away defeat: 0-6 v Stockport County (11-Sep-1920), 0-6 v Darlington (13-Feb-1926), 0-6 v Blackpool (11-Dec-1926), 0-6 v Middlesbrough (26-Feb-1927), 0-6 v Watford (20-Dec-1933), 0-6 v Bristol City (17-Sep-1947), 1-7 v Torquay Utd (16-Apr-1949), 1-7 v Notts County (01-Oct-1949), 1-7 v Stoke City (22-Sep-1956), 0-6 v Manchester City (26-Aug-1964), 0-6 v Huddersfield Town (28-Sep-1982)
Most points (3 for a win): 75, Division 4 (1988/89)
Most points (2 for a win): 66, Division 3(S) (1955/56)
Least points (3 for a win): 26, Division 2 (1994/95)
Least points (2 for a win): 21, Division 2 (1905/06) 21, Division 1 (1962/63)
Highest finish: 22, Division 1 (1962/63)
Lowest finish: 21, Division 3 (1995/96)

GOALS, GOALS, GOALS

Most goals scored (in a season): 106 (1955/56)
Fewest goals scored: 28 (1974/75)
Most goals conceded: 96 (1926/27)
Fewest goals conceded: 35 (1910/11), (1913/14)
Most clean sheets: 22 (1969/70)
Fewest clean sheets: 3 (1960/61)

O's beat Wales

On 26th May, 1996 Orient defeated Wales 2-1 in a friendly at Brisbane Road.

Just married

In 1995 Orient staged the first ever wedding ceremony at a football club. It was conducted on the pitch by former O's player and now man of the cloth, Alan Comfort.

O dear

It's said that England legend Peter Shilton was given the boot by Orient - because he couldn't the kick ball far enough.

ON THE RUN

Successive games unbeaten: 14 (30-Oct-1954)
Successive games without a win: 23 (06-Oct-1962)
Successive wins: 10 (21-Jan-1956)
Successive defeats: 9 (01-Apr-1995)
Successive draws: 6 (16-Sep-1972), (30-Nov-1974)
Successive games without scoring: 8 (19-Nov-1994)
Successive games without conceding: 6 (06-Feb-1971)

WIN, LOSE OR DRAW

Most wins (in a season): 29 (1955/56)
Fewest wins: 5 (1965/66)
Most draws: 20 (1974/75)
Fewest draws: 3 (1911/12)
Most defeats: 32 (1994/95)
Fewest defeats: 9 (1955/56), (1969/70), (1973/74)

THEIR LEAGUE RECORD

P	W	D	L	F	A
3462	1155	879	1428	4410	5051

LINCOLN CITY

HIGHS AND LOWS

Biggest home win: 11-1 v Crewe Alexandra (29-Sep-1951)
Biggest away win: 8-2 v Rotherham Town (02-Dec-1893), 6-0 v Burton Utd (23-Nov-1901), 6-0 v Darlington (02-Jan-1932)
Biggest home defeat: 0-6 v Barnet (04-Sep-1991)
Biggest away defeat: 3-11 v Manchester City (23-Mar-1895), 0-8 v Notts County (23-Jan-1897), 0-8 v Preston North End (28-Dec-1901), 1-9 v Wigan Borough (03-Mar-1923), 0-8 v Stoke City (23-Feb-1957)
Most points (3 for a win): 77, Division 3 (1981/82)
Most points (2 for a win): 74, Division 4 (1975/76)
Least points (3 for a win): 46, Division 3 (1985/86)
Least points (2 for a win): 21, Division 2 (1907/08)
Highest finish: 5, Division 2 (1901/02)
Lowest finish: 24, Division 4 (1966/67), (1986/87)

FIRST TIME

First League Game:
Away v Sheffield Utd (03-Sep-1892)
Result: Lost 2-4
Final position: 9th

KICKIN' OFF

Successive wins at start of season: 4 (1934/35), (1968/69), (1989/90)
Successive defeats at start of season: 3 (1959/60), (1992/93)
Successive unbeaten games at start of season: 7 (1901/02), (1950/51), (1989/90)

Home alone

In 1995-96 Lincoln went 621 minutes without conceding a goal at home, equalling a 64-year record.

GOALS, GOALS, GOALS

Most goals scored (in a season): 121 (1951/52)
Fewest goals scored: 28 (1910/11)
Most goals conceded: 101 (1919/20)
Fewest goals conceded: 25 (1980/81)
Most clean sheets: 25 (1980/81)
Fewest clean sheets: 1 (1892/93)

Tony Tops

Tony Emery has made the greatest number of League appearances for the club at 402, made between 1946 and 1959.

First out

In 1987, Lincoln became the first club to be relegated from the Football League, when automatic promotion from the Conference was introduced. They were promoted to the Football League as Conference Champions the following season.

ON THE RUN

Successive games unbeaten: 18 (11-Mar-1980)
Successive games without a win: 19 (22-Aug-1978)
Successive wins: 10 (01-Sep-1930)
Successive defeats: 12 (21-Sep-1896)
Successive draws: 5 (26-Dec-1977), (21-Feb-1981)
Successive games without scoring: 5 (23-Jan-1897), (15-Nov-1913), (10-Jan-1987)
Successive games without conceding: 5 (7 times)

WIN, LOSE OR DRAW

Most wins (in a season): 32 (1975/76)
Fewest wins: 7 (1892/93), (1910/11), (1978/79)
Most draws: 18 (1984/85)
Fewest draws: 3 (1892/93), (1907/08)
Most defeats: 29 (1964/65)
Fewest defeats: 4 (1975/76)

THEIR LEAGUE RECORD

P	W	D	L	F	A
3732	1360	876	1496	5582	5857

LIVERPOOL

FIRST TIME

First League Game: Away v Middlesbrough I. (02-Sep-1893)
Result: Won 2-0
Final position: 1st

KICKIN' OFF

Successive wins at start of season: 8 (1990/91)
Successive defeats at start of season: 8 (1899/00)
Successive unbeaten games at start of season: 29 (1987/88)

HIGHS AND LOWS

Biggest home win: 10-1 v Rotherham Town (18-Feb-1896), 9-0 v Crystal Palace (12-Sep-1989)
Biggest away win: 7-0 v Burton Swifts (29-Feb-1896) 7-0 v Crewe Alexandra (28-Mar-1896)
Biggest home defeat: 0-6 v Sunderland (19-Apr-1930)
Biggest away defeat: 0-8 v Huddersfield Town (10-Nov-1934), 1-9 v Birmingham City (11-Dec-1954)
Most points (3 for a win): 90, Division 1 (1987/88)
Most points (2 for a win): 68, Division 1 (1978/79)
Least points (3 for a win): 59, Premier (1992/93)
Least points (2 for a win): 28, Division 1 (1897/98) 28, Division 1 (1953/54)
Highest finish: 1, Division 1 (1900/01), (1905/06), (1921/22), (1922/23), (1946/47), (1963/64), (1965/66), (1972/73), (1975/76), (1976/77), (1978/79), (1979/80), (1981/82), (1982/83), (1983/84), (1985/86), (1987/88), (1989/90)
Lowest finish: 11, Division 2 (1954/55)

GOALS, GOALS, GOALS

Most goals scored (in a season): 106 (1895/96)
Fewest goals scored: 42 (1901/02), (1970/71)
Most goals conceded: 97 (1953/54)
Fewest goals conceded: 16 (1978/79)
Most clean sheets: 28 (1978/79)
Fewest clean sheets: 4 (1894/95), (1927/28), (1931/32), (1954/55)

Lights...camera... action

Anfield was the venue for the first ever Match Of The Day, broadcast in 1964, when Liverpool beat Arsenal 3-2 in a classic encounter.

Record breaker Rush

When Ian Rush scored a 59th minute goal against Rochdale in 1996, he broke Denis Law's post-war record of FA Cup goals with the 42nd of his career.

ON THE RUN

Successive games unbeaten: 31 (04-May-1987)
Successive games without a win: 14 (12-Dec-1953)
Successive wins: 12 (21-Apr-1990)
Successive defeats: 9 (29-Apr-1899)
Successive draws: 6 (19-Feb-1975)
Successive games without scoring: 5 (22-Dec-1906), (03-Jan-1948), (18-Dec-1971), (01-Sep-1993)
Successive games without conceding: 8 (30-Dec-1922)

WIN, LOSE OR DRAW

Most wins (in a season): 30 (1978/79)
Fewest wins: 9 (1903/04) (1953/54)
Most draws: 19 (1951/52)
Fewest draws: 5 (1898/99), (1899/1900), (1905/06), (1912/13), (1958/59), (1963/64)
Most defeats: 23 (1953/54)
Fewest defeats: 2 (1987/88)

THEIR LEAGUE RECORD

P	W	D	L	F	A
3726	1743	904	1079	6389	4745

LUTON TOWN

HIGHS AND LOWS

Biggest home win: 12-0 v Bristol Rovers (13-Apr-1936)
Biggest away win: 5-0 v Exeter City (21-Oct-1967)
Biggest home defeat: 1-6 v Leicester Fosse
(14-Jan-1899), 1-6 v Charlton Athletic (10-Feb-1962),
2-7 v Shrewsbury Town (10-Mar-1965), 0-5 v Manchester
Utd (12-Feb-1984)
Biggest away defeat: 0-9 v Small Heath (12-Nov-1898)
Most points (3 for a win): 88, Division 2 (1981/82)
Most points (2 for a win): 66, Division 4 (1967/68)
Least points (3 for a win): 37, Division 1 (1990/91)
Least points (2 for a win): 29, Division 2 (1962/63)
Highest finish: 7, Division 1 (1986/87)
Lowest finish: 17, Division 4 (1966/67)

Green issue

Luton's first game at Kenilworth Road in 1905 was known as the 'Green Game', because they played Plymouth who wore green, the referee was a Mr Green and the game was started by a local brewer called Green.

Wow Mal

Luton's most capped player is Mal Donaghy with 58 caps for Northern Ireland while at the club.

WIN, LOSE OR DRAW

Most wins (in a season): 27
(1936/37), (1967/68)
Fewest wins: 9 (1950/51)
(1959/60)
Most draws: 21 (1992/93)
Fewest draws: 4 (1897/98)
(1936/37)
Most defeats: 24 (1962/63)
(1964/65)
Fewest defeats: 4
(1981/82)

FIRST TIME

First League Game:
Away v Leicester Fosse
(04-Sep-1897)
Result: Drew 1-1
Final position: 8th

KICKIN' OFF

Successive wins at start of season: 3 (1933/34),
(1956/57), (1969/70),
(1981/82)
Successive defeats at start of season: 4 (1927/28)
Successive unbeaten games at start of season:
13 (1969/70)

GOALS, GOALS, GOALS

Most goals scored (in a season): 103 (1936/37)
Fewest goals scored: 38 (1991/92)
Most goals conceded: 95 (1898/99)
Fewest goals conceded: 35 (1921/22)
Most clean sheets: 20 (1921/22), (1969/70)
Fewest clean sheets: 2 (1898/99)

Bob a job

Luton's first full international player was Bob Hawkes for England in 1907. He was already an amateur international.

ON THE RUN

Successive games unbeaten: 19 (20-Jan-1968),
(08-Apr-1969)
Successive games without a win: 16 (09-Sep-1964)
Successive wins: 9 (22-Jan-1977)
Successive defeats: 8 (11-Nov-1899)
Successive draws: 5 (16-Feb-1929), (28-Aug-1971)
Successive games without scoring: 5 (23-Mar-1957),
(10-Apr-1973), (04-Apr-1994)
Successive games without conceding: 7
(13-Oct-1923), (16-Jan-1993)

THEIR LEAGUE RECORD

P	W	D	L	F	A
3072	1172	776	1124	4728	4481

MAN CITY

FIRST TIME

First League Game:
Home v Bootle
(03-Sep-1892)
Result: Won 7-0
Final position: 5th

KICKIN' OFF

Successive wins at start of season: 7 (1897/98)
Successive defeats at start of season: 5 (1901/02)
Successive unbeaten games at start of season: 11 (1914/15)

HIGHS AND LOWS

Biggest home win: 10-0 v Darwen (18-Feb-1899)
Biggest away win: 7-1 v Derby County (29-Jan-1938), 9-3 v Tranmere Rovers (26-Dec-1938)
Biggest home defeat: 2-7 v West Bromwich Alb. (01-Jan-1934), 1-6 v Middlesbrough (09-Mar-1938), 1-6 v Millwall (17-Sep-1938), 1-6 v Blackpool (23-Apr-1955), 1-6 v West Ham Utd (08-Sep-1962), 0-5 v Liverpool (10-Apr-1982)
Biggest away defeat: 2-10 v Small Heath (17-Mar-1894), 0-8 v Burton Wanderers (26-Dec-1894), 1-9 v Everton (03-Sep-1906), 0-8 v Wolverhampton W. (23-Dec-1933)
Most points (3 for a win): 82, Division 2 (1988/89)
Most points (2 for a win): 62, Division 2 (1946/47)
Least points (3 for a win): 39, Division 1 (1986/87)
Least points (2 for a win): 29, Division 1 (1949/50)
Highest finish: 1, Division 1 (1936/37), (1967/68)
Lowest finish: 14, Division 1 (1996/97)

GOALS, GOALS, GOALS

Most goals scored (in a season): 108 (1926/27)
Fewest goals scored: 36 (1949/50), (1986/87)
Most goals conceded: 102 (1962/63)
Fewest goals conceded: 34 (1976/77)
Most clean sheets: 22 (1976/77)
Fewest clean sheets: 2 (1893/94)

Nicky Summerbee

Shooting star

Nicky Sumerbee holds a place in the Guinness Book of Records after being timed as having the hardest shot in football at 87 mph. His blaster was seen on the Record Breakers TV show with SHOOT in attendance.

ON THE RUN

Successive games unbeaten: 22 (26-Dec-1936), (16-Nov-1946)
Successive games without a win: 17 (26-Dec-1979)
Successive wins: 9 (08-Apr-1912)
Successive defeats: 6 (10-Sep-1910), (12-Sep-1956), (30-Mar-1959), (05-Nov-1960), (09-Mar-1963)
Successive draws: 6 (05-Apr-1913)
Successive games without scoring: 6 (30-Jan-1971)
Successive games without conceding: 5 (20-Mar-1915), (28-Dec-1946), (23-Feb-1985)

WIN, LOSE OR DRAW

Most wins (in a season): 26 (1946/47), (1967/68)
Fewest wins: 8 (1893/94), (1949/50), (1986/87)
Most draws: 18 (1993/94)
Fewest draws: 3 (1892/93), (1894/95), (1959/60)
Most defeats: 22 (1958/59), (1959/60)
Fewest defeats: 5 (1895/96), (1898/99), (1902/03), (1965/66)

THEIR LEAGUE RECORD

P	W	D	L	F	A
3768	1525	914	1329	6168	5596

MAN UNITED

FIRST TIME

First League Game:
Away v Blackburn Rovers
(03-Sep-1892)
Result: Lost 3-4
Final position: 16th

KICKIN' OFF

Successive wins at start of season: 10 (1985/86)
Successive defeats at start of season: 12 (1930/31)
Successive unbeaten games at start of season: 15 (1985/86)

HIGHS AND LOWS

Biggest home win: 10-1 v Wolverhampton W.
(15-Oct-1892), 9-0 v Walsall Town S. (03-Apr-1895), 9-0
v Darwen (24-Dec-1898), 9-0 v Ipswich (04-Mar-1995)
Biggest away win: 7-0 v Grimsby Town (26-Dec-1899)
Biggest home defeat: 0-6 v Aston Villa (14-Mar-1914)
1-7 v Newcastle (10-Sep-1927), 0-6 v Huddersfield
(10-Sep-1930)
Biggest away defeat: 0-7 v Blackburn Rovers
(10-Apr-1926), 0-7 v Aston Villa (27-Dec-1930), 0-7 v
Wolverhampton W. (26-Dec-1931)
Most points (3 for a win): 92, Premier (1993/94)
Most points (2 for a win): 64, Division 1 (1956/57)
Least points (3 for a win): 48, Division 1 (1989/90)
Least points (2 for a win): 22, Division 1 (1930/31)
Highest finish: 1, Division 1 (1907/08), (1910/11),
(1951/52), (1955/56), (1956/57), (1964/65),
(1966/67)1, Premier (1992/93), (1993/94), (1995-96),
(1996/97)
Lowest finish: 20, Division 2 (1933/34)

GOALS, GOALS, GOALS

Most goals scored (in a season): 103 (1956/57),
(1958/59)
Fewest goals scored: 38 (1901/02), (1973/74)
Most goals conceded: 115 (1930/31)
Fewest goals conceded: 23 (1924/25)
Most clean sheets: 25 (1924/25)
Fewest clean sheets: 2 (1893/94)

Strange but true!

Ryan Giggs was on the books of Manchester City as a
youngster but their city rivals United managed to
persuade him to go to Old Trafford.

ON THE RUN

Successive games unbeaten: 26 (04-Feb-1956)
Successive games without a win: 16 (03-Nov-1928),
(19-Apr-1930)
Successive wins: 14 (15-Oct-1904)
Successive defeats: 14 (26-Apr-1930)
Successive draws: 6 (30-Oct-1988)
Successive games without scoring: 5 (22-Feb-1902),
(26-Jan-1924), (07-Feb-1981)
Successive games without conceding: 7 (15-Oct-1904),
(20-Sep-1924)

Ryan Giggs

WIN, LOSE OR DRAW

Most wins (in a season): 28
(1905/06), (1956/57)
Fewest wins: 7 (1930/31)
Most draws: 18 (1980/81)
Fewest draws: 4
(1899/1900), (1900/01),
(1934/35)
Most defeats: 27 (1930/31)
Fewest defeats: 4
(1905/06), (1993/94)

THEIR LEAGUE RECORD

P	W	D	L	F	A
3758	1691	924	1143	6329	5017

MANSFIELD

FIRST TIME
First League Game:
Home v Swindon Town
(29-Aug-1931)
Result: Won 3-2
Final position: 20th

KICKIN' OFF
Successive wins at start of
season: 6 (1962/63)
Successive defeats at start
of season: 3 (1983/84)
Successive unbeaten
games at start of season:
10 (1949/50) , (1962/63)

HIGHS AND LOWS
Biggest home win: 9-2 v Rotherham (27-Dec-1932), 8-1 v QPR (15-Mar-1965), 7-0 v Scunthorpe (21-Apr-1975)
Biggest away win: 5-1 v Chester (08-Mar-1952), 4-0 v Chesterfield (23-Sep-1961), 6-2 v Lincoln City (27-Mar-1963), 5-1 v Workington (26-Feb-1965), 4-0 v Crewe (16-Dec-1972), 4-0 v Hartlepool (03-Nov-1982), 4-0 v Chester (27-Dec-1983), 4-0 v Stockport (06-Apr-1984), 5-1 v Preston (01-May-1993), 4-0 v Wigan (18-Feb,1995)
Biggest home defeat: 1-7 v Reading (12-Mar-1932), 1-7 v Peterboro (26-Mar-1966), 1-7 v QPR. (24-Sep-1966)
Biggest away defeat: 1-8 v Walsall (19-Jan-1933), 0-7 v Crewe Alexandra (04-Feb-1933), 0-7 v Walsall (05-Oct-1935)
Most points (3 for a win): 81, Division 4 (1985/86)
Most points (2 for a win): 68, Division 4 (1974/75)
Least points (3 for a win): 38, Division 3 (1990/91)
Least points (2 for a win): 28, Division 3(S) (1946/47)
Highest finish: 21, Division 2 (1977/78)
Lowest finish: 20, Division 4 (1960/61), (1981/82)

GOALS, GOALS, GOALS
Most goals scored (in a season): 108 (1962/63)
Fewest goals scored: 41 (1971/72), (1984/85)
Most goals conceded: 112 (1959/60)
Fewest goals conceded: 38 (1984/85)
Most clean sheets: 20 (1974/75), (1976/77), (1984/85)
Fewest clean sheets: 3 (1931/32)

Top and bottom
Mansfield recorded their highest League win, 9-2 against Rotherham in 1932. Thirteen months later the boot was on the other foot as they suffered their heaviest League defeat, 8-1 against Walsall.

Strange but true
Decathlete and Olympic gold medallist Daley Thompson, the greatest athlete in the world in the 1980s, was Mansfield's unused substitute against Cardiff on 16th December, 1995.

ON THE RUN
Successive games unbeaten: 20 (14-Feb-1976)
Successive games without a win: 12 (06-Apr-1959), (03-Mar-1974), (10-Nov-1979)
Successive wins: 7 (28-Apr-1962), (13-Sep-1991)
Successive defeats: 7 (18-Jan-1947)
Successive draws: 5 (18-Oct-1986)
Successive games without scoring: 5 (04-Mar-1978)
Successive games without conceding: 6 (13-Oct-1984)

WIN, LOSE OR DRAW
Most wins (in a season): 28 (1974/75), (1976/77)
Fewest wins: 8 (1971/72), (1990/91)
Most draws: 20 (1971/72)
Fewest draws: 6 (1959/60), (1960/61), (1961/62)
Most defeats: 25 (1959/60)
Fewest defeats: 6 (1974/75)

THEIR LEAGUE RECORD

P	W	D	L	F	A
2648	965	687	996	3938	3931

MIDDLESBROUGH

FIRST TIME
First League Game:
Away v Lincoln City
(02-Sep-1899)
Result: Lost 0-3
Final position: 14th

KICKIN' OFF
Successive wins at start of season: 4 (1925/26),
(1993/94), (1994/95)
Successive defeats at start of season: 3 (1905/06),
(1926/27), (1984/85),
(1988/89)
Successive unbeaten games at start of season: 10 (1910/11)

HIGHS AND LOWS
Biggest home win: 9-0 v Brighton & Hove A.
(23-Aug-1958)
Biggest away win: 7-1 v Blackburn Rovers (29-Nov-1947), 7-1 v Derby County (29-Aug-1959)
Biggest home defeat: 0-5 v Bury (12-Feb-1910)
0-5 v Huddersfield Town (25-Aug-1962)
Biggest away defeat: 0-9 v Blackburn Rovers (06-Nov-1954)
Most points (3 for a win): 94, Division 3 (1986/87)
Most points (2 for a win): 65, Division 2 (1973/74)
Least points (3 for a win): 39, Division 1 (1981/82)
39, Division 1 (1988/89), Premier (1996/97)
Least points (2 for a win): 22, Division 1 (1923/24)
Highest finish: 3, Division 1 (1913/14)
Lowest finish: 2, Division 3 (1966/67), (1986/87)

GOALS, GOALS, GOALS
Most goals scored (in a season): 122 (1926/27)
Fewest goals scored: 34 (1981/82)
Most goals conceded: 91 (1953/54)
Fewest goals conceded: 30 (1973/74), (1986/87)
Most clean sheets: 27 (1986/87)
Fewest clean sheets: 4 (1927/28)

Fabrizio
Ravanelli

Absolutely Fab
Fabrizio Ravanelli became the most expensive player in the club's history when he moved from European Cup holders Juventus to Middlesbrough in the summer of 1997 for £7.5 million. The Italian scored a hat-trick on his Boro debut in the 3-3 draw with Liverpool.

ON THE RUN
Successive games unbeaten: 24 (08-Sep-1973)
Successive games without a win: 19 (03-Oct-1981)
Successive wins: 9 (16-Feb-1974)
Successive defeats: 8 (25-Aug-1954)
Successive draws: 8 (03-Apr-1971)
Successive games without scoring: 4 (11 times)
Successive games without conceding: 7 (07-Nov-1987)

WIN, LOSE OR DRAW
Most wins (in a season): 28 (1986/87)
Fewest wins: 7 (1923/24)
Most draws: 19 (1924/25)
Fewest draws: 2 (1925/26)
Most defeats: 27 (1923/24)
Fewest defeats: 4 (1973/74)

THEIR LEAGUE RECORD

P	W	D	L	F	A
3584	1360	864	1360	5461	5304

MILLWALL

FIRST TIME

First League Game:
Home v Bristol Rovers
(28-Aug-1920)
Result: Won 2-0
Final position: 7th

KICKIN' OFF

Successive wins at start of season: 6 (1934/35)
Successive defeats at start of season: 5 (1929/30)
Successive unbeaten games at start of season: 19 (1959/60)

HIGHS AND LOWS

Biggest home win: 9-1 v Torquay Utd (29-Aug-1927), 9-1 v Coventry City (19-Nov-1927)
Biggest away win: 6-1 v Crystal Palace (07-May-1927), 6-1 v Bristol Rovers (24-Dec-1927), 6-1 v Manchester City (17-Sep-1938), 6-1 v Ipswich Town (21-Mar-1953), 5-0 v Barrow (06-Feb-1965)
Biggest home defeat: 1-7 v Bury (21-Feb-1948)
Biggest away defeat: 1-8 v Plymouth Argyle (16-Jan-1932)
Most points (3 for a win): 90, Division 3 (1984/85)
Most points (2 for a win): 65, Division 3(S) (1927/28) 65, Division 3 (1965/66)
Least points (3 for a win): 26, Division 1 (1989/90)
Least points (2 for a win): 29, Division 2 (1947/48)
Highest finish: 10, Division 1 (1988/89)
Lowest finish: 9, Division 4 (1958/59)

GOALS, GOALS, GOALS

Most goals scored (in a season): 127 (1927/28)
Fewest goals scored: 38 (1921/22)
Most goals conceded: 100 (1955/56)
Fewest goals conceded: 30 (1920/21)
Most clean sheets: 25 (1920/21)
Fewest clean sheets: 5 (1989/90)

Home banker

In 1967, Millwall started a record run of 59 games unbeaten at home.

Desperate Den

Millwall's old ground, The Den, was closed five times by the FA for crowd disturbances - an unfortunate record for The Lions. Their new stadium, again known as The Den, is one of the smartest in the country.

Lord help us!

Millwall's first home was in the back garden of a local tavern called the Lord Nelson back in 1886.

ON THE RUN

Successive games unbeaten: 19 (22-Aug-1959)
Successive games without a win: 20 (26-Dec-1989)
Successive wins: 10 (10-Mar-1928)
Successive defeats: 11 (10-Apr-1929)
Successive draws: 5 (21-Sep-1929), (08-Dec-1951), (03-Oct-1959), (22-Dec-1973)
Successive games without scoring: 6 (20-Dec-1947), (5-Apr-1997)
Successive games without conceding: 11 (27-Feb-1926)

WIN, LOSE OR DRAW

Most wins (in a season): 30 (1927/28)
Fewest wins: 5 (1989/90)
Most draws: 18 (1921/22), (1922/23)
Fewest draws: 4 (1949/50)
Most defeats: 26 (1957/58)
Fewest defeats: 6 (1971/72)

THEIR LEAGUE RECORD

P	W	D	L	F	A
3052	1196	805	1051	4411	4119

NEWCASTLE

FIRST TIME
First League Game:
Away v Woolwich Arsenal
(02-Sep-1893)
Result: Drew 2-2
Final position: 4th

KICKIN' OFF
Successive wins at start of season: 11 (1992/93)
Successive defeats at start of season: 4 (1934/35)
Successive unbeaten games at start of season: 11 (1950/51), (1992/93), (1994/95)

HIGHS AND LOWS
Biggest home win: 13-0 v Newport County (05-Oct-1946)
Biggest away win: 6-0 v Everton (26-Oct-1912), 7-1 v Manchester Utd (10-Sep-1927), 6-0 v Walsall (29-Sep-1962)
Biggest home defeat: 1-9 v Sunderland (05-Dec-1908)
Biggest away defeat: 0-9 v Burton Wanderers (15-Apr-1895)
Most points (3 for a win): 96, Division 1 (1992/93)
Most points (2 for a win): 57, Division 2 (1964/65)
Least points (3 for a win): 31, Division 1 (1988/89)
Least points (2 for a win): 22, Division 1 (1977/78)
Highest finish: 1, Division 1 (1904/05), (1906/07), (1908/09), (1926/27)
Lowest finish: 20, Division 2 (1991/92)

GOALS, GOALS, GOALS
Most goals scored (in a season): 98 (1951/52)
Fewest goals scored: 30 (1980/81)
Most goals conceded: 109 (1960/61)
Fewest goals conceded: 35 (1969/70)
Most clean sheets: 20 (1947/48)
Fewest clean sheets: 3 (1933/34), (1960/61)

Strange but true!
Alan Shearer became the most expensive player in world football when he moved from Blackburn to Newcastle for £15 million in 1996. He finished the season with 25 Premiership goals, the third successive time he had led the top-flight goalcharts.

Alan Shearer

ON THE RUN
Successive games unbeaten: 14 (22-Apr-1950)
Successive games without a win: 21 (14-Jan-1978)
Successive wins: 13 (25-Apr-1992)
Successive defeats: 10 (23-Aug-1977)
Successive draws: 4 (14 times)
Successive games without scoring: 6 (31-Dec-1938), (29-Oct-1988)
Successive games without conceding: 6 (06-Mar-1982)

WIN, LOSE OR DRAW
Most wins (in a season): 29 (1992/93)
Fewest wins: 6 (1977/78)
Most draws: 17 (1990/91)
Fewest draws: 4 (1902/03), (1934/35)
Most defeats: 26 (1977/78)
Fewest defeats: 8 (1992/93), (1995/96), (1996/97)

THEIR LEAGUE RECORD

P	W	D	L	F	A
3750	1558	861	1331	6041	5377

NORTHAMPTON

FIRST TIME

First League Game:
Away v Grimsby Town
(28-Aug-1920)
Result: Lost 0-2
Final position: 14th

KICKIN' OFF

Successive wins at start of season: 7 (1955/56)
Successive defeats at start of season: 4 (1984/85)
Successive unbeaten games at start of season: 11 (1983/84)

HIGHS AND LOWS

Biggest home win: 10-0 v Walsall (05-Nov-1927)
Biggest away win: 5-0 v Brighton & Hove A.
(12-Apr-1963), 5-0 v Peterborough Utd (12-Oct-1985),
5-0 v Crewe Alexandra (28-Nov-1986), 5-0 v Chester City
(15-Aug-1987)
Biggest home defeat: 0-8 v Walsall (08-Apr-1947)
Biggest away defeat: 0-8 v Southampton (24-Dec-1921), 0-8 v Lincoln City (25-Oct-1980)
Most points (3 for a win): 99, Division 4 (1986/87)
Most points (2 for a win): 68, Division 4 (1975/76)
Least points (3 for a win): 38, Division 3 (1993/94)
Least points (2 for a win): 30, Division 2 (1966/67)
Highest finish: 21, Division 1 (1965/66)
Lowest finish: 23, Division 4 (1972/73), (1984/85)

GOALS, GOALS, GOALS

Most goals scored (in a season): 109 (1952/53), (1962/63)
Fewest goals scored: 40 (1972/73)
Most goals conceded: 92 (1965/66)
Fewest goals conceded: 40 (1975/76)
Most clean sheets: 19 (1975/76)
Fewest clean sheets: 3 (1965/66)

Cob a load of that!

In 1997, The Cobblers made their first Wembley appearance, beating Swansea 1-0 in the Third Division Play-off Final.

Strange but true

When Northampton beat Sutton Town 10-0 in an FA Cup tie in 1907-08, Herbert Chapman, who later took Huddersfield to a League Championship treble as manager, scored twice and had three other goals disallowed.

Bye bye

Northampton couldn't play home games in August at their old County Ground because Northants Cricket Club shared the stadium and had first use of the pitch in that month.

ON THE RUN

Successive games unbeaten: 21 (27-Sep-1986)
Successive games without a win: 18 (26-Mar-1969)
Successive wins: 8 (27-Aug-1960)
Successive defeats: 8 (26-Oct-1935)
Successive draws: 6 (18-Sep-1983)
Successive games without scoring: 7 (07-Apr-1939)
Successive games without conceding: 6 (03-Sep-1930)
(25-Oct-1975)

WIN, LOSE OR DRAW

Most wins (in a season): 30 (1986/87)
Fewest wins: 9 (1993/94)
Most draws: 19 (1987/88)
Fewest draws: 5 (1926/27), (1951/52), (1984/85)
Most defeats: 27 (1984/85)
Fewest defeats: 6 (1964/65)

THEIR LEAGUE RECORD

P	W	D	L	F	A
3096	1187	717	1192	4688	4613

NORWICH

HIGHS AND LOWS

Biggest home win: 10-2 v Coventry City (15-Mar-1930), 8-0 v Walsall (29-Dec-1951)
Biggest away win: 8-1 v Shrewsbury Town (13-Sep-1952)
Biggest home defeat: 1-6 v Bournemouth & BA (26-Dec-1946)
Biggest away defeat: 0-7 v Walsall (13-Sep-1930) 0-7 v Sheffield Wed. (19-Nov-1938)
Most points (3 for a win): 84, Division 2 (1985/86)
Most points (2 for a win): 64, Division 3(S) (1950/51)
Least points (3 for a win): 43, Premier (1994/95)
Least points (2 for a win): 28, Division 3(S) (1930/31), (1946/47)
Highest finish: 3, Premier (1992/93)
Lowest finish: 24, Division 3(S) (1956/57)

FIRST TIME

First League Game:
Away v Plymouth Argyle (28-Aug-1920)
Result: Drew 1-1
Final position: 16th

KICKIN' OFF

Successive wins at start of season: 4 (1988/89)
Successive defeats at start of season: 4 (1938/39), (1963/64)
Successive unbeaten games at start of season: 13 (1971/72)

Strange but true

To protect the area against German bombers during the war, two gun platforms were built in the club car park and manned by a guard.

GOALS, GOALS, GOALS

Most goals scored (in a season): 99 (1952/53)
Fewest goals scored: 36 (1972/73)
Most goals conceded: 100 (1946/47)
Fewest goals conceded: 36 (1971/72)
Most clean sheets: 20 (1974/75)
Fewest clean sheets: 5 (1928/29), (1946/47), (1963/64)

Birds Nest

Norwich's nickname, The Canaries, derives from the fact that they wore green and yellow kit and played at a ground called The Nest in 1906.

Model look

Norwich's new kit for the 1997-98 season was designed by top fashion designer Bruce Oldfield, a friend of club director and TV cook, Delia Smith. She had taken her place on the Canaries board the previous year.

ON THE RUN

Successive games unbeaten: 20 (31-Aug-1950)
Successive games without a win: 25 (22-Sep-1956)
Successive wins: 10 (23-Nov-1985)
Successive defeats: 7 (04-Sep-1935)
Successive draws: 7 (09-Dec-1978), (15-Jan-1994)
Successive games without scoring: 5 (21-Feb-1925), (12-Mar-1927), (12-Dec-1992)
Successive games without conceding: 4 (10 times)

WIN, LOSE OR DRAW

Most wins (in a season): 26 (1951/52)
Fewest wins: 7 (1973/74), (1978/79)
Most draws: 23 (1978/79)
Fewest draws: 5 (1938/39), (1981/82)
Most defeats: 24 (1930/31), (1938/39), (1946/47)
Fewest defeats: 6 (1933/34), (1971/72)

THEIR LEAGUE RECORD

P	W	D	L	F	A
2974	1086	802	1086	4273	4329

NOTTM FOREST

FIRST TIME

First League Game:
Away v Everton
(03-Sep-1892)
Result: Drew 2-2
Final position: 10th

KICKIN' OFF

Successive wins at start of
season: 4 (1950/51),
(1979/80)
Successive defeats at start
of season: 6 (1913/14)
Successive unbeaten
games at start of season:
16 (1978/79)

HIGHS AND LOWS

Biggest home win: 12-0 v Leicester Fosse (21-Apr-1909)
Biggest away win: 7-1 v Port Vale (02-Feb-1957)
7-1 v Sheffield Wed. (01-Apr-1995)
Biggest home defeat: 0-6 v The Wednesday (23-Apr-
1910), 1-7 v Birmingham City (07-Mar-1959)
Biggest away defeat: 0-8 v West Bromwich Alb.
(16-Apr-1900), 0-8 v Leeds City (29-Nov-1913),
0-8 v Birmingham (10-Mar-1920), 1-9 v Blackburn
Rovers (10-Apr-1937), 0-8 v Burnley (21-Nov-1959)
Most points (3 for a win): 83, Division 1 (1993/94)
Most points (2 for a win): 70, Division 3(S) (1950/51)
Least points (3 for a win): 34, Premier (1996/97)
Least points (2 for a win): 23, Division 2 (1913/14)
Highest finish: 1, Division 1 (1977/78)
Lowest finish: 4, Division 3(S) (1949/50)

GOALS, GOALS, GOALS

Most goals scored (in a season): 110 (1950/51)
Fewest goals scored: 29 (1924/25)
Most goals conceded: 90 (1936/37)
Fewest goals conceded: 24 (1977/78)
Most clean sheets: 25 (1977/78)
Fewest clean sheets: 3 (1897/98)

Strange but true

A referee's whistle was used for the first time in a game between Forest and Sheffield Norfolk in 1878.

A date to remember

When Forest's side won the League Championship in 1978 they went one full calendar year undefeated in the League.

For the record

Forest set a Premiership record of 25 games without defeat in 1995 before they were beaten by Newcastle 3-1 on the 23rd December.

ON THE RUN

Successive games unbeaten: 42 (26-Nov-1977)
Successive games without a win: 16 (21-Mar-1913)
Successive wins: 7 (24-Dec-1892), (20-Oct-1906),
(29-Aug-1921), (09-May-1979)
Successive defeats: 14 (21-Mar-1913)
Successive draws: 7 (29-Apr-1978)
Successive games without scoring: 6 (02-Sep-1970)
Successive games without conceding: 6
(26-Nov-1921), (19-Apr-1980)

WIN, LOSE OR DRAW

Most wins (in a season):
30 (1950/51)
Fewest wins: 6 (1924/25),
(1996/97)
Most draws: 18 (1969/70),
(1978/79)
Fewest draws: 4 (1893/94),
(1906/07)
Most defeats: 25 (1971/72)
Fewest defeats: 3
(1977/78), (1978/79)

THEIR LEAGUE RECORD

P	W	D	L	F	A
3766	1414	943	1409	5543	5494

NOTTS COUNTY

HIGHS AND LOWS

Biggest home win: 10-0 v Burslem Port Vale (26-Feb-1895), 11-1 v Newport County (15-Jan-1949)
Biggest away win: 8-1 v Accrington (12-Oct-1889)
Biggest home defeat: 0-7 v Preston North End (03-Nov-1888)
Biggest away defeat: 1-9 v Aston Villa (29-Sep-1888), 1-9 v Blackburn Rovers (16-Nov-1889), 0-8 v Newcastle Utd (26-Oct-1901), 0-8 v West Bromwich Alb. (25-Oct-1919), 1-9 v Portsmouth (09-Apr-1927)
Most points (3 for a win): 87, Division 3 (1989/90)
Most points (2 for a win): 69, Division 4 (1970/71)
Least points (3 for a win): 35, Division 2 (1996/97)
Least points (2 for a win): 23, Division 1 (1912/13)
Highest finish: 3, Division 1 (1890/91), (1900/01)
Lowest finish: 20, Division 4 (1966/67)

FIRST TIME

First League Game:
Away v Everton
(15-Sep-1888)
Result: Lost 1-2
Final position: 11th

KICKIN' OFF

Successive wins at start of season: 4 (1893/94), (1896/97), (1928/29)
Successive defeats at start of season: 5 (1963/64)
Successive unbeaten games at start of season: 18 (1930/31)

Strange but true

Only 300 fans watched a League game between Notts County and Crewe in 1894.

GOALS, GOALS, GOALS

Most goals scored (in a season): 107 (1959/60)
Fewest goals scored: 28 (1912/13)
Most goals conceded: 97 (1934/35)
Fewest goals conceded: 31 (1893/94), (1924/25)
Most clean sheets: 23 (1922/23)
Fewest clean sheets: 1 (1888/89)

Mills and boom

Paddy Mills scored five goals for County in a 9-0 win against Barnsley in 1927.

Pride of the County

County are thought to be the oldest existing professional club in the world and were founded in 1862. Their first ground was situated next to Nottingham Castle and club members arranged games between themselves before The Magpies moved on to Meadows Cricket Ground.

WIN, LOSE OR DRAW

Most wins (in a season): 30 (1970/71)
Fewest wins: 7 (1912/13), (1996/97)
Most draws: 18 (1968/69)
Fewest draws: 5 (1889/90), (1894/95), (1903/04), (1926/27), (1948/49)
Most defeats: 28 (1963/64)
Fewest defeats: 7 (1890/91), (1893/94), (1896/97), (1930/31), (1970/71), (1980/81)

ON THE RUN

Successive games unbeaten: 19 (26-Apr-1930)
Successive games without a win: 20 (3-Dec-1996)
Successive wins: 8 (17-Jan-1914)
Successive defeats: 7 (14-Sep-1912), (08-Apr-1933), (03-Sep-1983)
Successive draws: 5 (02-Dec-1978)
Successive games without scoring: 5 (30-Nov-1912), (25-Jan-1964), (29-Dec-1984)
Successive games without conceding: 6 (11-Mar-1969), (21-Oct-1970)

THEIR LEAGUE RECORD

P	W	D	L	F	A
3974	1471	973	1530	5766	5911

OLDHAM

FIRST TIME

First League Game:
Away v Stoke (07-Sep-1907)
Result: Won 3-1
Final position: 3rd

KICKIN' OFF

Successive wins at start of season: 5 (1929/30), (1990/91)
Successive defeats at start of season: 4 (1960/61)
Successive unbeaten games at start of season: 16 (1990/91)

GOALS, GOALS, GOALS

Most goals scored (in a season): 95 (1962/63)
Fewest goals scored: 35 (1922/23), (1924/25)
Most goals conceded: 95 (1934/35)
Fewest goals conceded: 39 (1909/10)
Most clean sheets: 17 (1923/24), (1924/25), (1952/53), (1973/74)
Fewest clean sheets: 3 (1955/56)

HIGHS AND LOWS

Biggest home win: 11-0 v Southport (26-Dec-1962)
Biggest away win: 6-0 v Darlington (27-Sep-1947)
Biggest home defeat: 0-6 v Aston Villa (27-Nov-1971)
Biggest away defeat: 4-13 v Tranmere Rovers (26-Dec-1935), 0-9 v Hull City (05-Apr-1958)
Most points (3 for a win): 88, Division 2 (1990/91)
Most points (2 for a win): 62, Division 3 (1973/74)
Least points (3 for a win): 40, Premier (1993/94)
Least points (2 for a win): 25, Division 2 (1953/54)
Highest finish: 2, Division 1 (1914/15)
Lowest finish: 23, Division 4 (1959/60)

Plastic-scene

The Latics are one of only four clubs to have had an artificial pitch installed in the Football League.

Strange but true

The first turf cut at Oldham's Boundary Park was done with a silver spade which is now kept in the VIP suite at the ground.

Roof-top support

In the club's early days, Boundary Park had a flat roof on which spectators used to stand. The Latics manager at the time, David Ashworth, who sported a bowler hat, would run up and down the roof watching the action. In one game, against Leeds in 1906, he ran straight off the edge and had to be dragged to safety.

Name change

Their nickname The Latics has evolved over the years from their original nickname, Athletic.

ON THE RUN

Successive games unbeaten: 20 (01-May-1990)
Successive games without a win: 17 (04-Sep-1920)
Successive wins: 10 (12-Jan-1974)
Successive defeats: 8 (27-Dec-1932), (15-Dec-1934)
Successive draws: 5 (26-Dec-1982)
Successive games without scoring: 6 (04-Feb-1922)
Successive games without conceding: 6 (26-Feb-1983), (23-Aug-1986)

WIN, LOSE OR DRAW

Most wins (in a season): 25 (1973/74), (1990/91)
Fewest wins: 8 (1953/54), (1959/60)
Most draws: 21 (1988/89)
Fewest draws: 4 (1958/59)
Most defeats: 26 (1934/35), (1958/59), (1959/60)
Fewest defeats: 8 (1909/10), (1990/91)

THEIR LEAGUE RECORD

P	W	D	L	F	A
3402	1253	862	1287	4941	5032

OXFORD UNITED

HIGHS AND LOWS

Biggest home win: 7-0 v Barrow (19-Dec-1964)
Biggest away win: 4-0 v Stockport County
(26-Apr-1968), 4-0 v Bristol City (10-Oct-1970), 4-0 v
Fulham (18-Oct-1980), 5-1 v Orient (04-Dec-1982), 5-1 v
Walsall (26-Dec-1988)
Biggest home defeat: 0-4 v Gillingham (20-Nov-1965),
0-4 v Southampton (25-Sep-1974), 0-4 v Watford (13-
May-1989), 0-4 v Charlton Athletic (12-Feb-1994)
Biggest away defeat: 0-6 v Liverpool (22-Mar-1986)
Most points (3 for a win): 95, Division 3 (1983/84)
Most points (2 for a win): 61, Division 4 (1964/65)
Least points (3 for a win): 31, Division 1 (1987/88)
Least points (2 for a win): 33, Division 2 (1968/69),
(1975/76)
Lowest finish: 18, Division 4 (1962/63), (1963/64)

FIRST TIME

First League Game:
Away v Barrow
(18-Aug-1962)
Result: Lost 2-3
Final position: 18th

KICKIN' OFF

**Successive wins at start of
season:** 4 (1982/83),
(1994/95)
**Successive defeats at start
of season:** 5 (1991/92)
**Successive unbeaten
games at start of season:** 9
(1983/84), (1994/95)

Brothers in arms

Former Manchester United
and Aston Villa manager
Ron Atkinson played in the
same Oxford side as his
brother Graham.

GOALS, GOALS, GOALS

Most goals scored (in a season): 91 (1983/84)
Fewest goals scored: 34 (1968/69)
Most goals conceded: 80 (1985/86), (1987/88)
Fewest goals conceded: 36 (1984/85)
Most clean sheets: 21 (1964/65)
Fewest clean sheets: 6 (1985/86), (1991/92)

Ground share

Sheep and horses used to
graze on Oxford's Manor
Ground in the 1920s and
they shared the pitch with
cricket, bowls and
tennis clubs.

To the Manor scorn

When Oxford drew 1-1 with Notts County in April 1996, it
was the first goal they had conceded at their Manor
Ground home in 10 hours, 44 minutes of play.

ON THE RUN

Successive games unbeaten: 20 (17-Mar-1984)
Successive games without a win: 27 (14-Nov-1987)
Successive wins: 6 (14-Jan-1967), (16-Mar-1968),
(04-Dec-1982), (06-Apr-1985)
Successive defeats: 7 (04-May-1991)
Successive draws: 5 (05-Sep-1962), (31-Oct-1964),
(24-Nov-1967), (07-Oct-1978)
Successive games without scoring: 6 (26-Mar-1988)
Successive games without conceding: 5 (21-Dec-1963)

WIN, LOSE OR DRAW

Most wins (in a season): 28
(1983/84)
Fewest wins: 6 (1987/88)
Most draws: 19 (1990/91)
Fewest draws: 7 (1972/73)
Most defeats: 23 (1993/94)
Fewest defeats: 7
(1983/84)

THEIR LEAGUE RECORD

P	W	D	L	F	A
1560	542	443	575	2021	2037

PETERBOROUGH

FIRST TIME

First League Game:
Home v Wrexham
(20-Aug-1960)
Result: Won 3-0
Final position: 1st

KICKIN' OFF

Successive wins at start of
season: 4 (1961/62)
Successive defeats at start
of season: 4 (1972/73)
Successive unbeaten
games at start of season: 8
(1973/74)

HIGHS AND LOWS

Biggest home win: 8-1 v Oldham Athletic
(26-Nov-1969), 7-0 v Barrow (09-Oct-1971)
Biggest away win: 6-0 v Stockport County
(04-Feb-1961), 7-1 v Mansfield Town (26-Mar-1966)
Biggest home defeat: 0-5 v Northampton Town
(12-Oct-1985)
Biggest away defeat: 0-7 v Tranmere Rovers
(29-Oct-1985)
Most points (3 for a win): 82, Division 4 (1981/82)
Most points (2 for a win): 66, Division 4 (1960/61)
Least points (3 for a win): 37, Division 1 (1993/94)
Least points (2 for a win): 36, Division 3 (1978/79)
Highest finish: 10, Division 1 (1992/93)
Lowest finish: 19, Division 4 (1972/73)

GOALS, GOALS, GOALS

Most goals scored (in a season): 134 (1960/61)
Fewest goals scored: 44 (1978/79)
Most goals conceded: 82 (1961/62)
Fewest goals conceded: 33 (1977/78)
Most clean sheets: 25 (1977/78)
Fewest clean sheets: 7 (1961/62), (1965/66), (1972/73)

Magnificent Seven

Mick Drewery kept seven consecutive clean sheets for
Posh from 6th October to 10th November 1973.

That's Posh

They are said to be nicknamed Posh after one of their
former managers, Pat Tirrel, was quoted as saying:
"I'm looking for posh players for a posh new team."

ON THE RUN

Successive games unbeaten: 17 (17-Dec-1960)
Successive games without a win: 17 (23-Sep-1978)
Successive wins: 9 (01-Feb-1992)
Successive defeats: 5 (31-Dec-1988), (13-Apr-1994),
(8-Oct-1996)
Successive draws: 8 (18-Dec-1971)
Successive games without scoring: 5 (18-Jan-1964)
Successive games without conceding: 7 (06-Oct-1973)

Paying the penalty

In 1967, Peterborough
United became the first
League club to be demoted
by the authorities after
offering irregular bonuses
to their players. They were
fourth in the division at the
time and had to play out the
rest of the League season
knowing they would be
relegated at the
end of it.

WIN, LOSE OR DRAW

Most wins (in a season): 28
(1960/61)
Fewest wins: 8 (1993/94)
Most draws: 18 (1975/76),
(1980/81), (1994/95)
Fewest draws: 6 (1961/62)
Most defeats: 25 (1993/94)
Fewest defeats: 8
(1960/61), (1973/74),
(1990/91)

THEIR LEAGUE RECORD

P	W	D	L	F	A
1702	646	486	570	2466	2270

PLYMOUTH

HIGHS AND LOWS

Biggest home win: 8-1 v Millwall (16-Jan-1932), 7-0 v Doncaster Rovers (05-Sep-1936)
Biggest away win: 8-1 v Hartlepool Utd (07-May-1994)
Biggest home defeat: 0-6 v Reading (25-Aug-1956)
Biggest away defeat: 0-9 v Stoke City (17-Dec-1960)
Most points (3 for a win): 87, Division 3 (1985/86)
Most points (2 for a win): 68, Division 3(S) (1929/30)
Least points (3 for a win): 46, Division 2 (1994/95)
Least points (2 for a win): 27, Division 2 (1967/68)
Highest finish: 4, Division 2 (1931/32), (1952/53)
Lowest finish: 4, Division 3 (1995/96)

FIRST TIME

First League Game:
Home v Norwich City
(28-Aug-1920)
Result: Drew 1-1
Final position: 11th

KICKIN' OFF

Successive wins at start of season: 4 (1925/26)
Successive defeats at start of season: 5 (1956/57)
Successive unbeaten games at start of season: 18 (1929/30)

Strange but true

On January 2nd, 1927 Plymouth beat Aberdare Athletic 6-5 away in a Division Three (South) match.

GOALS, GOALS, GOALS

Most goals scored (in a season): 107 (1925/26), (1951/52)
Fewest goals scored: 35 (1920/21)
Most goals conceded: 96 (1946/47)
Fewest goals conceded: 24 (1921/22)
Most clean sheets: 25 (1921/22)
Fewest clean sheets: 3 (1946/47)

Bother for Boro

Plymouth's 5-1 win over Scarborough in the 1996-97 season condemned Boro to their seventh straight League defeat - a club record.

Pilgrims Progress

The Pilgrims became only the sixth team outside the top two divisions to reach an FA Cup Semi-Final when they lost 1-0 to Watford in 1984.

Lee Phillips became Plymouth's youngest ever first team player when he made his debut in the 2-0 win over Gillingham on the 29th October, 1996 aged 16 years and 43 days.

WIN, LOSE OR DRAW

Most wins (in a season): 30 (1929/30)
Fewest wins: 8 (1949/50), (1963/64), (1976/77)
Most draws: 21 (1920/21)
Fewest draws: 5 (1946/47)
Most defeats: 24 (1955/56), (1967/68), (1991/92), (1994/95)
Fewest defeats: 4 (1929/30)

ON THE RUN

Successive games unbeaten: 22 (20-Apr-1929)
Successive games without a win: 13 (27-Apr-1963)
Successive wins: 9 (22-Mar-1930), (08-Mar-1986)
Successive defeats: 9 (26-Apr-1947), (12-Oct-1963)
Successive draws: 5 (09-Feb-1929)
Successive games without scoring: 5 (11-Mar-1939), (20-Sep-1947), (11-Mar-1950)
Successive games without conceding: 6 (08-Sep-1924)

THEIR LEAGUE RECORD

P	W	D	L	F	A
3062	1183	787	1092	4595	4320

PORT VALE

FIRST TIME

First League Game:
Away v Small Heath
(03-Sep-1892)
Result: Lost 1-5
Final position: 11th

KICKIN' OFF

Successive wins at start of season: 7 (1893/94)
Successive defeats at start of season: 4 (1979/80)
Successive unbeaten games at start of season: 18 (1969/70)

HIGHS AND LOWS

Biggest home win: 9-1 v Chesterfield (24-Sep-1932), 8-0 v Gateshead (26-Dec-1958)
Biggest away win: 6-0 v Fulham (28-Mar-1987)
Biggest home defeat: 0-10 v Sheffield Utd (10-Dec-1892)
Biggest away defeat: 0-10 v Notts County (26-Feb-1895)
Most points (3 for a win): 89, Division 2 (1992/93)
Most points (2 for a win): 69, Division 3(N) (1953/54)
Least points (3 for a win): 43, Division 3 (1983/84)
Least points (2 for a win): 22, Division 2 (1956/57)
Highest finish: 5, Division 2 (1930/31)
Lowest finish: 20, Division 4 (1979/80)

GOALS, GOALS, GOALS

Most goals scored (in a season): 110 (1958/59)
Fewest goals scored: 39 (1894/95), (1899/1900), (1922/23)
Most goals conceded: 106 (1935/36)
Fewest goals conceded: 21 (1953/54)
Most clean sheets: 30 (1953/54)
Fewest clean sheets: 3 (1956/57)

70 up

During the 1995-96 season, Vale completed a League double over arch rivals Stoke City, their first such twin success for 70 years.

Vale bare a Rudge!

Vale manager John Rudge is the second-longest serving manager at one club in the game behind Crewe's Dario Gradi. He took over at Vale Park in March 1984 , Gradi became boss at Crewe a year earlier.

Taylor raid!

Midfielder Ian Taylor became Port Vale's record sale when he left the Midlands club to join Sheffield Wednesday in August 1994 for a fee of £1 million.

ON THE RUN

Successive games unbeaten: 19 (05-May-1969)
Successive games without a win: 17 (07-Dec-1991)
Successive wins: 8 (08-Apr-1893)
Successive defeats: 9 (09-Mar-1957)
Successive draws: 6 (26-Apr-1981)
Successive games without scoring: 4 (11 times)
Successive games without conceding: 7 (11-Feb-1922)

WIN, LOSE OR DRAW

Most wins (in a season): 30 (1929/30)
Fewest wins: 8 (1956/57)
Most draws: 20 (1977/78)
Fewest draws: 4 (1893/94), (1894/95), (1895/96), (1905/06), (1928/29)
Most defeats: 28 (1956/57)
Fewest defeats: 3 (1953/54)

THEIR LEAGUE RECORD

P	W	D	L	F	A
3582	1291	932	1359	4945	5148

PORTSMOUTH

HIGHS AND LOWS

Biggest home win: 9-1 v Notts County (09-Apr-1927)
Biggest away win: 5-0 v Wolverhampton W. (14-Feb-1925), 5-0 v Leicester City (09-Nov-1929), 5-0 v Everton (01-Sep-1948), 5-0 v Newcastle Utd (06-Apr-1949), 5-0 v Bolton Wanderers (20-Sep-1952), 5-0 v Newport County (05-Feb-1962), 5-0 v Preston North End (10-Feb-1973)
Biggest home defeat: 0-5 v Birmingham City (15-Oct-1955)
Biggest away defeat: 0-10 v Leicester City (20-Oct-1928)
Most points (3 for a win): 91, Division 3 (1982/83)
Most points (2 for a win): 65, Division 3 (1961/62)
Least points (3 for a win): 35, Division 1 (1987/88)
Least points (2 for a win): 21, Division 1 (1958/59)
Highest finish: 1, Division 1 (1948/49), (1949/50)
Lowest finish: 7, Division 4 (1978/79)

FIRST TIME

First League Game:
Home v Swansea Town
(28-Aug-1920)
Result: Won 3-0
Final position: 12th

KICKIN' OFF

Successive wins at start of season: 5 (1979/80)
Successive defeats at start of season: 4 (1953/54)
Successive unbeaten games at start of season: 13 (1948/49)

Shining Knight

Alan Knight established a record number of League appearances for a goalkeeper with one club when he played his 601st game on 13th January 1996.

GOALS, GOALS, GOALS

Most goals scored (in a season): 91 (1979/80)
Fewest goals scored: 32 (1975/76)
Most goals conceded: 112 (1958/59)
Fewest goals conceded: 28 (1986/87)
Most clean sheets: 25 (1923/24)
Fewest clean sheets: 1 (1958/59)

Strange but true!

Pompey 'keeper Matthew Reilly was behind one of the rule changes in the early years . He played Gaelic football back in his native Ireland and was used to avoiding opponents by bouncing the ball. The FA then acted to ban 'keepers from using their hands outside the penalty area after seeing him in action.

What a bargain

Fratton Park, formerly a market garden, cost the club £4,950 to purchase back in 1898.

ON THE RUN

Successive games unbeaten: 15 (16-Apr-1921), (18-Apr-1924)
Successive games without a win: 25 (29-Nov-1958)
Successive wins: 7 (19-Apr-1980), (22-Jan-1983)
Successive defeats: 9 (27-Mar-1959), (02-Sep-1959), (02-Mar-1963), (21-Oct-1975)
Successive draws: 5 (28-Sep-1977)
Successive games without scoring: 6 (14-Jan-1939), (12-Oct-1974), (27-Dec-1993)
Successive games without conceding: 8 (26-Aug-1922)

WIN, LOSE OR DRAW

Most wins (in a season): 27 (1961/62), (1982/83)
Fewest wins: 6 (1958/59)
Most draws: 19 (1981/82)
Fewest draws: 6 (1928/29)
Most defeats: 27 (1958/59)
Fewest defeats: 7 (1921/22), (1923/24)

THEIR LEAGUE RECORD

P	W	D	L	F	A
3006	1117	775	1114	4446	4418

PRESTON

FIRST TIME
First League Game:
Home v Burnley
(08-Sep-1888)
Result: Won 5-2
Final position: 1st

KICKIN' OFF
Successive wins at start of season: 6 (1888/89)
Successive defeats at start of season: 5 (1924/25), (1929/30)
Successive unbeaten games at start of season: 22 (1888/89)

HIGHS AND LOWS
Biggest home win: 10-0 v Stoke (14-Sep-1889)
Biggest away win: 7-0 v Notts County (03-Nov-1888)
Biggest home defeat: 0-7 v Blackpool (01-May-1948)
Biggest away defeat: 0-7 v Nottingham Forest (09-Apr-1927)
Most points (3 for a win): 90, Division 4 (1986/87)
Most points (2 for a win): 61, Division 3 (1970/71)
Least points (3 for a win): 43, Division 4 (1985/86)
Least points (2 for a win): 26, Division 1 (1924/25)
Highest finish: 1, Division 1 (1888/89), (1889/90)
Lowest finish: 23, Division 4 (1985/86)

Strange but true
Deepdale was the last ground to see its plastic pitch removed when it was dug up in 1994. One of the club's former managers, John Beck, who preferred the long ball style of play, would instruct the groundstaff to put more sand in the corners of the plastic pitch to hold the ball up when it was whacked into that area.

GOALS, GOALS, GOALS
Most goals scored (in a season): 100 (1927/28), (1957/58)
Fewest goals scored: 37 (1924/25), (1972/73)
Most goals conceded: 100 (1984/85)
Fewest goals conceded: 33 (1912/13)
Most clean sheets: 20 (1977/78)
Fewest clean sheets: 3 (1900/01)

In at the start
Preston were one of the founder members of the Football League in 1888, and that season won the Championship without losing a single game!

ON THE RUN
Successive games unbeaten: 23 (08-Sep-1888)
Successive games without a win: 15 (14-Apr-1923)
Successive wins: 14 (25-Dec-1950)
Successive defeats: 8 (01-Oct-1983), (22-Sep-1984)
Successive draws: 6 (24-Feb-1979)
Successive games without scoring: 6 (08-Apr-1897), (19-Nov-1960)
Successive games without conceding: 6 (14-Sep-1901), (09-Sep-1972)

WIN, LOSE OR DRAW
Most wins (in a season): 26 (1950/51), (1957/58), (1986/87)
Fewest wins: 8 (1897/98)
Most draws: 19 (1979/80)
Fewest draws: 5 (1894/95), (1909/10), (1950/51), (1953/54)
Most defeats: 26 (1924/25), (1984/85)
Fewest defeats: 4 (1889/90), (1903/04), (1912/13)

THEIR LEAGUE RECORD

P	W	D	L	F	A
3948	1522	978	1448	5958	5697

QPR

HIGHS AND LOWS

Biggest home win: 8-0 v Merthyr Town (09-Mar-1929)
Biggest away win: 7-1 v Mansfield Town (24-Sep-1966)
Biggest home defeat: 0-5 v Barnsley (21-Jan-1950)
Biggest away defeat: 0-7 v Portsmouth (05-Jan-1924),
0-7 v Southend Utd (07-Apr-1928), 0-7 v Coventry City
(04-Mar-1933), 0-7 v Torquay Utd (22-Apr-1935), 0-7 v
Barnsley (04-Nov-1950), 1-8 v Mansfield Town (15-Mar-
1965), 1-8 v Manchester Utd (19-Mar-1969)
Most points (3 for a win): 85, Division 2 (1982/83)
Most points (2 for a win): 67, Division 3 (1966/67)
Least points (3 for a win): 33, Premier (1995/96)
Least points (2 for a win): 18, Division 1 (1968/69)
Highest finish: 2, Division 1 (1975/76)
Lowest finish: 22, Division 3(S) (1923/24), (1925/26)

FIRST TIME

First League Game:
Home v Watford
(28-Aug-1920)
Result: Lost 1-2
Final position: 3rd

KICKIN' OFF

Successive wins at start of season: 5 (1947/48)
Successive defeats at start of season: 2 (10 times)
Successive unbeaten games at start of season: 12 (1947/48)

On the move

Rangers' record of having 12 different grounds is more than any other League club. They have played at Welford's Field, London Scottish Ground, Brondesbury, Home Farm, Kensal Rise Green, Gun Club Wormwood Scrubs, Kilburn Cricket Ground, Kensal Rise Athletic Club, Latimer Road, Agricultural Society Park Royal, White City and Loftus Road.

GOALS, GOALS, GOALS

Most goals scored (in a season): 111 (1961/62)
Fewest goals scored: 37 (1923/24), (1925/26)
Most goals conceded: 95 (1968/69)
Fewest goals conceded: 28 (1971/72)
Most clean sheets: 22 (1920/21), (1971/72)
Fewest clean sheets: 1 (1968/69)

Breaking new ground

Former England boss Terry Venables was the manager at QPR when they became the first League club to have a plastic pitch installed in 1981.

ON THE RUN

Successive games unbeaten: 20 (03-Dec-1966), (11-Mar-1972)
Successive games without a win: 20 (07-Dec-1968)
Successive wins: 8 (07-Nov-1931)
Successive defeats: 9 (25-Feb-1969)
Successive draws: 6 (14-Dec-1957)
Successive games without scoring: 6 (14-Mar-1925), (18-Mar-1939)
Successive games without conceding: 7 (07-Sep-1946) (07-Mar-1967)

WIN, LOSE OR DRAW

Most wins (in a season): 26 (1947/48), (1966/67), (1982/83)
Fewest wins: 4 (1968/69)
Most draws: 18 (1991/92)
Fewest draws: 3 (1930/31)
Most defeats: 28 (1968/69)
Fewest defeats: 5 (1966/67), (1972/73)

THEIR LEAGUE RECORD

P	W	D	L	F	A
2986	1182	750	1054	4464	4135

READING

FIRST TIME

First League Game:
Away v Newport County
(28-Aug-1920)
Result: Won 1-0
Final position: 20th

KICKIN' OFF

Successive wins at start of
season: 13 (1985/86)
Successive defeats at start
of season: 5 (1930/31)
Successive unbeaten
games at start of season:
14 (1973/74), (1985/86)

HIGHS AND LOWS

Biggest home win: 10-2 v Crystal Palace (04-Sep-1946),
8-0 v Southport (22-Apr-1970)
Biggest away win: 7-1 v Mansfield Town (12-Mar-1932),
6-0 v Aldershot (12-Mar-1949), 6-0 v Plymouth Argyle
(25-Aug-1956)
Biggest home defeat: 1-6 v Bristol City (04-Jan-1930),
2-7 v Bristol City (04-Oct-1947), 0-5 v Aldershot
(20-Aug-1955), 1-6 v C.Palace (21-Sep-1996)
Biggest away defeat: 0-7 v Preston North End
(27-Aug-1928), 0-7 v Blackpool (10-Nov-1928), 1-8 v
Burnley (13-Sep-1930)
Most points (3 for a win): 94, Division 3 (1985/86)
Most points (2 for a win): 65, Division 4 (1978/79)
Least points (3 for a win): 42, Division 2 (1987/88)
Least points (2 for a win): 30, Division 2 (1930/31)
Highest finish: 2, Division 1 (1994/95)
Lowest finish: 16, Division 4 (1971/72)

GOALS, GOALS, GOALS

Most goals scored (in a season): 112 (1951/52)
Fewest goals scored: 36 (1922/23)
Most goals conceded: 96 (1930/31)
Fewest goals conceded: 35 (1978/79)
Most clean sheets: 26 (1978/79)
Fewest clean sheets: 5 (1953/54)

Strange but true!

The Royals' number one fan
is the spoon-bending
psychic Uri Geller, who
claims his presence can
affect his team's
performances.

Simod Said

The Simod Cup was designed for First and Second
Division clubs only, with Reading becoming victorious
after defeating First Division Luton 4-1 in 1988.

Shaka up

Reading's record sale is
Shaka Hislop for £1.575m
to Newcastle in 1995.

ON THE RUN

Successive games unbeaten: 19 (21-Apr-1973)
Successive games without a win: 14 (30-Apr-1927)
Successive wins: 13 (17-Aug-1985)
Successive defeats: 6 (26-Apr-1930), (10-Mar-1971),
(14-Apr-1989)
Successive draws: 4 (21-Sep-1929), (28-Feb-1935)
(19-Dec-1964) , (01-Apr-1978), (26-Sep-1989)
Successive games without scoring: 6 (13-Apr-1925)
Successive games without conceding: 11 (28-Mar-1979)

WIN, LOSE OR DRAW

Most wins (in a season): 29
(1951/52), (1985/86)
Fewest wins: 10 (1922/23),
(1987/88)
Most draws: 19 (1973/74),
(1989/90)
Fewest draws: 2 (1935/36)
Most defeats: 24 (1930/31),
(1976/77)
Fewest defeats: 7
(1978/79)

THEIR LEAGUE RECORD

P	W	D	L	F	A
3122	1253	775	1094	4756	4398

ROCHDALE

HIGHS AND LOWS

Biggest home win: 7-0 v Walsall (24-Dec-1921), 8-1 v Chesterfield (18-Dec-1926), 7-0 v Hartlepools Utd (02-Nov-1957)
Biggest away win: 7-0 v York City (14-Jan-1939)
Biggest home defeat: 0-6 v Barrow (26-Mar-1932), 0-6 v Wrexham (17-Oct-1936), 0-6 v Plymouth Argyle (24-Feb-1973)
Biggest away defeat: 0-8 v Wrexham (28-Sep-1929), 1-9 v Tranmere Rovers (25-Dec-1931), 0-8 v Leyton Orient (20-Oct-1987)
Most points (3 for a win): 67, Division 4 (1991/92)
Most points (2 for a win): 62, Division 3(N) (1923/24)
Least points (3 for a win): 46, Division 4 (1981/82), (1983/84)
Least points (2 for a win): 11, Division 3(N) (1931/32)
Highest finish: 2, Division 3(N) (1923/24), (1926/27)
Lowest finish: 24, Division 4 (1977/78), (1979/80)

FIRST TIME

First League Game:
Home v Accrington Stanley (27-Aug-1921)
Result: Won 6-3
Final position: 20th

KICKIN' OFF

Successive wins at start of season: 4 (1927/28)
Successive defeats at start of season: 4 (1946/47)
Successive unbeaten games at start of season: 9 (1925/26), (1991/92)

Rock on Tommy

Comedian Tommy Cannon of the famous 'Cannon and Ball' double act was once a director at Spotland.

GOALS, GOALS, GOALS

Most goals scored (in a season): 105 (1926/27)
Fewest goals scored: 33 (1979/80)
Most goals conceded: 135 (1931/32)
Fewest goals conceded: 26 (1923/24)
Most clean sheets: 26 (1923/24)
Fewest clean sheets: 1 (1931/32)

London falling

On the 21st October 1995, Dale won 4-0 at Barnet to record their first away win at a London club in their history.

Dale's loss

During the 1974-75 season, striker Alan Taylor left Dale for West Ham and proceeded to win them the FA Cup, scoring twice in the Quarter-Final and Semi-Final and then grabbing both goals in their 2-0 win over Fulham at Wembley.

ON THE RUN

Successive games unbeaten: 20 (15-Sep-1923)
Successive games without a win: 28 (14-Nov-1931)
Successive wins: 8 (29-Sep-1969)
Successive defeats: 17 (14-Nov-1931)
Successive draws: 6 (17-Aug-1968)
Successive games without scoring: 9 (14-Mar-1980)
Successive games without conceding: 5 (21-Sep-1968), (14-Feb-1976)

WIN, LOSE OR DRAW

Most wins (in a season): 27 (1925/26)
Fewest wins: 2 (1973/74)
Most draws: 20 (1968/69)
Fewest draws: 3 (1931/32)
Most defeats: 33 (1931/32)
Fewest defeats: 5 (1923/24)

THEIR LEAGUE RECORD

P	W	D	L	F	A
3058	1008	774	1276	4162	4860

ROTHERHAM

FIRST TIME

First League Game:
Home v Nottingham Forest
(30-Aug-1919)
Result: Won 2-0
Final position: 17th

KICKIN' OFF

Successive wins at start of
season: 6 (1948/49)
Successive defeats at start
of season: 5 (1967/68)
Successive unbeaten
games at start of season:
11 (1948/49)

HIGHS AND LOWS

Biggest home win: 8-0 v Oldham Athletic
(26-May-1947)
Biggest away win: 8-1 v Carlisle Utd (04-Dec-1948)
8-1 v Crewe Alexandra (08-Sep-1973)
Biggest home defeat: 0-5 v Bury (11-Dec-1920), 0-5 v
Chester (07-Jan-1933), 1-6 v Sheffield Utd
(01-Mar-1958), 2-7 v Bournemouth (10-Oct-1972)
Biggest away defeat: 1-11 v Bradford City (25-Aug-
1928)
Most points (3 for a win): 82, Division 4 (1988/89)
Most points (2 for a win): 71, Division 3(N) (1950/51)
Least points (3 for a win): 35, Division 2 (1996/97)
Least points (2 for a win): 21, Division 3(N) (1924/25)
Highest finish: 3, Division 2 (1954/55)
Lowest finish: 15, Division 4 (1973/74)

GOALS, GOALS, GOALS

Most goals scored (in a season): 114 (1946/47)
Fewest goals scored: 32 (1921/22)
Most goals conceded: 113 (1929/30)
Fewest goals conceded: 32 (1980/81)
Most clean sheets: 24 (1980/81)
Fewest clean sheets: 3 (1957/58)

Merry Millers

In 1950-51, during their Division Three (North)
title- winning season, The Millers from Rotherham
completed 15 League and Cup matches
without defeat.

ON THE RUN

Successive games unbeaten: 18 (04-Nov-1950), (13-
Oct-1969)
Successive games without a win: 14 (30-Mar-1934),
(08-Oct-1977)
Successive wins: 9 (02-Feb-1982)
Successive defeats: 8 (07-Apr-1956)
Successive draws: 6 (13-Oct-1969)
Successive games without scoring: 5 (04-Apr-1986)
Successive games without conceding: 7 (13-Feb-1982)

Wembley wonders

The Merry Millers enjoyed
Wembley success in 1996
when they defeated
Shrewsbury 2-0 in the
Final of the Auto
Windscreens Cup Final.
Nigel Jemson, a Wembley
goalscoring winner with
Nottingham Forest was
twice on target.
But the club were
relegated in 1997 after
seven defeats in their first
eight games.

WIN, LOSE OR DRAW

Most wins (in a season): 31
(1950/51)
Fewest wins: 7 (1924/25),
(1996-97)
Most draws: 16 (1970/71),
(1987/88), (1988/89)
Fewest draws: 4 (1931/32)
(1954/55)
Most defeats: 28 (1924/25)
Fewest defeats: 6
(1950/51)

THEIR LEAGUE RECORD

P	W	D	L	F	A
3088	1154	737	1197	4565	4661

SCARBOROUGH

HIGHS AND LOWS

Biggest home win: 4-0 v Bolton Wanderers
(29-Aug-1987)
Biggest away win: 4-0 v Newport County
(12-Apr-1988), 4-0 v Doncaster Rovers (23-Apr-1994)
Biggest home defeat: 0-4 v Barnet (26-Oct-1991)
Biggest away defeat: 0-5 v Chester (6-Apr-1996)
Most points (3 for a win): 77, Division 4 (1988/89)
Least points (3 for a win): 34, Division 3 (1994/95)
Highest finish: 5, Division 4 (1988/89)
Lowest finish: 23, Division 3 (1995/96)

FIRST TIME

First League Game:
Home v Wolverhampton W.
(15-Aug-1987)
Result: Drew 2-2
Final position: 12th

KICKIN' OFF

Successive wins at start of
season: None
Successive defeats at start
of season: None
Successive unbeaten
games at start of season: 6
(1996/97)

New Boys

Scarborough are relatively new to League football after
they won promotion to the big time via the GM Vauxhall
Conference Championship in 1987.

Six hitters

Boro's first League victims
in the FA Cup, whilst they
were members of the
Midland League, were
Lincoln City, beaten 6-4 on
13 December 1930 in a
Second Round tie.

GOALS, GOALS, GOALS

Most goals scored (in a season): 67 (1988/89)
Fewest goals scored: 39 (19995/96)
Most goals conceded: 73 (1989/90)
Fewest goals conceded: 48 (1987/88)
Most clean sheets: 16 (1988/89)
Fewest clean sheets: 6 (1992/93), (1994/95),
(1996-97)

Nearly there

Scarborough were denied a club record 10 games
without defeat when Hartlepool beat them 4-2 to record
their first win in nine games in November 1996.

ON THE RUN

Successive games unbeaten: 9 (24-Sep-1988),
(20-Jan-1990), (26-Dec-1990), 28-Sep-1996)
Successive games without a win: 16 (17-Sep-1994)
Successive wins: 3 (8 times)
Successive defeats: 7 (19-March-96)
Successive draws: 4 (21-Nov-1987), (08-Oct-1988),
(27-Jan-1990)
Successive games without scoring: 4 (12-Mar-1988),
(9-Mar, 1996)
Successive games without conceding: 3 (01-Feb-1991)

WIN, LOSE OR DRAW

Most wins (in a season): 21
(1988/89)
Fewest wins: 8 (1994/95),
(1995-96)
Most draws: 16 (1995-96)
Fewest draws: 8 (1993/94)
Most defeats: 24 (1994/95)
Fewest defeats: 11
(1988/89)

THEIR LEAGUE RECORD

P	W	D	L	F	A
444	149	120	225	583	631

SCUNTHORPE

FIRST TIME
First League Game:
Home v Shrewsbury Town
(19-Aug-1950)
Result: Drew 0-0
Final position: 12th

KICKIN' OFF
Successive wins at start of
season: 2 (1996/97)
Successive defeats at start
of season: 5 (1963/64)
Successive unbeaten
games at start of season: 9
(1982/83)

HIGHS AND LOWS
Biggest home win: 8-1 v Luton Town (24-Apr-1965),
7-0 v Northampton Town (16-Oct-1993)
Biggest away win: 8-1 v Torquay (28-Oct-1995)
Biggest home defeat: 2-7 v Wigan Athletic
(12-Mar-1982), 1-6 v Southend Utd (30-Sep-1983),
0-5 v Doncaster Rovers (15-Apr-1995)
Biggest away defeat: 0-8 v Carlisle Utd (25-Dec-1952)
Most points (3 for a win): 83, Division 4 (1982/83)
Most points (2 for a win): 66, Division 3(N) (1957/58)
Least points (3 for a win): 42, Division 4 (1981/82)
Least points (2 for a win): 29, Division 4 (1974/75)
Highest finish: 4, Division 2 (1961/62)
Lowest finish: 24, Division 4 (1974/75)

Great Eight
United's eight away goals in
their victory at Torquay
United on 28 October 1995
established a club record
for Scunthorpe.

GOALS, GOALS, GOALS
Most goals scored (in a season): 88 (1957/58)
Fewest goals scored: 33 (1972/73)
Most goals conceded: 87 (1967/68)
Fewest goals conceded: 37 (1971/72)
Most clean sheets: 23 (1971/72)
Fewest clean sheets: 5 (1967/68)

Botham strikes
The most famous player to appear at Glanford Park must
be England cricketing legend Ian Botham who made 11
appearances between the years 1979 and 1984 for the
club as a robust centre-forward.

Jack's a giant
Jack Brownsword holds
the record number of
appearances for the club
at 599 between 1950
and 1965.

ON THE RUN
Successive games unbeaten: 15 (30-Nov-1957),
(13-Nov-1971)
Successive games without a win: 14 (20-Apr-1974),
(22-Mar-1975)
Successive wins: 6 (24-Aug-1954), (06-Nov-1965),
(18-Oct-1969)
Successive defeats: 7 (27-Jan-1973)
Successive draws: 6 (02-Jan-1984)
Successive games without scoring: 7 (19-Apr-1975)
Successive games without conceding: 6 (27-Jan-1990)

WIN, LOSE OR DRAW
Most wins (in a season): 29
(1957/58)
Fewest wins: 7 (1974/75)
Most draws: 20 (1980/81)
Fewest draws: 7 (1961/62)
Most defeats: 26 (1972/73)
Fewest defeats: 9
(1957/58), (1982/83),
(1987/88)

THEIR LEAGUE RECORD

P	W	D	L	F	A
2121	758	588	775	2940	2983

SHEFFIELD UTD

HIGHS AND LOWS

Biggest home win: 10-0 v Burnley (19-Jan-1929)
Biggest away win: 10-0 v Burslem Port Vale (10-Dec-1892)
Biggest home defeat: 1-7 v Huddersfield Town (12-Nov-1927)
Biggest away defeat: 1-8 v Arsenal (12-Apr-1930), 2-9 v Arsenal (24-Dec-1932), 3-10 v Middlesbrough (18-Nov-1933), 0-7 v Tottenham Hotspur (12-Nov-1949)
Most points (3 for a win): 96, Division 4 (1981/82)
Most points (2 for a win): 60, Division 2 (1952/53)
Least points (3 for a win): 42, Premier (1993/94)
Least points (2 for a win): 22, Division 1 (1975/76)
Highest finish: 1, Division 1 (1897/98)
Lowest finish: 1, Division 4 (1981/82)

FIRST TIME

First League Game:
Home v Lincoln City
(03-Sep-1892)
Result: Won 4-2
Final position: 2nd

KICKIN' OFF

Successive wins at start of season: 8 (1903/04)
Successive defeats at start of season: 4 (1966/67)
Successive unbeaten games at start of season: 22 (1899/1900)

Strange but true

The Blades were founded in 1889, after members of Yorkshire County Cricket Club formed a football club to complement their cricket side at Bramall Lane.

GOALS, GOALS, GOALS

Most goals scored (in a season): 102 (1925/26)
Fewest goals scored: 33 (1975/76)
Most goals conceded: 101 (1933/34)
Fewest goals conceded: 38 (1969/70)
Most clean sheets: 20 (1981/82), (1983/84)
Fewest clean sheets: 3 (1898/99)

Dual role

Sheffield United's Bramall Lane ground has hosted both FA Cup Finals and Test Match cricket in its 108 year history

He ate all the pies!

Billy 'Fatty' Foulke was one of United's first heroes. He once punched a hole through a dressing-room door after he was upset by a refereeing decision. And legend has it that he once arrived at the team's hotel early and ate his meal - and those of six of his team-mates.

ON THE RUN

Successive games unbeaten: 22 (02-Sep-1899)
Successive games without a win: 19 (27-Sep-1975)
Successive wins: 8 (06-Feb-1893), (05-Sep-1903), (01-Feb-1958), (14-Sep-1960)
Successive defeats: 7 (19-Aug-1975)
Successive draws: 5 (17-Sep-1898), (27-Dec-1938), (05-Mar-1994)
Successive games without scoring: 6 (20-Oct-1990), (04-Dec-1993)
Successive games without conceding: 7 (20-Mar-1971)

WIN, LOSE OR DRAW

Most wins (in a season): 27 (1981/82)
Fewest wins: 6 (1920/21) (1975/76)
Most draws: 18 (1920/21)
Fewest draws: 5 (1893/94), (1902/03), (1913/14), (1951/52), (1969/70)
Most defeats: 26 (1975/76)
Fewest defeats: 4 (1899/1900), (1981/82)

THEIR LEAGUE RECORD

P	W	D	L	F	A
3852	1539	934	1379	6080	5721

SHEFFIELD WED

FIRST TIME

First League Game:
Away v Notts County
(03-Sep-1892)
Result: Won 1-0
Final position: 12th

KICKIN' OFF

Successive wins at start of
season: 7 (1904/05)
Successive defeats at start
of season: 4 (1971/72)
Successive unbeaten
games at start of season:
15 (1983/84)

HIGHS AND LOWS

Biggest home win: 8-0 v Sunderland (26-Dec-1911),
9-1 v Birmingham (13-Dec-1930)
Biggest away win: 6-0 v Nottingham Forest
(23-Apr-1910), 6-0 v West Ham Utd (08-Dec-1951)
Biggest home defeat: 1-7 v Nottingham Forest
(01-Apr-1995)
Biggest away defeat: 0-10 v Aston Villa (05-Oct-1912)
Most points (3 for a win): 88, Division 2 (1983/84)
Most points (2 for a win): 62, Division 2 (1958/59)
Least points (3 for a win): 42, Division 1 (1988/89)
Least points (2 for a win): 21, Division 2 (1974/75)
Highest finish: 1, Division 1 (1902/03), (1903/04),
(1928/29), (1929/30)
Lowest finish: 20, Division 3 (1975/76)

GOALS, GOALS, GOALS

Most goals scored (in a season): 106 (1958/59)
Fewest goals scored: 28 (1919/20)
Most goals conceded: 100 (1954/55)
Fewest goals conceded: 34 (1983/84)
Most clean sheets: 17 (1978/79)
Fewest clean sheets: 4 (1931/32)

Gimme Five

The 1902-03 season saw
Wednesday amazingly win
five trophies: the First
Division, Midland League,
Sheffield Challenge Cup,
Wharncliffe Charity Cup
and the Plymouth Bowl.

Long and short

In November 1898, Wednesday were probably involved
in the longest and shortest game in British football
history. They were beating Aston Villa 3-1 when the
game was abandoned after 79 minutes because of bad
light. The last 11 minutes were played five months later
with Wednesday adding another goal to eventually
run out 4-1 winners.

ON THE RUN

Successive games unbeaten: 19 (10-Dec-1960)
Successive games without a win: 20 (23-Oct-1954),
(11-Jan-1975)
Successive wins: 9 (23-Apr-1904)
Successive defeats: 7 (07-Jan-1893), (24-Oct-1992)
Successive draws: 5 (22-Dec-1973)
Successive games without scoring: 8 (08-Mar-1975)
Successive games without conceding: 5 (09-Nov-
1912), (03-Apr-1926), (21-Feb-1961), (04-Apr-1992)

Strange but true

In their early days at Olive
Grove, Wednesday were
nicknamed The Blades, now
the nickname of arch-rivals
Sheffield United.

WIN, LOSE OR DRAW

Most wins (in a season): 28
(1958/59)
Fewest wins: 5 (1974/75)
Most draws: 19 (1978/79)
Fewest draws: 4 (1894/95)
Most defeats: 26
(1919/20), (1974/75)
Fewest defeats: 6
(1983/84)

THEIR LEAGUE RECORD

P	W	D	L	F	A
3744	1469	934	1341	5734	5446

SHREWSBURY

FIRST TIME

First League Game:
Away v Scunthorpe Utd
(19-Aug-1950)
Result: Drew 0-0
Final position: 20th

KICKIN' OFF

Successive wins at start of season: 3 (1958/59)
Successive defeats at start of season: 4 (1973/74), (1982/83)
Successive unbeaten games at start of season: 6 (1957/58), (1961/62), (1978/79)

HIGHS AND LOWS

Biggest home win: 7-0 v Swindon Town (06-May-1955)
Biggest away win: 7-2 v Luton Town (10-Mar-1965)
Biggest home defeat: 1-8 v Norwich City (13-Sep-1952)
Biggest away defeat: 1-8 v Coventry City (22-Oct-1963), 0-7 v Bristol Rovers (21-Mar-1964)
Most points (3 for a win): 79, Division 3 (1993/94)
Most points (2 for a win): 62, Division 4 (1974/75)
Least points (3 for a win): 42, Division 2 (1988/89)
Least points (2 for a win): 31, Division 3 (1973/74)
Highest finish: 8, Division 2 (1983/84), (1984/85)
Lowest finish: 9, Division 3 (1992/93)

Seven up

November 25th 1995 saw Shrewsbury equal a club record of seven consecutive wins in all competitions, subsequently extended to seven in the League alone.

GOALS, GOALS, GOALS

Most goals scored (in a season): 101 (1958/59)
Fewest goals scored: 37 (1981/82)
Most goals conceded: 91 (1952/53)
Fewest goals conceded: 39 (1993/94)
Most clean sheets: 21 (1967/68)
Fewest clean sheets: 7 (1953/54), (1960/61), (1961/62), (1962/63), (1995/96)

Strange but true!

The Shrews have won the Welsh Cup five times, with the first of these coming as early as 1891.

King Arthur

Arthur Rowley took his tally of League goals to a record breaking 434 with his 152 strikes for Shrewsbury at the end of his career, hitting the net for The Shrews between 1958 and 1965.

Colin's best

Colin Griffin holds the Shrewsbury appearances record in the League at 406 between 1978 and 1989.

ON THE RUN

Successive games unbeaten: 16 (30-Oct-1993)
Successive games without a win: 17 (25-Jan-1992)
Successive wins: 7 (24-Sep-1955), 28-Oct-1995)
Successive defeats: 7 (26-Aug-1950), (25-Dec-1951), (17-Oct-1987)
Successive draws: 6 (09-Apr-1960), (30-Oct-1963)
Successive games without scoring: 6 (01-Jan-1991)
Successive games without conceding: 6 (12-Mar-1994)

WIN, LOSE OR DRAW

Most wins (in a season): 26 (1974/75)
Fewest wins: 8 (1988/89)
Most draws: 19 (1978/79)
Fewest draws: 5 (1979/80)
Most defeats: 25 (1973/74)
Fewest defeats: 6 (1978/79)

THEIR LEAGUE RECORD

P	W	D	L	F	A
2120	728	580	802	2891	3006

SOUTHAMPTON

FIRST TIME

First League Game:
Away v Gillingham
(28-Aug-1920)
Result: Drew 1-1
Final position: 2nd

KICKIN' OFF

Successive wins at start of season: 3 (1957/58), (1988/89)
Successive defeats at start of season: 4 (1925/26), (1927/28), (1938/39)
Successive unbeaten games at start of season: 7 (1950/51)

GOALS, GOALS, GOALS

Most goals scored (in a season): 112 (1957/58)
Fewest goals scored: 39 (1991/92)
Most goals conceded: 92 (1966/67)
Fewest goals conceded: 21 (1921/22)
Most clean sheets: 26 (1921/22)
Fewest clean sheets: 3 (1952/53)

HIGHS AND LOWS

Biggest home win: 8-0 v Northampton Town (24-Dec-1921)
Biggest away win: 6-0 v Carlisle Utd (22-Jan-1977)
Biggest home defeat: 0-6 v Plymouth Argyle (05-Dec-1931), 0-6 v Brentford (09-Mar-1959)
Biggest away defeat: 0-8 v Tottenham Hotspur (28-Mar-1936), 0-8 v Everton (20-Nov-1971)
Most points (3 for a win): 77, Division 1 (1983/84)
Most points (2 for a win): 61, Division 3(S) (1921/22) 61, Division 3 (1959/60)
Least points (3 for a win): 38, Premier (1995/96)
Least points (2 for a win): 29, Division 1 (1969/70)
Highest finish: 2, Division 1 (1983/84)
Lowest finish: 14, Division 3(S) (1955/56), (1958/59)

Deadly Davies

The 1966-67 season saw Ron Davies score exactly half of Southampton's 74 First Division goals, the first Saints player to achieve this League feat.

Extra Time

Saints' Cup-tie with Leeds in 1960 was eventful to say the least. The game kicked-off at 7.30pm, finished at 10.10pm with 90 minutes action, 62 minutes spent in darkness due to power failures, nine goals, two carried off by torchlight and Saints' winning goal finally coming an hour after the game was scheduled to end.

Riding High

As Southampton's ground, The Dell, was developed in its early years there was a special enclosure erected for the fans to store their bikes.

ON THE RUN

Successive games unbeaten: 19 (05-Sep-1921)
Successive games without a win: 20 (30-Aug-1969)
Successive wins: 6 (05-Sep-1964)
Successive defeats: 5 (8 times)
Successive draws: 7 (28-Dec-1994)
Successive games without scoring: 5 (26-Aug-1922), (01-Sep-1937)
Successive games without conceding: 8 (17-Apr-1922)

WIN, LOSE OR DRAW

Most wins (in a season): 26 (1959/60)
Fewest wins: 6 (1969/70)
Most draws: 18 (1924/25), (1972/73), (1994/95)
Fewest draws: 5 (1932/33)
Most defeats: 23 (1971/72), (1993/94)
Fewest defeats: 4 (1921/22)

THEIR LEAGUE RECORD

P	W	D	L	F	A
2946	1122	762	1062	4495	4303

SOUTHEND

HIGHS AND LOWS

Biggest home win: 7-0 v Queens Park R. (07-Apr-1928), 9-2 v Newport County (05-Sep-1936), 8-1 v Cardiff City (20-Feb-1937), 7-0 v Workington Town (29-Mar-1968)
Biggest away win: 5-0 v Newport County (23-Mar-1935), 5-0 v Exeter City (24-Aug-1957), 6-1 v Scunthorpe Utd (30-Sep-1983), 5-0 v Aldershot (09-Sep-1989)
Biggest home defeat: 0-4 v Watford (13-Sep-1924), 0-4 v C. Palace (26-Aug-1933), 0-4 v Bristol City (29-Apr-1953), 0-4 v Bury (29-Aug-1959), 0-4 v Bristol City (14-Sep-1964), 0-4 v Newport (04-Sep-1981), 0-4 v Northampton (06-Dec-1985), 0-4 v Northampton (26-Dec-1986), 0-4 v Watford (04-Feb-1995)
Biggest away defeat: 0-8 v Northampton Town (22-Mar-1924), 1-9 v Brighton & Hove A. (27-Nov-1965)
Most points (3 for a win): 85, Division 3 (1990/91)
Most points (2 for a win): 67, Division 4 (1980/81)
Least points (3 for a win): 39, Division 2 (1996/97)
Least points (2 for a win): 27, Division 3(S) (1921/22)
Highest finish: 12, Division 2 (1991/92)
Lowest finish: 20, Division 4 (1984/85)

FIRST TIME

First League Game:
Home v Brighton & Hove A. (28-Aug-1920)
Result: Won 2-0
Final position: 17th

KICKIN' OFF

Successive wins at start of season: 5 (1929/30), (1990/91)
Successive defeats at start of season: 4 (1992/93)
Successive unbeaten games at start of season: 15 (1931/32)

Back to their Roots!

When Southend's ground, Roots Hall, not known for an historic past, was excavated in 1914, diggers found Anglo-Saxon remains and Roman Viking coins.

GOALS, GOALS, GOALS

Most goals scored (in a season): 92 (1950/51)
Fewest goals scored: 34 (1921/22)
Most goals conceded: 86 (1996/97)
Fewest goals conceded: 31 (1980/81)
Most clean sheets: 25 (1980/81)
Fewest clean sheets: 5 (1932/33)

Stan the man

When Stan Collymore moved on to Nottm Forest in Southend's record sale at £2 million in 1993, Blues boss Barry Fry negotiated an extra £25,000 for the club if he scored 20 goals or more for Forest that season.

ON THE RUN

Successive games unbeaten: 16 (20-Feb-1932)
Successive games without a win: 17 (31-Dec-1983)
Successive wins: 7 (04-Oct-1924), (27-Apr-1990)
Successive defeats: 6 (21-Nov-1931), (05-Feb-1955), (29-Aug-1987)
Successive draws: 6 (30-Jan-1982)
Successive games without scoring: 6 (28-Oct-1933), (06-Apr-1979)
Successive games without conceding: 6 (08-Apr-1969)

WIN, LOSE OR DRAW

Most wins (in a season): 30 (1980/81)
Fewest wins: 8 (1921/22), (1996-97)
Most draws: 19 (1976/77)
Fewest draws: 4 (1925/26), (1965/66)
Most defeats: 26 (1965/66)
Fewest defeats: 9 (1980/81)

THEIR LEAGUE RECORD

P	W	D	L	F	A
3128	1172	763	1193	4539	4579

STOCKPORT

FIRST TIME

First League Game:
Away v Leicester Fosse
(01-Sep-1900)
Result: Drew 2-2
Final position: 17th

KICKIN' OFF

Successive wins at start of season: 4 (1921/22), (1949/50), (1976/77)
Successive defeats at start of season: 4 (1902/03), (1961/62)
Successive unbeaten games at start of season: 7 (1929/30), (1936/37), (1980/81)

GOALS, GOALS, GOALS

Most goals scored (in a season): 115 (1933/34)
Fewest goals scored: 27 (1969/70)
Most goals conceded: 97 (1925/26)
Fewest goals conceded: 21 (1921/22)
Most clean sheets: 23 (1921/22)
Fewest clean sheets: 5 (1900/1901), (1912/13), (1925/26)

Giantkillers

The 1996-97 season saw County reach the Semi-Finals of the Coca-Cola Cup where they fell to Premiership side Middlesbrough. Along the way they knocked out top-flight clubs Blackburn, West Ham and Southampton.

ON THE RUN

Successive games unbeaten: 18 (28-Jan-1933)
Successive games without a win: 15 (17-Mar-1989)
Successive wins: 8 (26-Dec-1927)
Successive defeats: 9 (19-Dec-1908)
Successive draws: 7 (04-May-1973), (17-Mar-1989)
Successive games without scoring: 7 (10-Mar-1923)
Successive games without conceding: 8 (02-May-1921)

HIGHS AND LOWS

Biggest home win: 13-0 v Halifax Town (06-Jan-1934)
Biggest away win: 7-1 v Bradford City (18-Sep-1965)
Biggest home defeat: 0-6 v Peterborough Utd (04-Feb-1961)
Biggest away defeat: 1-8 v Chesterfield (19-Apr-1902), 0-7 v Burton Utd (10-Oct-1903), 0-7 v Bristol City (20-Jan-1906), 0-7 v Fulham (08-Mar-1913), 0-7 v Port Vale (10-Apr-1954), 0-7 v Aldershot (22-Feb-1964), 0-7 v Hull City (29-Jan-1983)
Most points (3 for a win): 85, Division 2 (1993/94)
Most points (2 for a win): 64, Division 4 (1966/67)
Least points (3 for a win): 47, Division 4 (1984/85)
Least points (2 for a win): 23, Division 2 (1901/02) 23, Division 3 (1969/70)
Highest finish: 10, Division 2 (1905/06)
Lowest finish: 24, Division 4 (1964/65), (1973/74)

Count on Tony

On 26th December 1995, defender Tony Dinning kept a clean sheet when deputising for injured goalkeeper Neil Edwards during 55 minutes of a 2-0 win against Carlisle.

Hard work

Stockport played an amazing 67 games in the 1996-97 season.

WIN, LOSE OR DRAW

Most wins (in a season): 28 (1928/29), (1929/30)
Fewest wins: 6 (1969/70)
Most draws: 21 (1988/89)
Fewest draws: 2 (1946/47)
Most defeats: 29 (1964/65), (1969/70)
Fewest defeats: 5 (1936/37)

THEIR LEAGUE RECORD

P	W	D	L	F	A
3678	1371	884	1423	5215	5309

STOKE CITY

HIGHS AND LOWS

Biggest home win: 9-0 v Plymouth Argyle
(17-Dec-1960)
Biggest away win: 6-0 v Bury (13-Mar-1954)
Biggest home defeat: 1-6 v Tottenham Hotspur
(15-Sep-1951)
Biggest away defeat: 0-10 v Preston North End
(14-Sep-1889)
Most points (3 for a win): 93, Division 2 (1992/93)
Most points (2 for a win): 63, Division 3(N) (1926/27)
Least points (3 for a win): 17, Division 1 (1984/85)
Least points (2 for a win): 26, Division 1 (1906/07)
Highest finish: 4, Division 1 (1935/36), (1946/47)
Lowest finish: 14, Division 3 (1990/91)

FIRST TIME

First League Game:
Home v West Brom
(08-Sep-1888)
Result: Lost 0-2
Final position: 12th

KICKIN' OFF

Successive wins at start of
season: 5 (1905/06)
Successive defeats at start
of season: 4 (1906/07)
Successive unbeaten
games at start of season: 9
(1926/27)

Super Sheron

Former Manchester City
and Norwich striker Mike
Sheron scored in seven
successive League games
during the 1995-96 season,
the best sequence for the
club in modern times.

GOALS, GOALS, GOALS

Most goals scored (in a season): 92 (1926/27)
Fewest goals scored: 24 (1984/85)
Most goals conceded: 91 (1984/85)
Fewest goals conceded: 31 (1978/79)
Most clean sheets: 21 (1978/79)
Fewest clean sheets: 2 (1891/92)

Top cats

Two of England's greatest
'keepers, Peter Shilton and
Gordon Banks, both played
for the club during
the 1970s.

Old Boys

The Potters, behind Notts County, are the second oldest
League side in England and have played football at the
Victoria Ground for 119 years, the longest run at one
ground for any English League club.

ON THE RUN

Successive games unbeaten: 25 (05-Sep-1992)
Successive games without a win: 17 (15-Sep-1984),
(22-Apr-1989)
Successive wins: 8 (30-Mar-1895)
Successive defeats: 11 (06-Apr-1985)
Successive draws: 5 (01-Sep-1973), (21-Mar-1987)
Successive games without scoring: 8 (29-Dec-1984)
Successive games without conceding: 5
(12-Dec-1970), (16-Apr-1979)

WIN, LOSE OR DRAW

Most wins (in a season): 27
(1926/27), (1992/93)
Fewest wins: 3 (1889/90),
(1984/85)
Most draws: 19 (1989/90)
Fewest draws: 4 (1888/89),
(1889/90), (1891/92),
(1904/05)
Most defeats: 31 (1984/85)
Fewest defeats: 6
(1926/27), (1978/79)

THEIR LEAGUE RECORD

P	W	D	L	F	A
3622	1322	892	1408	5006	5226

SUNDERLAND

FIRST TIME

First League Game:
Home v Burnley
(13-Sep-1890)
Result: Lost 2-3
Final position: 7th

KICKIN' OFF

Successive wins at start of season: 4 (1894/95), (1903/04), (1910/11), (1925/26)
Successive defeats at start of season: 5 (1985/86)
Successive unbeaten games at start of season: 14 (1910/11)

GOALS, GOALS, GOALS

Most goals scored (in a season): 109 (1935/36)
Fewest goals scored: 30 (1969/70)
Most goals conceded: 97 (1957/58)
Fewest goals conceded: 35 (1899/00), (1901/02), (1974/75)
Most clean sheets: 26 (1995/96)
Fewest clean sheets: 3 (1952/53)

HIGHS AND LOWS

Biggest home win: 8-0 v Derby County (01-Sep-1894)
Biggest away win: 9-1 v Newcastle Utd (05-Dec-1908)
Biggest home defeat: 1-6 v Newcastle Utd (26-Dec-1955), 1-6 v Birmingham City (05-Apr-1958)
Biggest away defeat: 0-8 v The Wednesday (26-Dec-1911), 0-8 v West Ham Utd (19-Oct-1968), 0-8 v Watford (25-Sep-1982)
Most points (3 for a win): 93, Division 3 (1987/88)
Most points (2 for a win): 61, Division 2 (1963/64)
Least points (3 for a win): 34, Division 1 (1990/91)
Least points (2 for a win): 26, Division 1 (1969/70)
Highest finish: 1, Division 1 (1891/92), (1892/93), (1894/95), (1901/02), (1912/13), (1935/36)
Lowest finish: 1, Division 3 (1987/88)

Strange but true!

The Rokermen didn't have an English manager for 60 years before Alan Brown in 1957, so current supremo Peter Reid is somewhat of a rarity.

Roker-mights!

In the 1995-96 season, Sunderland established a club record of 18 undefeated League games beating their previous run of 16 in 1922-23. No surprise then that The Rokerites won the First Division title that year.

Saved!

Sunderland's Jim Montgomery produced arguably Wembley's greatest ever save in the 1973 Cup Final with Leeds.

ON THE RUN

Successive games unbeaten: 18 (10-Feb-1996)
Successive games without a win: 14 (16-Apr-1985)
Successive wins: 13 (14-Nov-1891)
Successive defeats: 9 (23-Nov-1976)
Successive draws: 6 (26-Mar-1949)
Successive games without scoring: 10 (27-Nov-1976)
Successive games without conceding: 6 (26-Dec-1901), (20-Dec-1902), (18-Jan-1964), (18-Dec-1982) (2-Apr-1996)

WIN, LOSE OR DRAW

Most wins (in a season): 27 (1987/88)
Fewest wins: 6 (1969/70)
Most draws: 18 (1954/55) (1994/95)
Fewest draws: 2 (1908/09)
Most defeats: 22 (1956/57), (1969/70), (1984/85), (1992/93)
Fewest defeats: 6 (1900/01), (1963/64)

THEIR LEAGUE RECORD

P	W	D	L	F	A
3852	1565	934	1353	6164	5588

SWANSEA CITY

HIGHS AND LOWS
Biggest home win: 8-0 v Hartlepool Utd (01-Apr-1978)
Biggest away win: 4-0 v Port Vale (21-Sep-1931), 4-0 v Torquay Utd (25-Sep-1948), 5-1 v Notts County (24-Sep-1955), 4-0 v Darlington (22-Jan-1977), 4-0 v Hartlepool Utd (31-Dec-1977), 5-1 v Wolverhampton W. (14-Sep-1985)
Biggest home defeat: 1-6 v Bradford PA. (14-Sep-1946), 1-6 v Workington (14-Sep-1965), 0-5 v Chester (26-Dec-1968), 1-6 v Reading (23-Sep-1989), 0-5 v Bristol City (20-Mar-1990), 1-6 v Wigan (06-Apr-1991)
Biggest away defeat: 0-7 v Tottenham Hotspur (03-Dec-1932), 1-8 v Fulham (22-Jan-1938), 0-7 v Bristol Rovers (02-Oct-1954), 0-7 v Workington (04-Oct-1965)
Most points (3 for a win): 73, Division 2 (1992/93)
Most points (2 for a win): 62, Division 3(S) (1948/49)
Least points (3 for a win): 29, Division 2 (1983/84)
Least points (2 for a win): 29, Division 2 (1946/47)
Highest finish: 6, Division 1 (1981/82)
Lowest finish: 22, Division 4 (1974/75)

FIRST TIME
First League Game:
Away v Portsmouth
(28-Aug-1920)
Result: Lost 0-3
Final position: 5th

KICKIN' OFF
Successive wins at start of season: 5 (1923/24)
Successive defeats at start of season: 4 (1931/32), (1950/51), (1985/86)
Successive unbeaten games at start of season: 7 (1926/27), (1948/49), (1968/69), (1978/79)

Euro Swans
Despite being a Third Division club, the Swans have made full use of being a Welsh side, making seven appearances in the European Cup-Winners' Cup with the last being back in 1991

GOALS, GOALS, GOALS
Most goals scored (in a season): 92 (1976/77)
Fewest goals scored: 36 (1983/84)
Most goals conceded: 99 (1957/58)
Fewest goals conceded: 34 (1948/49)
Most clean sheets: 21 (1924/25), (1968/69), (1969/70)
Fewest clean sheets: 3 (1959/60)

Strange but true!
Swansea's first game in Division Two was on 29th August 1925, and their first back in the First Division was on 29th August 1981. At one point they eventually reached the lofty heights of sixth place.

ON THE RUN
Successive games unbeaten: 19 (04-Feb-1961), (19-Oct-1970)
Successive games without a win: 15 (25-Mar-1989)
Successive wins: 8 (04-Feb-1961)
Successive defeats: 9 (26-Jan-1991)
Successive draws: 5 (23-Dec-1933), (26-Dec-1970), (28-Mar-1992), (05-Jan-1993)
Successive games without scoring: 6 (10-Feb-1996)
Successive games without conceding: 6 (16-Feb-1982)

WIN, LOSE OR DRAW
Most wins (in a season): 27 (1948/49)
Fewest wins: 7 (1983/84)
Most draws: 18 (1969/70)
Fewest draws: 4 (1932/33), (1950/51)
Most defeats: 27 (1983/84)
Fewest defeats: 7 (1948/49), (1969/70)

THEIR LEAGUE RECORD

P	W	D	L	F	A
3048	1122	732	1194	4359	4640

SWINDON TOWN

FIRST TIME
First League Game:
Home v Luton Town
(28-Aug-1920)
Result: Won 9-1
Final position: 4th

KICKIN' OFF
Successive wins at start of season: 6 (1963/64)
Successive defeats at start of season: 5 (1980/81)
Successive unbeaten games at start of season: 9 (1963/64), (1995-96)

HIGHS AND LOWS
Biggest home win: 9-1 v Luton Town (28-Aug-1920), 8-0 v Newport County (26-Dec-1938), 8-0 v Bury (08-Dec-1979)
Biggest away win: 7-1 v Watford (06-Sep-1951)
Biggest home defeat: 1-6 v Watford (01-Feb-1936), 0-5 v Nottingham Forest (14-Jan-1950), 1-6 v Newcastle Utd (28-Nov-1964), 0-5 v Liverpool (22-Aug-1993), 0-5 v Leeds Utd (07-May-1994)
Biggest away defeat: 0-9 v Torquay Utd (08-Mar-1952)
Most points (3 for a win): 102, Division 4 (1985/86)
Most points (2 for a win): 64, Division 3 (1968/69)
Least points (3 for a win): 30, Premier (1993/94)
Least points (2 for a win): 25, Division 2 (1973/74)
Highest finish: 22, Premier (1993/94)
Lowest finish: 17, Division 4 (1983/84)

GOALS, GOALS, GOALS
Most goals scored (in a season): 100 (1926/27)
Fewest goals scored: 34 (1955/56)
Most goals conceded: 105 (1932/33)
Fewest goals conceded: 34 (1995/96)
Most clean sheets: 23 (1968/69)
Fewest clean sheets: 4 (1993/94)

Strange but true!
Despite winning the Second Division Play-off Final in 1991 with a 1-0 win over Sunderland, the club were initially relegated to the old Third Division, then re-admitted to the Second Division on appeal, after the FA found them guilty of financial irregularities. Their place in the top-flight was taken by Sunderland.

Strange but true!
Although Town are currently nicknamed The Robins because of their red shirt colour, they were originally known as 'The Moonrakers' after an old Wiltshire legend.

Long John
John Trollope holds the club record for League appearances with a staggering 770 between 1960 and 1980.

ON THE RUN
Successive games unbeaten: 22 (12-Jan-1986)
Successive games without a win: 19 (17-Apr-1993)
Successive wins: 8 (06-Nov-1926), (12-Jan-1986)
Successive defeats: 6 (13-Apr-1932), (31-Dec-1966), (03-May-1980), (02-May-1993)
Successive draws: 6 (22-Nov-1991)
Successive games without scoring: 5 (16-Nov-1963), (26-Apr-1966)
Successive games without conceding: 6 (17-Aug-1968)

WIN, LOSE OR DRAW
Most wins (in a season): 32 (1985/86)
Fewest wins: 5 (1993/94)
Most draws: 17 (1967/68), (1995/96)
Fewest draws: 4 (1950/51)
Most defeats: 25 (1956/57)
Fewest defeats: 4 (1995/96)

THEIR LEAGUE RECORD

P	W	D	L	F	A
3094	1167	810	1117	4584	4472

TORQUAY UNITED

HIGHS AND LOWS

Biggest home win: 9-0 v Swindon Town (08-Mar-1952)
Biggest away win: 6-1 v Newport County
(25-Dec-1935)
Biggest home defeat: 1-8 v Scunthorpe (28-Oct-1995)
Biggest away defeat: 1-9 v Millwall (29-Aug-1927),
2-10 v Fulham (07-Sep-1931), 2-10 v Luton Town
(02-Sep-1933)
Most points (3 for a win): 77, Division 4 (1987/88)
Most points (2 for a win): 60, Division 4 (1959/60)
Least points (3 for a win): 30, Division 4 (1995/96)
Least points (2 for a win): 30, Division 3(S) (1927/28)
30, Division 3(S) (1937/38)
Highest finish: 2, Division 3(S) (1956/57)
Lowest finish: 24, Division 4 (1984/85), (1985/86),
(1996/97)

FIRST TIME

First League Game:
Home v Exeter City
(27-Aug-1927)
Result: Drew 1-1
Final position: 22nd

KICKIN' OFF

**Successive wins at start of
season:** 3 (1949/50),
(1981/82)
**Successive defeats at start
of season:** 4 (1929/30),
(1953/54)
**Successive unbeaten
games at start of season:**
14 (1990/91)

Strange but true!

The idea of creating a
Torquay club was agreed
by old boys of Torquay
College and Torbay College,
while sitting in Princess
Gardens listening to
the band.

Torquay were saved from
relegation from the League
in 1996 because
Conference Champs
Stevenage didn't have a
ground up to League status

GOALS, GOALS, GOALS

Most goals scored (in a season): 89 (1956/57)
Fewest goals scored: 38 (1937/38), (1984/85)
Most goals conceded: 106 (1931/32)
Fewest goals conceded: 41 (1987/88)
Most clean sheets: 19 (1965/66)
Fewest clean sheets: 2 (1927/28)

Early Exit

Gulls supporters never get too excited when their side
starts its domestic Cup campaigns, due to the fact that
they have never been beyond the FA Cup Fourth Round
and the League Cup Third Round.

ON THE RUN

Successive games unbeaten: 15 (14-Sep-1960),
(05-May-1990)
Successive games without a win: 17 (05-Mar-1938)
Successive wins: 6 (14-Nov-1953), (21-Sep-1990)
Successive defeats: 8 (26-Mar-1948), (29-Sep-1971),
(30-Sep-1995)
Successive draws: 8 (25-Oct-1969)
Successive games without scoring: 7 (08-Jan-1972)
Successive games without conceding: 5 (30-Apr-
1966), (13-Jan-1990)

WIN, LOSE OR DRAW

Most wins (in a season):
26 (1959/60)
Fewest wins: 5 (1995/96)
Most draws: 18 (1986/87),
(1990/91)
Fewest draws: 5 (1980/81)
Most defeats: 27
(1985/86), (1195/96)
Fewest defeats: 9
(1993/94)

THEIR LEAGUE RECORD

P	W	D	L	F	A
2822	982	719	1121	3880	4340

TOTTENHAM

FIRST TIME

First League Game:
Home v Wolverhampton W.
(01-Sep-1908)
Result: Won 3-0
Final position: 2nd

KICKIN' OFF

Successive wins at start of
season: 11 (1960/61)
Successive defeats at start
of season: 4 (1912/13),
(1974/75)
Successive unbeaten
games at start of season:
16 (1960/61)

HIGHS AND LOWS

Biggest home win: 9-0 v Bristol Rovers (22-Oct-1977)
Biggest away win: 5-0 v Coventry City (30-Aug-1919),
5-0 v Plymouth Argyle (07-May-1949), 6-1 v Stoke City
(15-Sep-1951), 6-1 v West Ham Utd (25-Aug-1962),
5-0 v Millwall (29-Apr-1989)
Biggest home defeat: 0-6 v Sunderland (19-Dec-1914),
0-6 v Arsenal (06-Mar-1935)
Biggest away defeat: 0-7 v Liverpool (02-Sep-1978)
Most points (3 for a win): 77, Division 1 (1984/85)
Most points (2 for a win): 70, Division 2 (1919/20)
Least points (3 for a win): 45, Premier (1993/94)
Least points (2 for a win): 28, Division 1 (1914/15)
Highest finish: 1, Division 1 (1950/51), (1960/61)
Lowest finish: 12, Division 2 (1929/30)

GOALS, GOALS, GOALS

Most goals scored (in a season): 115 (1960/61)
Fewest goals scored: 38 (1987/88)
Most goals conceded: 95 (1958/59)
Fewest goals conceded: 32 (1908/09), (1919/20)
Most clean sheets: 21 (1970/71)
Fewest clean sheets: 4 (1926/27)

Ian Walker

Preston tribute

In 1899, Spurs changed
their kit to white shirts
and blue shorts, as a
tribute to Preston, the
most successful team of
that era.

Just like dad

Tottenham 'keeper Ian
Walker is the son of former
Colchester stopper and
now Norwich boss, Mike
Walker. He is also a part
time model.

ON THE RUN

Successive games unbeaten: 22 (31-Aug-1949)
Successive games without a win: 16 (29-Dec-1934)
Successive wins: 13 (23-Apr-1960)
Successive defeats: 7 (01-Jan-1994)
Successive draws: 5 (01-Feb-1969), (20-Sep-1975)
Successive games without scoring: 6 (28-Dec-1985)
Successive games without conceding: 5 (22-Apr-1967),
(24-Jan-1987), (17-Dec-1994)

WIN, LOSE OR DRAW

Most wins (in a season): 32
(1919/20)
Fewest wins: 8 (1914/15)
Most draws: 17 (1968/69)
Fewest draws: 4 (1960/61)
Most defeats: 22 (1934/35)
Fewest defeats: 4 (1919/20)

THEIR LEAGUE RECORD

P	W	D	L	F	A
3226	1347	792	1087	5339	4564

TRANMERE

HIGHS AND LOWS

Biggest home win: 11-1 v Durham City (07-Jan-1928)
Biggest away win: 5-0 v Hartlepools Utd (14-Nov-1931)
Biggest home defeat: 3-9 v Manchester City
(26-Dec-1938), 1-7 v Bury (01-Oct-1960)
Biggest away defeat: 0-8 v Grimsby Town
(14-Sep-1925), 0-8 v Bradford City (06-Mar-1929), 0-8 v
Lincoln City (21-Apr-1930), 0-8 v Bury (10-Jan-1970)
Most points (3 for a win): 80, Division 4 (1988/89)
80, Division 3 (1989/90)
Most points (2 for a win): 60, Division 4 (1964/65)
Least points (3 for a win): 50, Division 4 (1982/83)
50, Division 4 (1986/87)
Least points (2 for a win): 17, Division 2 (1938/39)
Highest finish: 4, Division 1 (1992/93)
Lowest finish: 21, Division 4 (1980/81)

FIRST TIME

First League Game:
Home v Crewe Alexandra
(27-Aug-1921)
Result: Won 4-1
Final position: 18th

KICKIN' OFF

**Successive wins at start of
season:** 3 (1930/31),
(1969/70), (1977/78)
**Successive defeats at start
of season:** 4 (1962/63)
**Successive unbeaten
games at start of season:** 9
(1923/24), (1935/36)

At the start

Rovers were formed by
the players of Belmont and
Lyndhurst Wanderers
Cricket Club in 1884.
Although they nearly folded
in 1899 when half the side
left to join a rival club, they
survived to go on and win
the 'Combination' title in
1908 and the Lancashire
Combination in 1914,
eventually joining the
Football League in 1921.

GOALS, GOALS, GOALS

Most goals scored (in a season): 111 (1930/31)
Fewest goals scored: 39 (1938/39)
Most goals conceded: 115 (1960/61)
Fewest goals conceded: 41 (1937/38)
Most clean sheets: 20 (1970/71), (1988/89)
Fewest clean sheets: 4 (1936/37), (1938/39), (1956/57)

Strange but true!

Prenton Park amazingly played an important role in the
Allies' victory in the Second World War. The car park
was used as a base for sending up black smoke screens
to confuse the German aircraft.

WIN, LOSE OR DRAW

Most wins (in a season):
27 (1964/65)
Fewest wins: 6 (1938/39),
(1978/79)
Most draws: 22 (1970/71)
Fewest draws: 3 (1928/29),
(1984/85)
Most defeats: 31 (1938/39)
Fewest defeats: 8
(1988/89)

ON THE RUN

Successive games unbeaten: 18 (16-Mar-1970)
Successive games without a win: 16 (08-Nov-1969)
Successive wins: 9 (26-Oct-1964), (09-Feb-1990)
Successive defeats: 8 (29-Oct-1938)
Successive draws: 5 (25-Oct-1976)
Successive games without scoring: 5 (26-Dec-1969)
Successive games without conceding: 6 (25-Aug-1973)

THEIR LEAGUE RECORD

P	W	D	L	F	A
3074	1183	737	1154	4662	4510

WALSALL

FIRST TIME

First League Game:
Home v Darwen
(03-Sep-1892)
Result: Lost 1-2
Final position: 12th

KICKIN' OFF

Successive wins at start of season: 3 (1898/99)
Successive defeats at start of season: 6 (1952/53)
Successive unbeaten games at start of season: 13 (1979/80)

HIGHS AND LOWS

Biggest home win: 10-0 v Darwen (04-Mar-1899)
Biggest away win: 8-0 v Northampton Town (08-Apr-1947)
Biggest home defeat: 0-7 v Chelsea (04-Feb-1989)
Biggest away defeat: 0-12 v Small Heath (17-Dec-1892), 0-12 v Darwen (26-Dec-1896)
Most points (3 for a win): 83, Division 3 (1994/95)
Most points (2 for a win): 65, Division 4 (1959/60)
Least points (3 for a win): 31, Division 2 (1988/89)
Least points (2 for a win): 24, Division 3(S) (1952/53)
Highest finish: 6, Division 2 (1898/99)
Lowest finish: 16, Division 4 (1990/91)

Middle name

When Walsall Swifts, formed in 1877, and Walsall Town, formed in 1879, amalgamated in 1888, there was a dispute over which club should keep its name. The solution was simple, Walsall Football Club was formed.

GOALS, GOALS, GOALS

Most goals scored (in a season): 102 (1959/60)
Fewest goals scored: 40 (1900/01), (1953/54), (1989/90)
Most goals conceded: 118 (1952/53)
Fewest goals conceded: 40 (1947/48), (1994/95)
Most clean sheets: 19 (1947/48), (1974/75)
Fewest clean sheets: 1 (1892/93)

First class

Front runner Michael Ricketts scored with his first touch of the ball in his first League game after coming on as a substitute in the 68th minute against Brighton on 4th May 1996, his only appearance of the season.

In a Harry!

Colin Harrison holds the record number of League appearances for Walsall at 467.

ON THE RUN

Successive games unbeaten: 21 (06-Nov-1979)
Successive games without a win: 18 (15-Oct-1988)
Successive wins: 7 (04-Nov-1933), (10-Oct-1959)
Successive defeats: 15 (29-Oct-1988)
Successive draws: 5 (29-Sep-1979), (07-May-1988)
Successive games without scoring: 5 (08-Oct-1927) (25-Aug-1954), (17-Mar-1971), (21-Apr-1979), (05-Mar-1991)
Successive games without conceding: 6 (30-Mar-1959), (28-Dec-1974)

WIN, LOSE OR DRAW

Most wins (in a season): 28 (1959/60), (1960/61)
Fewest wins: 5 (1892/93)
Most draws: 18 (1971/72), (1979/80)
Fewest draws: 3 (1892/93), (1893/94), (1921/22), (1931/32)
Most defeats: 29 (1952/53), (1953/54)
Fewest defeats: 5 (1979/80)

THEIR LEAGUE RECORD

P	W	D	L	F	A
3294	1175	788	1331	4859	5153

WATFORD

HIGHS AND LOWS

Biggest home win: 8-0 v Sunderland (25-Sep-1982)
Biggest away win: 6-1 v Swindon Town (01-Feb-1936),
5-0 v Newport County (15-Feb-1936), 5-0 v Gillingham
(11-Jan-1969), 5-0 v Lincoln City (13-Sep-1978),
5-0 v Wolverhampton W. (03-Dec-1983)
Biggest home defeat: 1-7 v Swindon Town
(06-Sep-1951)
Biggest away defeat: 1-8 v Aberdare Athletic
(02-Jan-1926), 0-7 v Port Vale (15-Sep-1947), 1-8 v
Crystal Palace (23-Sep-1959)
Most points (3 for a win): 80, Division 2 (1981/82)
Most points (2 for a win): 71, Division 4 (1977/78)
Least points (3 for a win): 32, Division 1 (1987/88)
Least points (2 for a win): 19, Division 2 (1971/72)
Highest finish: 2, Division 1 (1982/83)
Lowest finish: 15, Division 4 (1958/59)

FIRST TIME

First League Game:
Away v Queens Park R.
(28-Aug-1920)
Result: Won 2-1
Final position: 6th

KICKIN' OFF
**Successive wins at start of
season:** 4 (1988/89)
**Successive defeats at start
of season:** 4 (1933/34),
(1934/35)
**Successive unbeaten
games at start of season:** 7
(1923/24)

Luther missit
Former Watford star
Luther Blissett arrived at
AC Milan's San Siro ground
after joining the Italian club
in 1984 and said "where's
the dog track?"

GOALS, GOALS, GOALS

Most goals scored (in a season): 92 (1959/60)
Fewest goals scored: 24 (1971/72)
Most goals conceded: 89 (1925/26)
Fewest goals conceded: 34 (1968/69)
Most clean sheets: 25 (1968/69)
Fewest clean sheets: 5 (1947/48)

Pop in
Pop superstar Elton John
was chairman of the club
when they reached the
1984 FA Cup Final and is
still at Vicarage Road
today.

Foundations laid
There are conflicting stories regarding the foundation of
the club but the most likely suggestion is that Watford
was formed as Watford Rovers in 1891. Another version
suggest the amalgamation of West Herts and Watford's
St. Mary's.

ON THE RUN

Successive games unbeaten: 22 (1-Oct-1996)
Successive games without a win: 19 (27-Nov-1971)
Successive wins: 7 (17-Nov-1934), (26-Dec-1977)
Successive defeats: 9 (18-Dec-1971), (26-Dec-1972)
Successive draws: 7 (30-Nov-1996))
Successive games without scoring: 7 (18-Dec-1971)
Successive games without conceding: 8 (24-Sep-1949)

WIN, LOSE OR DRAW

Most wins (in a season): 30
(1977/78)
Fewest wins: 5 (1971/72)
Most draws: 18 (1921/22)
Fewest draws: 5
(1946/47), (1982/83)
Most defeats: 28 (1971/72)
Fewest defeats: 5
(1977/78)

THEIR LEAGUE RECORD

P	W	D	L	F	A
3078	1147	801	1130	4412	4308

WEST BROM

FIRST TIME

First League Game:
Away v Stoke
(08-Sep-1888)
Result: Won 2-0
Final position: 6th

KICKIN' OFF

Successive wins at start of season: 4 (1930/31), (1932/33), (1947/48), (1992/93)
Successive defeats at start of season: 5 (1960/61)
Successive unbeaten games at start of season: 9 (1953/54)

HIGHS AND LOWS

Biggest home win: 12-0 v Darwen (04-Apr-1892)
Biggest away win: 8-0 v Wolver (27-Dec-1893)
Biggest home defeat: 0-5 v Preston (26-Dec-1888), 1-6 v Nottingham Forest (20-Oct-1900), 0-5 v Bolton Wanderers (26-Dec-1923), 1-6 v Sunderland (23-Oct-1937), 0-5 v Nottingham Forest (08-Feb-1984), 0-5 v Liverpool (23-Mar-1985)
Biggest away defeat: 0-7 v Bolton (07-Dec-1889), 1-8 v Sunderland (22-Oct-1892), 1-8 v Notts County (19-Nov-1892), 1-8 v Derby County (25-Dec-1896), 1-8 v Port Vale (09-Mar-1929), 3-10 v Stoke City (04-Feb-1937), 0-7 v Wolverhampton W. (16-Mar-1963), 0-7 v Manchester Utd (08-Apr-1970), 0-7 v Ipswich (06-Nov-1976)
Most points (3 for a win): 85, Division 2 (1992/93)
Most points (2 for a win): 60, Division 1 (1919/20)
Least points (3 for a win): 24, Division 1 (1985/86)
Least points (2 for a win): 28, Division 1 (1972/73)
Highest finish: 1, Division 1 (1919/20)
Lowest finish: 7, Division 3 (1991/92)

GOALS, GOALS, GOALS

Most goals scored (in a season): 105 (1929/30)
Fewest goals scored: 35 (1900/01), (1985/86)
Most goals conceded: 98 (1936/37)
Fewest goals conceded: 27 (1908/09)
Most clean sheets: 22 (1975/76)
Fewest clean sheets: 2 (1889/90)

In the bag

October 1995 was a historic month for The Baggies because not only did they record their 100th home win but they also gained their 500th away victory.

Strange but true!

One of Albion's first real stars was John 'Baldy' Reynolds who made his name during the 1890's. Remarkably he managed to win five caps for Northern Ireland then go on and gain eight caps with England!

ON THE RUN

Successive games unbeaten: 17 (07-Dec-1901), (07-Sep-1957)
Successive games without a win: 13 (11-May-1985)
Successive wins: 11 (05-Apr-1930)
Successive defeats: 11 (28-Oct-1995)
Successive draws: 5 (20-Feb-1915), (30-Sep-1961), (05-Apr-1980), (05-Feb-1983), (20-Apr-1991)
Successive games without scoring: 4 (16 times)
Successive games without conceding: 6 (08-Apr-1950)

WIN, LOSE OR DRAW

Most wins (in a season): 28 (1919/20)
Fewest wins: 4 (1985/86)
Most draws: 19 (1979/80)
Fewest draws: 4 (1893/94), (1894/95), (1902/03)
Most defeats: 26 (1985/86), (1919/20)
Fewest defeats: 6 (1908/09)

THEIR LEAGUE RECORD

P	W	D	L	F	A
3910	1524	949	1437	6171	5810

WEST HAM

HIGHS AND LOWS

Biggest home win: 8-0 v Rotherham United (08-Mar-1958), 8-0 v Sunderland (19-Oct-1968)
Biggest away win: 6-0 v Leicester City (15-Feb-1923)
Biggest home defeat: 0-6 v Sheffield Wed. (08-Dec-1951), 2-8 v Blackburn Rovers (26-Dec-1963)
Biggest away defeat: 0-7 v Barnsley (01-Sep-1919), 0-7 v Everton (22-Oct-1927), 0-7 v Sheffield Wed. (28-Nov-1959)
Most points (3 for a win): 88, Division 1 (1992/93)
Most points (2 for a win): 66, Division 2 (1980/81)
Least points (3 for a win): 38, Division 1 (1988/89) 38, Division 1 (1991/92)
Least points (2 for a win): 31, Division 1 (1931/32)
Highest finish: 3, Division 1 (1985/86)
Lowest finish: 20, Division 2 (1932/33)

FIRST TIME

First League Game:
Home v Lincoln City
(30-Aug-1919)
Result: Drew 1-1
Final position: 7th

KICKIN' OFF

Successive wins at start of season: 5 (1983/84)
Successive defeats at start of season: 3 (1938/39), (1962/63), (1966/67), (1971/72), (1977/78)
Successive unbeaten games at start of season: 21 (1990/91)

Strange but true

Former England defender Alvin Martin scored a remarkable hat-trick in West Ham's 8-1 win against Newcastle in 1987. Each goal came against a different goalkeeper, the first being Martin Thomas, the second outfield substitute Chris Hepworth and finally, England striker Peter Beardsley was left to pick the ball out of the net.

GOALS, GOALS, GOALS

Most goals scored (in a season): 101 (1957/58)
Fewest goals scored: 37 (1991/92)
Most goals conceded: 107 (1931/32)
Fewest goals conceded: 29 (1980/81)
Most clean sheets: 22 (1980/81)
Fewest clean sheets: 3 (1931/32)

Irons in the fire!

Thames Ironworks FC, later to become West Ham United, were forced to close in 1900 due to financial problems, but their players helped in the building of HMS Warrior, the very first ironclad warship.

ON THE RUN

Successive games unbeaten: 27 (27-Dec-1980)
Successive games without a win: 17 (31-Jan-1976)
Successive wins: 9 (19-Oct-1985)
Successive defeats: 9 (28-Mar-1932)
Successive draws: 5 (07-Sep-1968)
Successive games without scoring: 5 (01-May-1971)
Successive games without conceding: 5 (11-Nov-1922), (29-Sep-1923), (18-Apr-1981), (23-Nov-1985), (26-Dec-1990)

WIN, LOSE OR DRAW

Most wins (in a season): 28 (1980/81)
Fewest wins: 9 (1987/88) (1991/92)
Most draws: 18 (1968/69)
Fewest draws: 4 (1934/35), (1964/65), (1982/83)
Most defeats: 23 (1931/32)
Fewest defeats: 4 (1980/81)

THEIR LEAGUE RECORD

P	W	D	L	F	A
2980	1136	733	1111	4560	4442

WIGAN

FIRST TIME
First League Game:
Away v Hereford Utd
(19-Aug-1978)
Result: Drew 0-0
Final position: 6th

KICKIN' OFF
Successive wins at start of season: 2 (1985/86)
Successive defeats at start of season: 5 (1994/95)
Successive unbeaten games at start of season: 7 (1987/88)

HIGHS AND LOWS
Biggest home win: 7-1 v Scarborough (11-Mar-1997)
Biggest away win: 7-2 v Scunthorpe Utd (12-Mar-1982), 6-1 v Swansea City (06-Apr-1991)
Biggest home defeat: 0-5 v Bristol Rovers (26-Feb-1983)
Biggest away defeat: 1-6 v Bristol Rovers (03-Mar-1990)
Most points (3 for a win): 91, Division 4 (1981/82)
Most points (2 for a win): 55, Division 4 (1978/79) 55, Division 4 (1979/80)
Least points (3 for a win): 41, Division 2 (1992/93)
Least points (2 for a win): 47, Division 4 (1980/81)
Highest finish: 4, Division 3 (1985/86), (1986/87)
Lowest finish: 19, Division 3 (1993/94)

GOALS, GOALS, GOALS
Most goals scored (in a season): 84 (1996/97)
Fewest goals scored: 43 (1992/93)
Most goals conceded: 72 (1982/83), (1992/93)
Fewest goals conceded: 46 (1981/82)
Most clean sheets: 18 (1978/79), (1983/84), (1985/86)
Fewest clean sheets: 8 (1979/80)

Spain reigns
During the 1995-96 season, Wigan became the first English club to field three Spanish players in the Football League, with two of them finishing as leading scorers for the club. The three skilful senors were Isidro Diaz, Roberto Martinez and Jesus Seba.

Glory at last for Latics
The 1996-97 Third Division title was The Latics' first ever Championship trophy. They previously had won the Freight Rover trophy in 1985.

ON THE RUN
Successive games unbeaten: 21 (24-Oct-1981)
Successive games without a win: 14 (09-May-1989)
Successive wins: 6 (22-Feb-1986), (26-Dec-1987)
Successive defeats: 7 (06-Apr-1993)
Successive draws: 4 (24-Nov-1984), (09-May-1989)
Successive games without scoring: 4 (12-Mar-1983), (15-Apr-1995)
Successive games without conceding: 5 (14-Oct-1978)

WIN, LOSE OR DRAW
Most wins (in a season): 26 (1981/82), (1996-97)
Fewest wins: 10 (1992/93)
Most draws: 14 (1984/85), (1985/86), (1988/89), (1989/90), (1991/92)
Fewest draws: 9 (1982/83), (1990/91)
Most defeats: 25 (1992/93)
Fewest defeats: 7 (1981/82)

THEIR LEAGUE RECORD

P	W	D	L	F	A
866	343	225	298	1196	1115

WIMBLEDON

HIGHS AND LOWS

Biggest home win: 6-0 v Newport County (03-Sep-1983)
Biggest away win: 5-0 v Southport (17-Apr-1978), 6-1 v Torquay Utd (28-Feb-1979), 5-0 v Crystal Palace (24-Feb-1985)
Biggest home defeat: 1-5 v Arsenal (27-Aug-1988)
Biggest away defeat: 1-7 v Aston Villa (11-Feb-1995)
Most points (3 for a win): 98, Division 4 (1982/83)
Most points (2 for a win): 61, Division 4 (1978/79)
Least points (3 for a win): 51, Division 1 (1988/89)
Least points (2 for a win): 34, Division 3 (1979/80)
Highest finish: 6, Division 1 (1986/87), (1993/94)
Lowest finish: 13, Division 4 (1977/78)

FIRST TIME

First League Game:
Home v Halifax Town (20-Aug-1977)
Result: Drew 3-3
Final position: 13th

KICKIN' OFF

Successive wins at start of season: None
Successive defeats at start of season: 3 (1992/93), (1196/97)
Successive unbeaten games at start of season: 13 (1978/79)

GOALS, GOALS, GOALS

Most goals scored (in a season): 97 (1983/84)
Fewest goals scored: 47 (1989/90)
Most goals conceded: 81 (1979/80)
Fewest goals conceded: 37 (1985/86)
Most clean sheets: 18 (1980/81), (1985/86)
Fewest clean sheets: 6 (1995/96)

Multi-talented

Dean Holdsworth started his career alongside his twin brother David at Watford before joining first Brentford and then Wimbledon. He was The Dons' top scorer in a season on a number of occasions and is in demand as a media personality and part-time model for fashion company Top Man, as well as for his soccer talents.

Dean Holdsworth

WIN, LOSE OR DRAW

Most wins (in a season): 29 (1982/83)
Fewest wins: 10 (1979/80)
Most draws: 16 (1977/78), (1989/90)
Fewest draws: 9 (1980/81), (1983/84), (1986/87), (1988/89)
Most defeats: 22 (1979/80)
Fewest defeats: 6 (1982/83)

ON THE RUN

Successive games unbeaten: 22 (15-Jan-1983)
Successive games without a win: 14 (23-Feb-1980)
Successive wins: 7 (09-Apr-1983), (07-Sep-1996)
Successive defeats: 4 (03-Apr-1982), (19-Sep-1987), (01-Oct-1994)
Successive draws: 4 (03-Mar-1984), (19-Apr-1988), (26-Dec-1991), (29-Apr-1995)
Successive games without scoring: 5 (13-Apr-1995)
Successive games without conceding: 4 (07-Feb-1981) (22-Mar-1981), (23-Apr-1983), (26-Aug-1985), (30-Jan-1993)

THEIR LEAGUE RECORD

P	W	D	L	F	A
846	337	237	272	1225	1119

WOLVES

FIRST TIME

First League Game:
Home v Aston Villa
(08-Sep-1888)
Result: Drew 1-1
Final position: 3rd

KICKIN' OFF

Successive wins at start of season: 6 (1949/50)
Successive defeats at start of season: 3 (1894/95), (1964/65), (1970/71), (1978/79), (1985/86)
Successive unbeaten games at start of season: 12 (1949/50), (1992/93)

HIGHS AND LOWS

Biggest home win: 10-1 v Leicester City (15-Apr-1938), 9-0 v Fulham (16-Sep-1959)
Biggest away win: 9-1 v Cardiff City (03-Sep-1955)
Biggest home defeat: 0-8 v West Bromwich Alb. (27-Dec-1893)
Biggest away defeat: 0-9 v Derby County (10-Jan-1891), 1-10 v Newton Heath (15-Oct-1892)
Most points (3 for a win): 92, Division 3 (1988/89)
Most points (2 for a win): 64, Division 1 (1957/58)
Least points (3 for a win): 29, Division 1 (1983/84)
Least points (2 for a win): 23, Division 1 (1905/06)
Highest finish: 1, Division 1 (1953/54), (1957/58), (1958/59)
Lowest finish: 4, Division 4 (1986/87)

GOALS, GOALS, GOALS

Most goals scored (in a season): 115 (1931/32)
Fewest goals scored: 27 (1983/84)
Most goals conceded: 99 (1905/06)
Fewest goals conceded: 27 (1923/24)
Most clean sheets: 23 (1923/24)
Fewest clean sheets: 3 (1889/90)

Wright ahead

Wolves legend Billy Wright made a grand total of 105 appearances for England, with 70 of those being in consecutive games.

Ever present Wolves

From 26th October 1938 to April 6th, 1963, England played 148 internationals and Wolves were represented in every one of those games.

Tipton Terror

Steve Bull is nicknamed the Tipton Terror after hitting over 230 League goals for Wolves. He was born in the town.

ON THE RUN

Successive games unbeaten: 20 (24-Nov-1923)
Successive games without a win: 19 (01-Dec-1984)
Successive wins: 8 (13-Mar-1915), (04-Feb-1967), (14-Mar-1987), (15-Oct-1988)
Successive defeats: 8 (05-Dec-1981)
Successive draws: 5 (06-Sep-1969)
Successive games without scoring: 7 (02-Feb-1985)
Successive games without conceding: 8 (31-Aug-1982)

WIN, LOSE OR DRAW

Most wins (in a season): 28 (1957/58), (1958/59)
Fewest wins: 6 (1983/84)
Most draws: 19 (1990/91)
Fewest draws: 4 (1888/89), (1891/92), (1892/93), (1904/05), (1964/65)
Most defeats: 25 (1964/65), (1983/84), (1984/85), (1985/86)
Fewest defeats: 3 (1923/24),

THEIR LEAGUE RECORD

P	W	D	L	F	A
3920	1593	893	1434	6437	5946

WREXHAM

HIGHS AND LOWS

Biggest home win: 10-1 v Hartlepools Utd
(03-Mar-1962)
Biggest away win: 6-0 v Rochdale (17-Oct-1936),
6-0 v Chesterfield (11-Sep-1976)
Biggest home defeat: 2-6 v Stoke City (26-Feb-1927),
0-4 v Crewe Alexandra (14-Sep-1938), 0-4 v Chester
(26-May-1947), 0-4 v Rotherham United (18-Sep-1948),
2-6 v York City (21-Aug-1954), 0-4 v Oldham Athletic
(18-Sep-1963), 1-5 v Tranmere Rovers (29-Sep-1965),
0-4 v Chelsea (15-Nov-1980), 0-4 v Bradford City (02-
Apr-1983), 0-4 v York City (29-Dec-1990), 2-6 v Burnley
(12-Oct-1991)
Biggest away defeat: 0-9 v Brentford (15-Oct-1963)
Most points (3 for a win): 80, Division 3 (1992/93)
Most points (2 for a win): 61, Division 4 (1969/70)
61, Division 3 (1977/78)
Least points (3 for a win): 40, Division 4 (1990/91)
Least points (2 for a win): 32, Division 3(N) (1925/26),
(1949/50), 32, Division 3 (1963/64)
Highest finish: 15, Division 2 (1978/79)
Lowest finish: 24, Division 4 (1965/66), (1990/91)

FIRST TIME

First League Game:
Home v Hartlepools Utd
(27-Aug-1921)
Result: Lost 0-2
Final position: 12th

KICKIN' OFF

**Successive wins at start of
season:** 3 (1923/24),
(1935/36), (1973/74)
**Successive defeats at start
of season:** 6 (1951/52)
**Successive unbeaten
games at start of season:**
10 (1928/29)

Strange but true!

The Robins are the oldest
Welsh club still in
existence. They were
founded by a group of local
businessmen initially to
play a 17-a-side game
against an Insurance team.
In 1875 they were among
the founders of the
Welsh FA.

GOALS, GOALS, GOALS

Most goals scored (in a season): 106 (1932/33)
Fewest goals scored: 37 (1923/24)
Most goals conceded: 107 (1963/64)
Fewest goals conceded: 42 (1978/79)
Most clean sheets: 19 (1973/74)
Fewest clean sheets: 5 (1933/34), (1965/66)

Paying the price

Welsh international midfielder Mickey Thomas was
arrested during his spell at Wrexham for allegedly
passing on forged £10 notes to youth team players.

ON THE RUN

Successive games unbeaten: 16 (03-Sep-1966)
Successive games without a win: 14 (08-Dec-1923),
(04-Mar-1950)
Successive wins: 7 (10-Oct-1961), (04-Mar-1978)
Successive defeats: 9 (02-Oct-1963)
Successive draws: 5 (12-Jan-1935), (29-Oct-1966)
Successive games without scoring: 6 (04-Apr-1951),
(12-Sep-1973)
Successive games without conceding: 6 (12-Apr-1968)

WIN, LOSE OR DRAW

Most wins (in a season): 26
(1969/70)
Fewest wins: 10 (1923/24),
(1949/50), (1990/91)
Most draws: 20 (1966/67),
(1986/87)
Fewest draws: 5 (1933/34)
Most defeats: 27 (1963/64)
Fewest defeats: 8
(1977/78), (1992/93)

THEIR LEAGUE RECORD

P	W	D	L	F	A
3050	1151	758	1141	4596	4484

WYCOMBE

FIRST TIME

First League Game:
Away v Carlisle Utd
(14-Aug-1993)
Result: Drew 2-2
Final position: 4th

KICKIN' OFF

Successive wins at start of season: 2 (1994/95)
Successive defeats at start of season: None
Successive unbeaten games at start of season: 6 (1993/94)

HIGHS AND LOWS

Biggest home win: 5-0 v Burnley (15-Apr-1997)
Biggest away win: 3-0 v Doncaster Rovers (19-Mar-1994)
Biggest home defeat: 2-5 v Colchester Utd (18-Sep-1993), 0-3 v Birmingham City (18-Mar-1995)
Biggest away defeat: 0-3 v Mansfield Town (12-Feb-1994), 1-4 v Stockport (24-Sep-1994), 1-4 v Wrexham (05-Nov-1994), 3-6 v Peterborough (28-Sept-1996)
Most points (3 for a win): 78, Division 2 (1994/95)
Least points (3 for a win): 55, Division 2 (1996/97)
Highest finish: 6, Division 2 (1994/95)
Lowest finish: 4, Division 3 (1993/94)

Strange but true!

Football commentator Alan Parry is on the board at Adams Park, the ground where Leicester manager Martin O'Neill began his managerial career.

GOALS, GOALS, GOALS

Most goals scored (in a season): 67 (1993/94)
Fewest goals scored: 51 (1996/97)
Most goals conceded: 59 (1995/96)
Fewest goals conceded: 46 (1994/95)
Most clean sheets: 19 (1994/95)
Fewest clean sheets: 9 (1995/96)

Follow the leader

Wycombe Wanderers are said to have been originally named after the famous FA Cup winning side of the 1880s, The Wanderers, who visited the town of High Wycombe for a FA Cup tie against the first Wycombe club back in 1877.

Strange but true!

Wanderers are now one of only four clubs in the Football League, the others being Barnet, Scarborough and Crewe, who have never finished as Champions or runners-up in any of the League divisions.

ON THE RUN

Successive games unbeaten: 7 (19-Nov-1994)
Successive games without a win: 8 (21-Feb-1995)
Successive wins: 4 (03-Jan-1994), (26-Feb-1994)
Successive defeats: 3 ((5 times)
Successive draws: 4 (16-Sept-1995)
Successive games without scoring: 5 (11-Mar-1995)
Successive games without conceding: 4 (13-Aug-1994)

WIN, LOSE OR DRAW

Most wins (in a season): 21 (1994/95)
Fewest wins: 15 (1993/94), (1995/96), (1996/97)
Most draws: 15 (1994/95), (1995/96)
Fewest draws: 10 (1996/97)
Most defeats: 21 (1996/97)
Fewest defeats: 10 (1993/94), (1994/95)

THEIR LEAGUE RECORD

P	W	D	L	F	A
180	70	53	57	241	214

YORK CITY

HIGHS AND LOWS

Biggest home win: 9-1 v Southport (02-Feb-1957)
Biggest away win: 5-0 v Blackpool (28-Dec-1993), 5-0 v Blackpool (18-Apr-1995)
Biggest home defeat: 0-7 v Rochdale (14-Jan-1939)
Biggest away defeat: 0-12 v Chester (01-Feb-1936)
Most points (3 for a win): 101, Division 4 (1983/84)
Most points (2 for a win): 62, Division 4 (1964/65)
Least points (3 for a win): 33, Division 3 (1987/88)
Least points (2 for a win): 27, Division 3 (1965/66)
Highest finish: 15, Division 2 (1974/75)
Lowest finish: 24, Division 4 (1980/81)

FIRST TIME

First League Game:
Away v Wigan Borough
(31-Aug-1929)
Result: Won 2-0
Final position: 6th

KICKIN' OFF

Successive wins at start of season: 4 (1992/93)
Successive defeats at start of season: 5 (1987/88)
Successive unbeaten games at start of season: 8 (1984/85)

Well done Jack-son

Barry Jackson holds the record number of appearances for York City with 481 games played between 1958 and 1970.

Strange but true

York amazingly finished the 1996-97 season with a near identical record to their previous campaign. Both times they finished one place above the relegation zone, won 13 games, drew 13 and lost 20, ending up with 52 points!

GOALS, GOALS, GOALS

Most goals scored (in a season): 96 (1983/84)
Fewest goals scored: 39 (1975/76)
Most goals conceded: 106 (1965/66)
Fewest goals conceded: 38 (1973/74)
Most clean sheets: 20 (1983/84), (1993/94)
Fewest clean sheets: 4 (1932/33)

City slickers

City knocked out Premiership Champions Manchester United in the Coca-Cola Cup during 1995-96, but had to wait until the last match of the season to avoid relegation. They beat United 3-0 at Old Trafford, the only time The Reds suffered a home defeat all season.

ON THE RUN

Successive games unbeaten: 21 (10-Sep-1973)
Successive games without a win: 17 (04-May-1987)
Successive wins: 7 (31-Oct-1964)
Successive defeats: 8 (14-Nov-1966)
Successive draws: 6 (26-Dec-1992)
Successive games without scoring: 7 (28-Aug-1972)
Successive games without conceding: 11 (01-Oct-1973)

WIN, LOSE OR DRAW

Most wins (in a season): 31 (1983/84)
Fewest wins: 8 (1987/88), (1991/92)
Most draws: 19 (1973/74)
Fewest draws: 6 (1930/31), (1932/33), (1934/35), (1964/65)
Most defeats: 29 (1987/88)
Fewest defeats: 6 (1973/74)

THEIR LEAGUE RECORD

P	W	D	L	F	A
2730	967	679	1084	3980	4101

MACCLESFIELD

HIGHS AND LOWS

Biggest win: 15-0 v Chester St Marys (15-Feb-1886)
Biggest defeat: 1-13 v Tranmere Rovers Reserves (03-May-1929)
Record goalscorer: Albert Valentine, 84 (1933-34)
Record transfer fee paid: £10,000 to Birmingham for Ryan Price (1995)
Record transfer fee received: £40,000 from Sheffield United for Mike Lake (1988)
Biggest attendance: 9,003 v Winsford United (04-Feb-1948)

Strange but true

From the mid-19th century until 1874, Macclesfield Town Football Club played under rugby rules before moving into their current Moss Rose ground in 1891.

Mac Magic

Macclesfield boss Sammy McIlroy earned the tag 'the last of the Busby Babes' after becoming the final major signing by the legendary Man United manager at Old Trafford. The Northern Ireland star enjoyed a very successful career at United and scored the club's dramatic equaliser in their FA Cup Final clash with Arsenal in 1979 before Alan Sunderland scored an even more dramatic winner for The Gunners.

CLEAN SHEETS

Games without conceding a goal in Vauxhall Conference in 1996-97 season

Macclesfield	23
Kidderminster	19
Telford	16
Slough	14
Hednesford	13

GOALS, GOALS, GOALS

Successive games with goals in Vauxhall Conference 1996-97

Kidderminster	33
Macclesfield	20
Morecambe	14
Rushden & D	14
Woking	12

Record breakers

Macclesfield headed the Vauxhall Conference table on the 5th November, 1994 and were never toppled from that lofty position all season. They set a League record of 10 successive victories and at one stage held a 22 point lead over their nearest rivals. Their boss Sammy McIlroy lifted a record four Manager of the Month awards as well as the Manager of the Year trophy.

HOW THEY FINISHED
GM VAUXHALL CONFERENCE 1996-97

	P	W	D	Lt	F	A	Pts
Macclesfield	42	27	9	6	80	30	90
Kidderminster	42	26	7	9	84	42	85
Stevenage	42	24	10	8	87	53	82
Morecambe	42	19	9	14	69	56	66
Woking	42	18	10	14	71	63	64
Northwich	42	17	12	13	61	54	63
Farnborough	42	16	13	13	58	53	61
Hednesford	42	16	12	14	52	50	60
Telford	42	16	10	16	46	56	58
Gateshead	42	15	11	16	59	63	56
Southport	42	15	10	17	51	61	55
Rushden & D	42	14	11	17	61	63	53
Stalybridge	42	14	10	18	53	58	52
Kettering	42	14	9	19	53	62	51
Hayes	42	12	14	16	54	55	50
Slough	42	12	14	16	62	65	50
Dover	42	12	14	16	57	68	50
Welling	42	13	9	20	50	60	48
Halifax	42	12	12	18	55	74	48
Bath	42	12	11	19	53	80	47
Bromsgrove	42	12	5	25	41	67	41
Altrincham	42	9	12	21	49	73	39

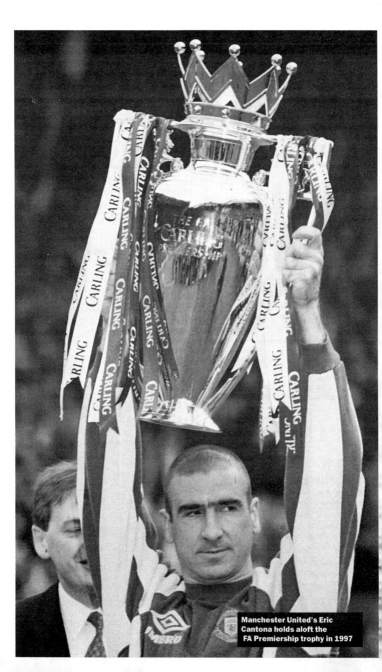

Manchester United's Eric Cantona holds aloft the FA Premiership trophy in 1997

HONOURS
CLUB-BY-CLUB

ARSENAL
● **Division One**
Champions 1930-31, 1932-33, 1933-34, 1934-35, 1937-38, 1947-48, 1952-53, 1970-71, 1988-89, 1990-91
Runners-up 1925-26, 1931-32, 1972-73
● **Division Two**
Runners-up 1903-04

ASTON VILLA
● **FA Premier League**
Runners-up 1992-93
● **Division One**
Champions 1893-94, 1895-96, 1896-97, 1898-99, 1889-1900, 1909-10, 1980-81
Runners-up 1888-89, 1902-03, 1907-08, 1910-11, 1912-13, 1913-14, 1930-31, 1932-33, 1989-90
● **Division Two**
Champions 1937-38, 1959-60
Runners-up 1974-75, 1987-88
● **Division Three**
Champions 1971-72

BARNET
● None

BARNSLEY
● **Division Two**
Runners-up 1996-97

BIRMINGHAM
● **Division Two**
Champions 1892-93, 1920-21, 1947-48, 1954-55, 1994-95
Runners-up 1893-94, 1900-01, 1902-03, 1971-72, 1984-85
● **Division Three**
Runners-up 1991-92

Division Three (N)
Champions 1933-34, 1938-39, 1954-55
Runners-up 1953-54
● **Division Three**
Runners-up 1980-81
● **Division Four**
Runners-up 1967-68

BLACKBURN
● **FA Premier League**
Champions 1994-95
Runners-up 1993-94
● **Division One**
Champions 1911-12, 1913-14
● **Division Two**
Champions 1938-39
Runners-up 1957-58
● **Division Three**
Champions 1974-75
Runners-up 1979-80

BLACKPOOL
● **Division One**
Runners-up 1955-56

Since 1992-93, with the inception of the Premier League, the First Division has been the old Second, the Second Division the old Third, and the Third Division the old Fourth.

Alan Shearer took Blackburn to the League title in 1995

● **Division Two**
Champions 1929-30
Runners-up 1936-37, 1969-70
● **Division Four**
Runners-up 1984-85

BOLTON
● **Division One**
Champions 1996-97
● **Division Two**
Champions 1908-09, 1977-78
Runners-up 1899-1900, 1904-05,
1910-11, 1934-35, 1992-93
● **Division Three**
Champions 1972-73

BOURNEMOUTH
● **Division Three**
Champions 1986-87
● **Division Three (S)**
Runners-up 1947-48
● **Division Four**
Runners-up 1970-71

BRADFORD CITY
● **Division Two**
Champions 1907-08
● **Division Three**
Champions 1984-85
● **Division Three (N)**
Champions 1928-29
● **Division Four**
Runners-up 1981-82

BRENTFORD
● **Division Two**
Champions 1934-35
Runners-up 1994-95
● **Division Three**
Champions 1991-92
● **Division Three (S)**
Champions 1932-33
Runners-up 1929-30, 1957-58
● **Division Four**
Champions 1962-63

BRIGHTON
● **Division Two**
Runners-up 1978-79
● **Division Three (S)**
Champions 1957-58
Runners-up 1953-54, 1955-56
● **Division Three**
Runners-up 1971-72, 1976-77,
1987-88
● **Division Four**
Champions 1964-65

BRISTOL CITY
● **Division One**
Runners-up 1906-07
● **Division Two**
Champions 1905-06
Runners-up 1975-76
● **Division Three (S)**
Champions 1922-23, 1926-27, 1954-55
Runners-up 1937-38
● **Division Three**
Runners-up 1964-65, 1989-90

BRISTOL ROVERS
● **Division Three (S)**
Champions 1952-53
● **Division Three**
Champions 1989-90
Runners-up 1973-74

BURNLEY
● **Division One**
Champions 1920-21, 1959-60
Runners-up 1919-20, 1961-62
● **Division Two**
Champions 1897-98, 1972-73
Runners-up 1912-13, 1946-47
● **Division Three**
Champions 1981-82
● **Division Four**
Champions 1991-92

BURY
● **Division Two**
Champions 1894-95, 1996-97
Runners-up 1923-24
● **Division Three**
Champions 1960-61
Runners-up 1967-68

CAMBRIDGE
● **Division Three**
Champions 1990-91
Runners-up 1977-78
● **Division Four**
Champions 1976-77

CARDIFF CITY
● **Division One**
Runners-up 1923-24
● **Division Two**
Runners-up 1920-21, 1951-52, 1959-60
● **Division Three (S)**
Champions 1946-47
● **Division Three**
Champions 1992-93
Runners-up 1975-76, 1982-83
● **Division Four**
Runners-up 1987-88

CARLISLE UNITED
● **Division Three**
Champions 1964-65, 1994-95
Runners-up 1981-82
● **Division Four**
Runners-up 1963-64

CHARLTON
● **Division One**
Runners-up 1936-37
● **Division Two**
Runners-up 1935-36, 1985-86
● **Division Three (S)**
Champions 1928-29, 1934-35

CHELSEA
● **Division One**
Champions 1954-55
● **Division Two**
Champions 1983-84, 1988-89

Runners-up 1906-07, 1911-12,
1929-30, 1962-63, 1976-77

CHESTER CITY
● **Division Three**
Runners-up 1993-94
● **Division Three (N)**
Runners-up 1935-36
● **Division Four**
Runners-up 1985-86

CHESTERFIELD
● **Division Three (N)**
Champions 1930-31; 1935-36
Runners-up 1933-34
● **Division Four**
Champions 1969-70, 1984-85

COLCHESTER
● **Division Four**
Runners-up 1961-62

COVENTRY CITY
● **Division Two**
Champions 1966-67
● **Division Three**
Champions 1963-64
● **Division Three (S)**
Champions 1935-36
Runners-up 1933-34
● **Division Four**
Runners-up 1958-59

CREWE
● None

CRYSTAL PALACE
● **Division One**
Champions 1993-94

Gordon Strachan and the
1992 League Championship
trophy won with Leeds

● **Division Two**
Champions 1978-79
Runners-up 1968-69
● **Divsion Three**
Runners-up 1963-64
● **Division Three (S)**
Champions 1920-21
Runners-up 1928-29, 1930-31,
1938-39
● **Division Four**
Runners-up 1960-61

DARLINGTON
● **Division Three (N)**
Champions 1924-25
Runners-up 1921-22
● **Division Four**
Champions 1990-91
Runners-up 1965-66

DERBY COUNTY
● **Division One**
Champions 1971-72, 1974-75
Runners-up 1895-96; 1929-30,
1935-36, 1995-96
● **Division Two**
Champions 1911-12, 1914-15,
1968-69, 1986-87; Runners-up
1925-26
● **Division Three (N)**
Champions 1956-57
Runners-up 1955-56

DONCASTER
● **Division Three (N)**
Champions 1934-35, 1946-47,
1949-50
Runners-up 1937-38, 1938-39
● **Division Four**
Champions 1965-66, 1968-69
Runners-up 1983-84

EVERTON
● **Division One**
Champions 1890-91, 1914-15,
1927-28, 1931-32, 1938-39,
1962-63, 1969-70, 1984-85,
1986-87
Runners-up 1889-90, 1894-95,
1901-02, 1904-05, 1908-09,
1911-12, 1985-86
● **Division Two**
Champions 1930-31
Runners-up 1953-54

EXETER CITY
● **Division Three (S)**
Runners-up 1932-33
● **Division Four**
Champions 1989-90
Runners-up 1976-77

FULHAM
● **Division Two**
Champions 1948-49
Runners-up 1958-59
● **Division Three (S)**
Champions 1931-32
● **Division Three**
Runners-up 1970-71, 1996-97

GILLINGHAM
● **Division Three**
Runners-up 1995-96
● **Division Four**
Champions 1963-64
Runners-up 1973-74

GRIMSBY
● **Division Two**
Champions 1900-01, 1933-34
Runners-up 1928-29
● **Division Three (N)**
Champions 1925-26, 1955-56
Runners-up 1951-52
● **Division Three**
Champions 1979-80
Runners-up 1961-62
● **Division Four**
Champions 1971-72
Runners-up 1978-79, 1989-90

HARTLEPOOL
● **Division Three (N)**
Runners-up 1956-57

HEREFORD
● **Division Three**
Champions 1975-76
● **Division Four**
Runners-up 1972-73

HUDDERSFIELD
● **Division One**
Champions 1923-24, 1924-25, 1925-26
Runners-up 1926-27, 1927-28, 1933-34
● **Division Two**
Champions 1969-70
Runners-up 1919-20, 1952-53
● **Division Four**
Champions 1979-80

HULL CITY
● **Division Three (N)**
Champions 1932-33, 1948-49
● **Division Three**
Champions 1965-66
Runners-up 1958-59
● **Division Four**
Runners-up 1982-83

IPSWICH TOWN
● **Division One**
Champions 1961-62
Runners-up 1980-81, 1981-82
● **Division Two**
Champions 1960-61, 1967-68, 1991-92
● **Division Three (S)**
Champions 1953-54, 1956-57

LEEDS UNITED
● **Division One**
Champions 1968-69, 1973-74, 1991-92
Runners-up 1964-65, 1965-66, 1969-70, 1970-71, 1971-72
● **Division Two**
Champions 1923-24, 1963-64, 1989-90
Runners-up 1927-28, 1931-32, 1955-56

Champs in 1985 - Everton's
Andy Gray and Peter Reid

LEICESTER CITY
● **Division One**
Runners-up 1928-29
● **Division Two**
Champions 1945-25, 1936-37, 1953-54, 1956-57, 1970-71, 1979-80
Runners-up 1907-08

LEYTON ORIENT
● **Division Two**
Runners-up 1961-62

● **Division Three**
Champions 1969-70
● **Division Three (S)**
Champions 1955-56
Runners-up 1954-55

LINCOLN CITY
● **Division Three (N)**
Champions 1931-32, 1947-48,
1951-52; Runners-up 1927-28,
1930-31, 1936-37
● **Division Four**
Champions 1975-76
Runners-up 1980-81

LIVERPOOL
● **Division One**
Champions 1900-01, 1905-06,
1921-22, 1922-23, 1946-47,
1963-64, 1965-66, 1972-73,
1975-76, 1976-77, 1978-79, 1979-
80, 1981-82, 1982-83, 1983-84,
1985-86, 1987-88, 1989-90
Runners-up 1898-99, 1909-10,
1968-69, 1973-74, 1974-75, 1977-
78, 1984-85, 1986-87, 1988-89,
1990-91
● **Division Two**
Champions 1893-94, 1895-96,
1904-05, 1961-62

LUTON TOWN
● **Division Two**
Champions 1981-82
Runners-up 1954-55, 1973-74
● **Division Three**
Runners-up 1969-70
● **Division Four**
Champions 1967-68
● **Division Three (S)**
Champions 1936-37
Runners-up 1935-36

MAN CITY
● **Division One**
Champions 1936-37, 1967-68
Runners-up 1903-04, 1920-21,
1976-77
● **Division Two**
Champions 1898-99, 1902-03,
1909-10, 1927-28, 1946-47,
1965-66
Runners-up 1895-96, 1950-51,
1987-88

MAN UTD
● **FA Premier League**
Champions 1992-93, 1993-94,
1995-96, 1996-97
Runners-up 1994-95
● **Division One**
Champions 1907-08, 1910-11,
1951-52, 1955-56, 1956-57,
1964-65, 1966-67
Runners-up 1946-47, 1947-48,
1948-49, 1950-51, 1958-59,
1963-64, 1967-68, 1979-80,
1987-88, 1991-92
● **Division Two**
Champions 1935-36, 1974-75
Runners-up 1896-97, 1905-06,
1924-25, 1937-38

MANSFIELD
● **Division Three**
Champions 1976-77
● **Division Four**
Champions 1974-75
● **Division Three (N)**
Runners-up 1950-51

MIDDLESBROUGH
● **Division One**
Champions 1994-95
● **Division Two**
Champions 1926-27, 1928-29,
1973-74

Runners-up 1901-02, 1991-92
● **Division Three**
Runners-up 1966-67, 1986-87

MILLWALL
● **Division Two**
Champions 1987-88
● **Division Three (S)**
Champions 1927-28, 1937-38
Runners-up 1952-53
● **Division Three**
Runners-up 1965-66, 1984-85
● **Division Four**
Champions 1961-62
Runners-up 1964-65

NEWCASTLE
● **FA Premier League**
Runners-up 1995-96, 1996-97
● **Division One**
Champions 1904-05, 1906-07,
1908-09, 1926-27, 1992-93
● **Division Two**
Champions 1964-65
Runners-up 1897-98, 1947-48

NORTHAMPTON
● **Division Two**
Runners-up 1964-65
● **Division Three**
Champions 1962-63
● **Division Three (S)**
Runners-up 1927-28, 1949-50
● **Division Four**
Champions 1986-87
Runners-up 1975-76

NORWICH CITY
● **Division Two**
Champions 1971-72, 1985-86
● **Division Three (S)**

Champions 1933-34
● **Division Three**
Runners-up 1959-60

NOTTM FOREST
● **Division One**
Champions 1977-78
Runners-up 1966-67, 1978-79
● **Division Two**
Champions 1906-07, 1921-22
Runners-up 1956-57
● **Division Three (S)**
Champions 1950-51

NOTTS COUNTY
● **Division Two**
Champions 1896-97, 1913-14,
1922-23
Runners-up 1894-95, 1980-81
● **Division Three (S)**
Champions 1930-31, 1949-50
Runners-up 1936-37
● **Division Three**
Runners-up 1972-73
● **Division Four**
Champions 1970-71
Runners-up 1959-60

OLDHAM
● **Division One**
Runners-up 1914-15
● **Division Two**
Champions 1990-91
Runners-up 1909-10
● **Division Three (N)**
Champions 1952-53
● **Division Three**
Champions 1973-74
● **Division Four**
Runners-up 1962-63

OXFORD UNITED
● Division Two
Champions 1984-85
Runners-up 1995-96
● Division Three
Champions 1967-68, 1983-84

PETERBOROUGH
● Division Four
Champions 1960-61, 1973-74

PLYMOUTH
● Division Three (S)
Champions 1929-30, 1951-52
Runners-up 1921-22, 1922-23,
1923-24, 1924-25, 1925-26,
1926-27
● Division Three
Champions 1958-59
Runners-up 1974-75; 1985-86

PORTSMOUTH
● Division One
Champions 1948-49, 1949-50
● Division Two
Runners-up 1926-27, 1986-87
● Division Three (S)
Champions 1923-24
● Division Three
Champions 1961-62, 1982-83

PORT VALE
● Division Two
Runners-up 1993-94
● Division Three (N)
Champions 1929-30, 1953-54
Runners-up 1952-53
● Division Four
Champions 1958-59

PRESTON
● Division One
Champions 1888-89, 1889-90
Runners-up 1890-91, 1891-92,
1892-93, 1905-06, 1952-53,
1957-58
● Division Two
Champions 1903-04, 1912-13,
1950-51
Runners-up 1914-15, 1933-34
● Division Three
Champions 1970-71, 1995-96
● Division Four
Runners-up 1986-87

QPR
● Division One
Runners-up 1975-76
● Division Two
Champions 1982-83
Runners-up 1967-68, 1972-73
● Division Three (S)
Champions 1947-48
Runners-up 1946-47
● Division Three
Champions 1966-67

READING
● Division One
Runners-up 1994-95
● Division Two
Champions 1993-94
● Division Three
Champions 1985-86
● Division Three (S)
Champions 1925-26
Runners-up 1931-32, 1934-35,
1948-49, 1951-52
● Division Four
Champions 1978-79

ROCHDALE
● **Division Three (N)**
Runners-up 1923-24, 1926-27

ROTHERHAM
● **Division Three**
Champions 1980-81
● **Division Three (N)**
Champions 1950-51
Runners-up 1946-47, 1947-48,
1948-49
● **Division Four**
Champions 1988-89
Runners-up 1991-92

SCARBOROUGH
● None

SCUNTHORPE
● **Division Three (N)**
Champions 1957-58

SHEFFIELD UTD
● **Division One**
Champions 1897-98
Runners-up 1896-97, 1899-1900
● **Division Two**
Champions 1952-53
Runners-up 1892-93, 1938-39,
1960-61, 1970-71, 1989-90
● **Division Four**
Champions 1981-82

SHEFFIELD WED
● **Division One**
Champions 1902-03, 1903-04,
1928-29, 1929-30
Runners-up 1960-61
● **Division Two**
Champions 1899-1900, 1925-26,

1951-52, 1955-56, 1958-59
Runners-up 1949-50, 1983-84

SHREWSBURY
● **Division Three**
Champions 1978-79, 1993-94
● **Division Four**
Runners-up 1974-75

SOUTHAMPTON
● **Division One**
Runners-up 1983-84
● **Division Two**
Runners-up 1965-66, 1977-78
● **Division Three (S)**
Champions 1921-22
Runners-up 1920-21
● **Division Three**
Champions 1959-60

SOUTHEND
● **Division Three**
Runners-up 1990-91
● **Division Four**
Champions 1980-81
Runners-up 1971-72, 1977-78

STOCKPORT
● **Division Two**
Runners-up 1996-97
● **Division Three (N)**
Champions 1921-22, 1936-37
Runners-up 1928-29, 1929-30
● **Division Four**
Champions 1966-67
Runners-up 1990-91

STOKE CITY
● **Division Two**
Champions 1932-33, 1962-63,
1992-93

Runners-up 1921-22
● **Division Three (N)**
Champions 1926-27

SUNDERLAND
● **Division One**
Champions 1891-92, 1892-93, 1894-95, 1901-02, 1912-13, 1935-36, 1995-96
Runners-up 1893-94, 1897-98, 1900-01, 1922-23, 1934-35
● **Division Two**
Champions 1975-76
Runners-up 1963-64, 1979-80
● **Division Three**
Champions 1987-88

SWANSEA CITY
● **Division Three (S)**
Champions 1924-25, 1948-49

SWINDON TOWN
● **Division Two**
Champions 1995-96
● **Division Three**
Runners-up 1962-63, 1968-69
● **Division Four**
Champions 1985-86

TORQUAY UNITED
● **Division Three (S)**
Runners-up 1956-57

TOTTENHAM
● **Division One**
Champions 1950-51, 1960-61
Runners-up 1921-22, 1951-52, 1956-57, 1962-63
● **Division Two**
Champions 1919-20, 1949-50
Runners-up 1908-09, 1932-33

TRANMERE
● **Division Three (N)**
Champions 1937-38
● **Division Four**
Runners-up 1988-89

WALSALL
● **Division Three**
Runners-up 1960-61, 1994-95
● **Division Four**
Champions 1959-60
Runners-up 1979-80

WATFORD
● **Division One**
Runners-up 1982-83
● **Division Two**
Runners-up 1981-82
● **Division Three**
Champions 1968-69
Runners-up 1978-79
● **Division Four**
Champions 1977-78

WEST BROM
● **Division One**
Champions 1919-20
Runners-up 1924-25, 1953-54
● **Division Two**
Champions 1901-02, 1910-11
Runners-up 1930-31, 1948-49

WEST HAM
● **Division Two**
Champions 1957-58, 1980-81
Runners-up 1922-23, 1990-91

WIGAN ATHLETIC
● **Division Three**
Champions 1996-97

WIMBLEDON
● **Division Three**
Runners-up 1983-84
● **Division Four**
Champions 1982-83

WOLVES
● **Division One**
Champions 1953-54, 1957-58, 1958-59
Runners-up 1937-38, 1938-39, 1949-50, 1954-55, 1959-60
● **Division Two**
Champions 1931-32, 1976-77
Runners-up 1966-67, 1982-83
● **Division 3 (N)**
Champions 1923-24
● **Division Three**
Champions 1988-89

● **Division Four**
Champions 1987-88

WREXHAM
● **Division Three**
Champions 1977-78
● **Division Three (N)**
Runners-up 1932-33
● **Division Four**
Runners-up 1969-70

WYCOMBE
● None

YORK CITY
● **Division Four**
Champions 1983-84

Bolton celebrate their promotion to the Premiership after winning the First Division title in 1996-97